회화잡는 주제별 영단어 12000

회화잡는 주제별 영단어 12000

2018년 2월 15일 초판 01쇄 발행
2025년 3월 15일 초판 13쇄 발행

지은이 이서영
발행인 손건
편집기획 김상배, 장수경
마케팅 이언영
디자인 이성세
제작 최승용
인쇄 선경프린테크

발행처 **LanCom** 랭컴
주소 서울시 영등포구 영신로34길 19
등록번호 제 312-2006-00060호
전화 02) 2636-0895
팩스 02) 2636-0896
홈페이지 www.lancom.co.kr

ⓒ 랭컴 2018
ISBN 979-11-88112-55-5 13740

이 책의 저작권은 저자에게 있습니다. 저자와 출판사의 허락없이
내용의 일부를 인용하거나 발췌하는 것을 금합니다.

회화 잡는 주제별 영단어 12000

이서영 지음

LanCom
Language & Communication

이 책의 내용

Part 01 기본어휘

01 숫자
숫자 전반 10
기수 13
서수 15
도량형 17

02 시간과 연월일
시간 19
때 23
월 25
계절 26
요일 27
기념일 28

Part 02 일상생활

01 하루
하루의 생활 32

02 입는 것(衣)
의복 35
화장과 청결 40
액세서리 43
잡화 46
색 48

03 먹는 것(食)
식사 전반 51
식당 52
요리 일반 54
디저트와 과자류 58
음료 60
주류 61
식재료 63
조미료 65
조리법 67
맛을 나타내는 형용사 70
기타 71

04 주거(住)
주거 전반 73
주거의 구조 75
가구와 세간 79
가전제품 81
부엌용품 85
기타 가사용품 89

Part 03 인체와 건강

01 인체
인체 전반 92
인체의 명칭 93

02 건강

생리적 현상 104
체력 106

03 질병
병과 증상 108
의료 116
병원 119
약품 122

Part 04 가족과 인간관계

01 가족
가족관계 128

02 인간관계
인생과 결혼 132

03 교제와 사교
이성과의 교제 137
트러블 140
방문·초대 142

Part 05 사회

01 사회
사회 일반 146
복지 147

범죄와 사건 149
종교 154

02 사고와 재해
사고 159
재해 162

Part 06 정보와 교통

01 정보통신과 미디어
전화 168
우편 171
매스미디어 173
컴퓨터와 인터넷 177

02 교통과 건설
도로 교통 182
열차 188
항공 190
선박 192

03 지리
세계의 대륙과 지역 194
세계의 여러 나라 196
세계의 여러 나라 사람 200

Part 07 자연과 과학

01 자연과 자연현상
자연 전반	204
날씨	210
시간의 변화	214

02 과학
테크놀로지	216
우주와 천체	217

03 환경과 에너지
환경문제	221

04 생물
동물	224
조류	228
곤충	230
어류	233
조개류	235

05 식물
식물 전반	237
야채	241
과일	244
견과류	246
곡물	247

Part 08 교육과 문화

01 교육과 학교
교육	252
학교	254
학문	256
수업·커리큘럼	259
문구와 사무용품	263

02 문화
문화 일반	266
예술·음악	268
취미	273
오락	276

03 스포츠와 레저
스포츠	278

04 여행
여행과 관광	285
숙박	289
쇼핑	290

Part 09 정치와 경제

01 정치
정치 일반	298
국가	303

선거 306

02 법률
법과 재판 309

03 국제관계
외교 314
군사와 무기 316

04 경제
산업 일반 321

05 직장과 일
기업 324
회사조직 328
고용 331
직업 334

06 경제와 돈
경제 전반 341
주식과 채권 347
금융(은행) 349
세금 352

Part 10 언어생활

01 부사적인 표현
부사어 356
의태어와 의성어 361

02 동작 표현
동작을 나타내는 말 363

03 수량
수와 양을 나타내는 표현 368

04 물건에 관한 표현
물건에 관한 표현 373

Part 11 감정과 화술

01 성질과 상태
모습과 체격 378
도형 380

02 감정과 감각
감정을 나타내는 명사 382
감정을 나타내는 동사와 형용사 385
감각 391
성격과 태도 393

03 화술
의사소통 399
토론 406
판단 411

구 성 및 특 징

1　크게 11가지 주제별로 엮은 사전식 영단어장

일상생활에서 많이 쓰이는 단어 위주로 숫자와 시간을 나타내는 기본어휘, 먹는 것, 입는 것, 주거 생활과 관련된 일상 단어, 가족과 인간관계, 사회, 정보와 교통, 자연과 과학, 교육과 문화, 정치와 경제, 언어생활 등 총 11개의 주제로 분류하여 표제단어와 각 단어의 구(句)에 활용된 어휘를 포함 약 12,000여 단어를 수록하였습니다. 전문적인 상급 어휘는 제외하고 언어 본래의 기능인 커뮤니케이션 능력에 중점을 두어 기본적인 식사, 여행, 일상생활의 대화가 가능하도록 단어를 선별하였습니다. 무작위로 배열한 단어장을 공부하고 나서 금방 쉽게 잊어버렸던 경험이 있을 것입니다. 이 책은 주제별로 유의미한 단어들을 묶어 학습함으로써 암기의 효율을 높이고 지루하지 않게 공부할 수 있습니다.

2　기억력을 높이는 알짜 구절을 통해 초스피드 암기

구(句)는 서로 관련된 몇 개의 단어가 모여서 이루어진 형태로 단어의 가장 중요한 의미, 형태, 용법, 연어까지 응축되어 있습니다. 구를 통한 학습은 단어를 가장 빠르고 명확하게 익힐 수 있는 방법입니다. 구안에서 단어가 어떤 뜻으로 쓰였는지 정확히 파악하고 짧은 구절 암기를 통해 빠르고 오랫동안 기억할 수 있습니다. 단어만 따로 써가면서 외우거나 긴 문장을 억지로 힘들게 외우지 말고 일상과 관련된 단어의 구절부터 학습해 보시기 바랍니다.

PART 01

기본
어휘

01 숫자

■ 숫자 전반

number
[nʌ́mbə:r]

n. 수, 숫자
odd number 홀수 / even number 짝수

calculation
[kæ̀lkjəléiʃən]

n. 계산
make[do] a calculation 계산하다

addition
[ədíʃən]

n. 덧셈
easy additions 쉬운 덧셈 (문제)

subtraction
[səbtrǽkʃən]

n. 뺄셈
addition and subtraction 가감

multiplication
[mʌ̀ltəplikéiʃ-ən]

n. 곱셈
the multiplication sign 곱셈 기호

division
[divíʒən]

n. 나눗셈
children learning to do multiplication and division 곱셈과 나눗셈을 배우는 아이들

arithmetic
[ərίθmətik]

n. 산수
mental arithmetic 암산

square
[skwɛːr]

n. 제곱

extract the square root 제곱근을 구하다

decimal
[désəməl]

n. 소수

to 5 places of decimals 소수점 (5)자리까지

fraction
[frǽkʃ-ən]

n. 분수

common[vulgar] fraction 보통 분수

round (off)
[raund]

n. 반올림하다

round off the numbers to two decimal places 소수 둘째 자리에서 반올림하다

diameter
[daiǽmitər]

n. 지름, 직경

3 inches in diameter 지름이 3인치

number
[nʌ́mbəːr]

n. 번호

a serial number 일련 번호

average
[ǽvəridʒ]

n. 평균

be above[below] the average
평균 이상[이하]이다

distance
[dístəns]

n. 거리

measure a distance 거리를 재다

size
[saiz]

n. 크기

a shoe of ~size 4A 사이즈 4A의 구두

height
[hait]

n. 높이

at a height of 3,000 meters 3,000m의 고도

length
[leŋkθ]

n. 길이

the length of a line 선의 길이

weight
[weit]

n. 무게

gain weight 체중이 늘다

bulk
[bʌlk]

n. 크기, 부피

a ship of great bulk 큰 배

thickness
[θíknis]

n. 두께

to a thickness of ten centimeters
10cm의 두께로

circumference
[sərkʌ́mfərəns]

n. 원주, 둘레

the circumference of a pond 연못의 둘레

depth
[depθ]

n. 깊이

sound the depth 깊이를 재다

width
[widθ]

n. 넓이

have a width of 6 feet 넓이가 여섯 자다

area
[ɛ́əriə]

n. 면적

the gross area 총면적

volume
[válju:m]

n. 크기, 분량

the volume of a box 상자의 용량

speed
[spi:d]

n. 속도

maximum speed 최고 속도

■ 기수

cardinal number [káːrdənl nʌ́mbəːr] *n.* 기수

one [wʌn] *n.* 하나

two [tú] *n.* 둘

three [θriː] *n.* 셋

four [fɔːr] *n.* 넷

five [faiv] *n.* 다섯

six [siks] *n.* 여섯

seven [sév-ən] *n.* 일곱

eight [eit] *n.* 여덟

nine [nain] *n.* 아홉

ten [ten] *n.* 열

eleven [ilévən] *n.* 열하나

twelve [twelv]	*n.* 열둘
thirteen [θə̀ːrtíːn]	*n.* 열셋
fourteen [fɔ́ːrtíːn]	*n.* 열넷
fifteen [fiftíːn]	*n.* 열다섯
sixteen [síkstíːn]	*n.* 열여섯
seventeen [sév-əntíːn]	*n.* 열일곱
eighteen [éitíːn]	*n.* 열여덟
nineteen [náintíːn]	*n.* 열아홉
twenty [twénti]	*n.* 스물
thirty [θɔ́ːrti]	*n.* 서른
forty [fɔ́ːrti]	*n.* 마흔
hundred [hʌ́ndrəd]	*n.* 백
thousand [θáuz-ənd]	*n.* 천

ten thousand [ten θáuz-ənd]	*n.* 만
million [míljən]	*n.* 백만
billion [bíljən]	*n.* 십억

■ 서수

ordinal number [ɔ́ːrdənəl nʌ́mbəːr]	*n.* 서수
first [fəːrst]	*n.* 첫 번째
second [sék-ənd]	*n.* 두 번째
third [θəːrd]	*n.* 세 번째
fourth [fɔːrθ]	*n.* 네 번째
fifth [fifθ]	*n.* 다섯 번째
sixth [siksθ]	*n.* 여섯 번째
seventh [sév-ənθ]	*n.* 일곱 번째
eighth [eitθ]	*n.* 여덟 번째

ninth [nainθ]	*n.* 아홉 번째
tenth [tenθ]	*n.* 열 번째
eleventh [ilévənθ]	*n.* 열한 번째
twelfth [twelfθ]	*n.* 열두 번째
thirteenth [θə̀ːrtíːnθ]	*n.* 열세 번째
fourteenth [fɔ́ːrtíːnθ]	*n.* 열네 번째
fifteenth [fiftíːnθ]	*n.* 열다섯 번째
sixteenth [síkstíːnθ]	*n.* 열여섯 번째
seventeenth [sév-əntíːnθ]	*n.* 열일곱 번째
eighteenth [éitíːnθ]	*n.* 열여덟 번째
nineteenth [náintíːnθ]	*n.* 열아홉 번째
twentieth [twéntiiθ]	*n.* 스무 번째
thirtieth [θə́ːrtiiθ]	*n.* 서른 번째
fortieth [fɔ́ːrtiiθ]	*n.* 마흔 번째

hundredth [hʌ́ndrədθ]	*n.* 백 번째
thousandth [θáuzəndθ]	*n.* 천 번째
ten thousandth [ten θáuzəndθ]	*n.* 만 번째
millionth [míljənθ]	*n.* 백만 번째
billionth [bíljənθ]	*n.* 십억 번째

■ 도량형

millimeter [míləmìːtər]	*n.* 밀리미터 30 millimeters of rain 30밀리미터의 강우
centimeter [séntəmìːtər]	*n.* 센티미터 to a thickness of 10 centimeters 10센티미터의 두께로
meter [míːtər]	*n.* 미터 five meters long 길이 5미터
kilometer [kilámitər]	*n.* 킬로미터 at a speed of 60 kilometers for hour 시속 60km의 속도로
mile [mail]	*n.* 마일 run at sixty miles per hour 시속 60마일로 달리다

gram
[græm]

n. 그램

200 grams of cheese 치즈 200g

milligram
[míləgræm]

n. 밀리그램

add 10 milligrams of salt to water
물에 소금 10mg을 넣다

kilogram
[kíləgræm]

n. 킬로그램

weigh 60 kilograms 체중이 60kg이다

ton
[tʌn]

n. 톤

per ton 톤당(當)

square meter
[skwɛəːr míːtər]

n. 제곱미터

9 square meters of carpet
9 제곱미터 짜리 카펫

hectare
[héktɛər]

n. 헥타르

40 hectares of golf courses
40헥타아르의 골프코스

acre
[éikər]

n. 에이커

plow up an acre of the field
1에이커의 밭을 갈아 엎다

liter
[líːtər]

n. 리터

drink 2 liters water a day
하루에 2리터의 물을 마시다

knot
[nɑt]

n. 노트

a ship good for 30 knots
30노트를 낼 수 있는 배

02 시간과 연월일

■ 시간

first
[fəːrst]
a. 처음의
for the first time 처음으로

end
[end]
n. 끝
be at an end 끝나다, 다하다

recently
[ríːsəntli]
ad. 최근
a book recently published 최근에 출판된 책

lately
[léitli]
ad. 요즘에, 최근
till lately 최근까지

last
[lɑːst]
a. 마지막의
the last day of the vacation
휴가의 맨 마지막 날

past
[pæst]
n. 과거 *a.* 과거의
for the past two years 과거 2년간

present
[prézənt]
n. 현재
for the present 현재로서는, 당분간

future [fjúːtʃəːr]	*n.* 미래 *a.* 미래의 in the near future 가까운 미래에	
once [wʌns]	*ad.* 이전에, 일찍이 once upon a time 옛날에	
morning [mɔ́ːrniŋ]	*n.* 아침, 오전 in the morning 아침에	
noon [nuːn]	*n.* 정오, 한낮 at noon 정오에	
afternoon [æftərnúːn]	*n.* 오후 in the afternoon 오후에	
evening [íːvniŋ]	*n.* 저녁 in the evening 저녁에	
night [nait]	*n.* 밤 at night 밤에	
midnight [mídnàit]	*n.* 자정, 한밤중 at midnight 한밤중에	
tonight [tənáit]	*n.* 오늘 밤 at eight o'clock tonight 오늘 밤 8시에	
time [taim]	*n.* 시간 waste time 시간을 소비하다	
o'clock [əklɑk]	*n.* ~시, 정각 at 5 o'clock 5시에	

hour
[áuər]
n. 시간, 1시간
half an hour 반시간, 30분

minute
[mínit]
n. 분
in 5 minutes 5분 후에

second
[sék-ənd]
n. 초
in a second 곧, 바로

quarter
[kwɔ́ːrtər]
n. 15분, 4분의
1 at quarter to three 3시 15분에

half
[hæf]
n. 30분
at half past ten 10시 30분에

previous
[príːviəs]
a. 이전의
a previous engagement 선약

forever
[fərévəːr]
ad. 영원히
remain unchanged forever 영구불변하다

forward
[fɔ́ːrwəːrd]
ad. 앞으로
from this time forward 금후

ever
[évər]
ad. 이전에, 언제나
ever since 그 후 내내

later
[léitəːr]
ad. 나중에
sooner or later 조만간, 언젠가는

next
[nekst]
ad. 다음에
next month 다음 달

someday [sʌ́mdèi]	*ad.* 언젠가(미래) someday soon 가까운 날에
sometimes [sʌ́mtàimz]	*ad.* 때때로 sometimes happen 때때로 일어나다
date [deit]	*n.* 날짜 the date of one's birth 생년월일
century [séntʃuri]	*n.* 세기, 100년 in the 19th century 19세기에
era [íərə]	*n.* 시대, 연대 the Victorian era 빅토리아 여왕 시대
now [nau]	*ad.* 지금 from now on 이후로는, 앞으로는
ago [əgóu]	*a. ad.* ~전에, 이전에 a long time ago 오래 전에
since [sins]	*ad.* ~이래로 since then 그때 이후로, 그때부터
until [əntíl]	*prep.conj.* ~까지(=till) until tomorrow morning 내일 아침까지
period [píəriəd]	*n.* 기간 a period of change 변화기
moment [móumənt]	*n.* 순간 at the moment 바로 지금

permanent
[pə́:rmənənt]

a. 영구한, 영원의
a permanent residence 영구거주

constant
[kánstənt]

a. 불변의, 일정의
at constant speed 일정한 속도로

temporary
[témpərèri]

a. 임시의, 일시의
a temporary residence 임시 처소

fast
[fæst]

a. 빠른
a fast reading 속독

rapid
[rǽpid]

a. 빠른
a rapid growth 급성장

early
[ə́:rli]

ad. 이른, 빠른
early in the morning 아침 일찍

slow
[slou]

a. 느린, 더딘
a slow train 완행열차

late
[leit]

a. 늦은
late in the morning 아침 느지막이

■ 때

year
[jiə:r]

n. 해, 년
last year 작년

yearly
[jíə:rli]

a. ad. 매년(의)
the yearly mean 연평균

annual
[ǽnjuəl]

a. 1년의, 연간의

an annual salary 연봉

month
[mʌnθ]

n. 달

the monthly mean 월평균

monthly
[mʌ́nθli]

a. ad. 매달(의)

at the end of the month 월말에

day
[dei]

n. 하루, 낮

take a day off 하루 쉬다

daily
[déili]

a. 매일의

daily life 일상생활

today
[tədéi]

n. 오늘

today's newspaper 오늘 신문

yesterday
[jéstərdèi]

n. 어제

the day before yesterday 그저께

tomorrow
[təmɔ́:rou]

n. 내일

the day after tomorrow 모레

week
[wi:k]

n. 1주

the news of the week 주간 뉴스

weekly
[wí:kli]

a. ad. 매주(의)

a weekly magazine 주간지

weekend
[wí:kènd]

n. 주말

a weekend journey 주말여행

■ 월

calendar
[kǽləndər]

n. 달력

lunar calendar 음력 / solar calendar 양력

January
[dʒǽnjuèri]

n. 일월

on the 1st of January 1월 1일에

February
[fébruèri]

n. 이월

February has 29 days in a leap year
윤년에는 2월이 29일 있다.

March
[mɑ:rtʃ]

n. 삼월

late in March 3월 하순에

April
[éiprəl]

n. 사월

at the end of April 4월 말에

May
[mei]

n. 오월

from April to May 4월에서 5월까지

June
[dʒu:n]

n. 유월

at the begining of June 6월 초에

July
[dʒu:lái]

n. 칠월

on July 10 7월 10일에

August
[ɔ́:gəst]

n. 팔월

on August 3 8월 3일에

September
[səptémbər]

n. 구월

a letter dated September 10
9월 10일 날짜로 된 편지

October
[ɑktóubər]

n. 시월

a child born in October 10월생의 아이

November
[nouvémbəːr]

n. 십일월

in November 11월에

December
[disémbər]

n. 십이월

the December number (잡지의) 12월호

season
[síːz-ən]

n. 계절, 철

the four seasons 사계절

■ 계절

spring
[spriŋ]

n. 봄

in the spring of 2002 2002년의 봄에

summer
[sʌ́mər]

n. 여름

the coming summer vacation 올 여름 휴가

autumn
[ɔ́ːtəm]

n. 가을

fine autumn weather 맑은 가을 날씨

winter
[wíntəːr]

n. 겨울

pass the winter 겨울을 나다

summer solstice
[sʌ́mər sɑ́lstis]

n. 하지

point of summer solstice 하지점

winter solstice
[wíntəːr sɑ́lstis]

n. 동지

red-bean gruel taken on the winter solstice 동지팥죽

autumn equinox
[ɔ́ːtəm íːkwənɑ̀ks]

n. 추분

autumn equinox tide (해양과학) 추분조(秋分潮)

spring equinox
[spriŋ íːkwənɑ̀ks]

n. 춘분

the Spring[Vernal] Equinox Day
춘분의 날

■ 요일

Sunday
[sʌ́ndei]

n. 일요일

on Sunday afternoon 일요일 오후에

Monday
[mʌ́ndei]

n. 월요일

on Monday morning 월요일 아침에

Tuesday
[tjúːzdei]

n. 화요일

Tuesday of this week 금주 화요일

Wednesday
[wénzdèi]

n. 수요일

last Wednesday 지난 주 수요일

Thursday
[θə́ːrzdei]

n. 목요일

next Thursday 다음 주 목요일

Friday [fráidei]	*n.* 금요일 Black Friday 추수감사절 연휴 이후 첫 금요일
Saturday [sǽtəːrdei]	*n.* 토요일 Saturday-to-Monday 토요일부터 월요일까지의

■ 기념일

anniversary [æ̀nəvə́ːrsəri]	*n.* 기념일 one's wedding anniversary 결혼기념일 silver wedding anniversary 은혼식 golden wedding anniversary 금혼식
birthday [bə́ːrθdèi]	*n.* 생일 the 60th anniversary of one's birth 환갑
ceremony [sérəmòuni]	*n.* 식, 의식 a marriage ceremony 결혼식
Easter [íːstər]	*n.* 부활절 an Easter egg 부활절의 달걀
Halloween [hæ̀ləwín]	*n.* 할로윈 give a Halloween party 할로윈 파티를 열다
Christmas [krísməs]	*n.* 크리스마스 white Christmas 눈이 내린 크리스마스
year-end party [jíəːr énd páːrti]	*n.* 송년파티 hold a year-end party 송년회를 열다

farewell party
[fɛ̀ərwél pá:rti]

n. 송별회

miss a farewell party 송별회에 빠지다

welcome party
[wélkəm pá:rti]

n. 환영회

attend a welcome party 환영회에 참석하다

surprise party
[sərpráiz pá:rti]

n. 깜짝파티

give a surprise party 깜짝 파티를 열다

housewarming party
[hauswɔ́ərmiŋ pá:rti]

n. 집들이

give a housewarming party 집들이를 하다

PART 02

일상
생활

01 하루

■ 하루의 생활

lie
[lai]
v. 눕다
lie in bed 침대에 눕다

sit
[sit]
v. 앉다
sit on a chair 의자에 앉다

stand
[stænd]
v. 서다
stand straight 똑바로 서다

sleep
[sli:p]
v. 잠자다
sleep well 잘 자다

get up
[get ʌp]
v. 자리에서 일어나다
get up at 6:30 6시 30분에 일어나다

rest
[rest]
v. 쉬다, 휴식하다
rest for 20 minutes 20분 쉬다

put
[put]
v. 두다, 놓아두다
put a glass on the table
식탁위에 유리컵을 놓다

push
[puʃ]

v. 밀다, 누르다

push the button 버튼을 누르다

bring
[briŋ]

v. 가져오다, 데려오다

bring a friend to the party
친구를 파티에 데려오다

take
[teik]

v. 취하다, 데리고 가다

take a dog for a walk 개를 산책에 데려가다

carry
[kǽri]

v. 휴대하다, 가지고 있다

carry a camera in a bag
카메라를 가방에 가지고 다니다

make
[meik]

v. 만들다, 제작하다

make coffee 커피를 만들다

create
[kriéit]

v. 창조하다, 만들다

create jobs 일자리를 창출하다

open
[óupən]

v. 열다

open the window 창문을 열다

close
[klouz]

v. 닫다

close the window 창문을 닫다

turn
[təːrn]

v. 돌리다, 회전하다

turn right 우회전하다

break
[breik]

v. 부수다, 깨뜨리다

break a window 창문을 깨뜨리다

use [juːz]	*v.* 쓰다, 사용하다 **use a cellular phone** 휴대 전화를 사용하다
keep [kiːp]	*v.* 유지하다, 계속하다 **keep silence** 침묵을 지키다
throw [θrou]	*v.* 던지다 **throw a bone to a dog** 개에게 뼈다귀를 던져주다
collect [kəlékt]	*v.* 모으다, 수집하다 **collect information** 정보를 수집하다

02 입는 것(衣)

의복

clothes
[klouðz]
n. 의복
custom clothes 맞춤복

ready-to wear
[réadi tu wɛəːr]
a. 기성복의
ready-to wear clothing 기성복

suit
[suːt]
n. 양복(한 벌 정장)
a suit of clothes 옷 한 벌

casual
[kǽʒuəl]
a. 캐주얼한
prefer casual wear 캐주얼한 복장을 좋아하다

jacket
[dʒǽkit]
n. 상의
a life jacket 구명 재킷

blouse
[blaus, blauz]
n. 블라우스
a green silk blouse 초록색 실크 블라우스

coat
[kout]
n. 코트(웃옷)
put on a coat 코트를 입다

sweater
[swétər]

n. 스웨터

a handwoven sweater 손으로 짠 스웨터

turtleneck
[tə́:rtlnèk]

n. 목티

a turtleneck sweater 터틀넥의 스웨터

cardigan
[ká:rdigən]

n. 카디건

a cotton cardigan 면 카디건

vest
[vest]

n. 조끼

a bullet-proof vest 방탄조끼

skirt
[skə:rt]

n. 치마

a pleated skirt 주름치마

trousers
[tráuzə:rz]

n. 바지

a coat with trousers to match 바지와 어울리는 웃옷

pants
[pænts]

n. 바지

a short pants 반바지

underwear
[ʌ́ndərwèər]

n. 속옷

thermal underwear 보온 내의

bra
[brɑ:]

n. 브래지어

an A-cup bra A컵의 브래지어

pajamas
[pədʒɑ́:məz]

n. 잠옷

a suit[pair] of pajamas 파자마 한 벌

02 입는 것

swimsuit
[swímsùːt]
n. 수영복
a one-piece swimsuit 원피스 수영복

overalls
[óuvərɔ̀ːlz]
n. 멜빵작업바지
a pair of overalls 한 벌의 작업 바지

uniform
[júːnəfɔ̀ːrm]
n. 유니폼
a nurse's uniform 간호원 유니폼

jeans
[dʒiːnz]
n. 청바지
a faded pair of blue jeans
색이 빠진 청바지 한 벌

shirt
[ʃəːrt]
n. 셔츠
a medium-sized shirt M사이즈의 셔츠

tight
[tait]
a. 꼭 끼는
a skin-tight dress 몸에 꼭 들러붙는 드레스

loose
[luːs]
a. 헐거운
loose-fitting clothes 헐거운 옷

stocking
[stákiŋ]
n. 스타킹
nylon stockings 나일론 스타킹

pantyhose
[pǽntihòuz]
n. 팬티스타킹
wear a pantyhose 팬티스타킹을 신다

high heels
[hai hiːlz]
n. 하이힐
wear high hills 뾰족구두를 신다

shoes
[ʃuːs]

n. 구두

ready-made shoes 기성화

sneakers
[sníːkəːrs]

n. 운동화

play tennis in sneakers
운동화를 신고 테니스 하다

sandals
[sǽndls]

n. 샌들

rubber-soled sandals 고무창을 댄 샌들

boots
[buːts]

n. 부츠

lace-up boots 끈으로 매게 된 부츠

socks
[sɑks]

n. 양말

pull on socks 양말을 신다

wear
[wɛəːr]

v. 입다

wear black 검은 옷을 입고 있다

take off
[teikɔːf]

v. 벗다

take off one's coat 상의를 벗다

change
[tʃeindʒ]

v. 바꾸다, 갈아입다

change shirts 셔츠를 갈아입다

try on
[traiɑn]

v. 입어보다

try on a new suit 새옷을 입어보다

dress
[dres]

v. 옷을 입다

be dressed up 옷을 잘 차려 입고 있다

collar
[kálər]

n. 깃, 칼라

a stand-upcollar 세운 칼라

pocket
[pákit]

n. 주머니

an empty pocket 무일푼(인 사람)

button
[bʌ́tn]

n. 단추

lose a button 단추를 잃다

belt
[belt]

n. 허리띠

a belt buckle 벨트 고리

fashionable
[fǽʃənəbəl]

a. 유행의

fashionable clothes 유행하는 의상

formal
[fɔ́ːrm-əl]

a. 정식(장)의

wear formal attire 정장하다

tailor
[téiləːr]

n. 재단사, 재봉사

tailor shop 양복점

size
[saiz]

n. 크기, 치수

size the clothes into three classes
의복을 3단계로 분류하다

sleeve
[sliːv]

n. 소매

long-sleeved 긴소매의
short-sleeved 반소매의

sleeveless
[slíːvlis]

a. 민소매

a sleeveless sweater 민소매 스웨터

material [mətí-əriəl]
n. 재료, 소재
cut material with scissors 가위로 옷감을 베다

textile [tékstail, -til]
n. 직물, 옷감
a textile factory 직물공장

texture [tékstʃəːr]
n. 피륙, 천
smooth texture 부드러운 천

■ 화장과 청결

make-up [meikʌp]
n. 화장
make-up base 기초화장

cosmetics [kazmétiks]
n. 화장품
hypoallergenic cosmetics 저자극성 화장품

lotion [lóuʃən]
n. 로션
moisturizing lotion 보습 로숀

lipstick [lípstìk]
n. 립스틱
wear lipstick 립스틱을 바르다

cream [kriːm]
n. 크림
a skin cream 영양 크림

foundation [faundéiʃ-ən]
n. 파운데이션
put on foundation cream 파운데이션을 바르다

eye shadow [aiʃǽdou]
n. 아이섀도
put on eye shadow 아이섀도를 하다

mascara
[mæskǽrə]

n. 마스카라

apply a coat of mascara
마스카라를 한 꺼풀 바르다

drier
[dráiər]

n. 드라이기

a hair drier 헤어드라이어

manicure
[mǽnəkjùə:r]

v. 매니큐어를 하다

manicure one's nail 손톱에 매니큐어를 하다

toothbrush
[tú:θbrʌ̀ʃ]

n. 칫솔

brush one's teeth 칫솔로 이를 닦다

toothpaste
[tú:θpèist]

n. 치약

squeeze toothpaste out 치약을 짜내다

soap
[soup]

n. 비누

soap bubbles 비누 거품

shampoo
[ʃæmpú:]

n. 샴푸

body shampoo 바디샴푸

skin
[skin]

n. 피부

skin care 피부미용관리

wash
[wɑʃ]

v. 씻다 *n.* 씻기

have a wash and brush up
세수하고 머리 빗다

bath
[bæθ]

n. 목욕

take a bath 목욕하다

shower
[ʃáuə:r]

n. 샤워

shower gel 샤워 젤

towel
[táu-ə]

n. 수건

a bath towel 목욕 수건

beauty salon
[bjú:ti səlán]

n. 미용실

go to the beauty salon 미용실에 가다

barbershop
[bá:rbərʃàp]

n. 이발소

at the barbershop 이발소에서

permanent
[pá:rmənənt]

n. 파마

go to the beauty parlor for a permanent
파마하러 미장원에 가다

cut
[kʌt]

v. 자르다

have hair cut 머리를 커트하다

hair spray
[hɛər sprei]

n. 헤어스프레이

spray-on hair lacquer 분무용 헤어스프레이

brush
[brʌʃ]

n. 솔

a shoe brush 구둣솔

trim
[trim]

v. 손질하다

trim one's nails 손톱을 깎다

massage
[məsá:ʒ]

v. 마사지하다

massage oil into the skin
피부에 오일을 발라 마사지하다

mirror
[mírə]

n. 거울

look into a mirror 거울을 보다

shave
[ʃeiv]

v. 면도하다

shave a customer 손님을 면도해 주다

perfume
[pə́ːrfjuːm]

n. 향수

put on perfume 향수를 바르다

■ 액세서리

accessory
[æksésəri]

n. 액세서리

accessories to go with this dress
이 옷에 어울리는 액세서리

real
[ríː-əl]

a. 진짜의

real pearls 진짜 진주

fake
[feik]

a. 가짜의

fake jewelry 모조 보석

precious
[préʃəs]

a. 귀중한, 값비싼

precious garments 값비싼 의상.

jewel
[dʒúːəl]

n. 보석

a jewel box 보석 상자

diamond
[dáiəmənd]

n. 다이아몬드

a diamond ring 다이아몬드 반지

gold
[gould]

n. 금

a gold bracelet 금팔찌

silver
[sílvəːr]

n. 은

solid silver 순은

ring
[riŋ]

n. 반지

a wedding ring 결혼반지

bracelet
[bréislit]

n. 팔찌

wear a golden bracelet 금팔찌를 끼다

wrist watch
[rist watʃ]

n. 손목시계

a gold wrist watch 금 손목시계

handbag
[hǽndbæ̀g]

n. 핸드백

an alligator handbag 악어 핸드백

brooch
[broutʃ]

n. 브로치

a gold brooch 금 브로치

tie
[tái]

n. 넥타이

tie pin 넥타이핀

scarf
[skaːrf]

n. 스카프

a silk scarf 실크 스카프

shawl
[ʃɔːl]

n. 숄

a silk shawl interwoven with gold
금이 섞인 비단 숄

earrings
[íərìŋz]

n. 귀걸이

silver earrings 은 귀걸이

necklace
[néklis]

n. 목걸이

wear a necklace. 목걸이를 하다

treasure
[tréʒər]

n. 보물

a treasure chest 보물 상자

emerald
[émərəld]

n. 에메랄드

a brooch of diamonds and emeralds
다이아몬드와 에메랄드로 된 브로치

ruby
[rúːbi]

n. 루비

a ruby ring 루비 반지

pearl
[pəːrl]

n. 진주

a pearl necklace 진주 목걸이

coral
[kɔ́ːrəl]

n. 산호

red coral 홍산호

crystal
[krístl]

n. 수정

crystal ware 크리스털 세공

ivory
[áivəri]

n. 상아

imitation ivory 모조 상아

pendant
[péndənt]

n. 펜던트

take a pendent off 펜던트를 풀다

■ 잡화

bag
[bæg]

n. 가방

a shopping-bag 쇼핑백

hat
[hæt]

n. (테가 있는) 모자

a straw hat 밀짚모자

cap
[kæp]

n. (테가 없는) 모자

a baseball cap 야구 모자

glasses
[glǽsiz]

n. 안경

wear strong glasses 도수가 높은 안경을 끼다

cigarette
[sìgərét]

n. 담배

light a cigarette 담배에 불을 붙이다

ashtray
[ǽʃtrèi]

n. 재떨이

empty an ashtray 재떨이를 비우다

handkerchief
[hǽŋkərtʃif]

n. 손수건

linen handkerchiefs 린넨으로 된 손수건

umbrella
[ʌmbrélə]

n. 우산

put up an umbrella 우산을 받다

parasol
[pǽrəsɔ̀ːl]

n. 양산

open a parasol 양산을 펴다

necktie
[néktài]

n. 넥타이

tie a necktie 넥타이를 매다

glove
[glʌv]

n. 장갑

woolen gloves 털장갑

wallet
[wálit]

n. 지갑 (=purse)

a leather wallet 가죽 지갑

comb
[koum]

n. 빗

a pocket comb 휴대용 빗

mirror
[mírər]

n. 거울

a hand mirror 손거울

suitcase
[súːtkèis]

n. 여행가방

a man with a suitcase 여행가방을 가진 사람

muffler
[mʌ́fləːr]

n. 머플러

a woolen muffler 모직 머플러

fan
[fæn]

n. 부채

fold a fan 부채를 접다

electric fan
[iléktrik fæn]

n. 선풍기

turn off an electric fan 선풍기를 끄다

belt
[belt]

n. 벨트

a leather belt 가죽벨트

contact lens
[kántækt lenz]

n. 콘택트렌즈

wear contact lenses 콘택트렌즈를 끼다

ribbon
[ríbən]

n. 리본

put on a ribbon 리본을 달다

sunglasses
[sʌ́nglæ̀siz]

n. 선글라스

designer sunglasses
유명 디자이너가 만든 선글라스

■ 색

red
[red]

n. 빨간색

a red car 빨간 자동차

blue
[bluː]

n. 파란색

deep blue sea 검푸른 바다

light blue
[lait bluː]

n. 하늘색

light blue eyes 연한 푸른색 눈동자

navy blue
[néivi bluː]

n. 짙은 청색

a navy blue suit 짙은 청색 정장

white
[hwait]

n. 흰색

a white lily 흰나리

black
[blæk]

n. 검정색

black clouds 먹구름

yellow
[jélou]

n. 노란색

yellowing autumn leaves
가을 잎을 노랗게 물들이는

green
[griːn]

n. 녹색

green bananas 설익은 바나나

light green [lait gri:n]	*n.* 연두색	dress in light green 연두색 옷을 입다
orange [ɔ́(:)rindʒ]	*n.* 오렌지색	a pale shade of orange 연한 주황색 색조
pink [piŋk]	*n.* 핑크색	dressed in pink 분홍색 옷을 입은
purple [pə́:rpəl]	*n.* 보라색	dye purple 자줏빛으로 물들이다
brown [braun]	*n.* 갈색	brown eyes 갈색 눈동자
gold [gould]	*n.* 금색	pure gold 순금
golden [góuldən]	*a.* 금빛의	golden hair 금빛 머리
silver [sílvəːr]	*n.* 은색	the silver moon 은빛 달
gray [grei]	*n.* 회색	a grey suit 회색 양복
beige [beiʒ]	*a.* 베이지색의	a beige carpet 베이지색 카펫
cream [kri:m]	*n.* 크림색	paint cream 크림색으로 칠하다

bright
[brait]

a. 밝은

bright sunshine 밝은 햇빛

dark
[dɑːrk]

a. 어두운, 짙은

dark eyes 검은[다갈색] 눈

bluish
[blúːiʃ]

a. 푸르스름한

eyes of **bluish** green 청록색 눈동자

먹는 것(食)

■ 식사 전반

cooking
[kúkiŋ]

n. 요리
home cooking 가정 요리

nutrition
[nju:tríʃ-ən]

n. 영양
inadequate nutrition 불충분한 영양

food
[fu:d]

n. 음식
tempting food 미각을 돋우는 음식

fast
[fæst]

n. 단식
go on a fast of five days
5일간의 단식을 시작하다

abstinence
[ǽbstənəns]

n. 금주
total abstinence 절대 금주

drinking
[dríŋkiŋ]

n. 음주
drinking habit 술버릇

overdrinking
[òuvərdríŋkíŋ]

n. 과음
overdrinking oneself 과음하여 탈나다

hangover
[hǽŋòuvər]

n. 숙취

suffer from hangover 숙취로 고생하다

overeating
[òuvərí:tiŋ]

n. 과식

sickness arising from overeating
과식에서 오는 병

■ 식당

meal
[mi:l]

n. 식사, 끼니

have[take] a meal 식사하다

menu
[ménju]

n. 메뉴, 식단

make out a menu 식단을 짜다

restaurant
[rést-ərənt]

n. 음식점, 식당

eat at Japanese restaurant
일식요리점에서 식사하다

cafe
[kæféi]

n. 카페

go to cafe for coffee 커피 마시러 카페에 가다

buffet
[bəféi]

n. 뷔페

buffet lunch 뷔페식 점심 식사

breakfast
[brékfəst]

n. 아침식사

have a good breakfast
충분한 아침 식사를 하다

lunch
[lʌntʃ]

n. 점심식사

out to lunch 점심 먹으러 외출 중인

dinner
[dínər]

n. 저녁식사

give a dinner 저녁을 한턱내다

snack
[snæk]

n. 간식

have a snack 간식을 들다
night snack 밤참

eat out
[íːt aut]

v. 외식하다

eat out once a week 일주일에 한번 외식하다

epicure
[épikjùər]

n. 미식가, 식도락가

an epicure of the wine bottle 와인 미식가

food coupon
[fuːd kjúːpɑn]

n. 식권

buy a month's worth of meal coupons
한 달 치 식권을 사다

wet towel
[wet táu-əl]

n. 물수건

rub one's hands on the wet towel
물수건으로 손을 잘 닦다

recommendation
[rèkəmendéiʃən]

n. 추천요리

chef's recommendation 주방장 추천요리

specialty
[spéʃəlti]

n. 특선요리

the specialty of the house 그 집의 특선요리

order
[ɔ́ːrdər]

n. 주문

give a order 주문하다

appetizer
[ǽpitàizər]

n. 전채, 식욕을 돋우는 것

appetizer wine 식욕을 돋우는 술

waiter
[wéitəːr]

n. 웨이터, 종업원

ask the waiter for the bill
종업원에게 계산서를 달라고 하다

tip
[tip]

n. 팁

give a tip to a waitress 여종업원에게 팁을 주다

dessert
[dizə́ːrt]

n. 후식, 디저트

have an ice cream for dessert
후식으로 아이스크림을 먹다

■ 요리 일반

boiled rice
[bɔild rais]

n. 밥

boil rice 밥을 짓다

side dish
[said diʃ]

n. 반찬

materials for making side dishes
반찬거리

lunch box
[lʌntʃ baks]

n. 도시락

prepare a lunch box 도시락을 싸다

rice cake
[rais keik]

n. 떡

stuff a rice cake 떡에 소를 박다

gruel
[grúːəl]

n. 귀리죽

boil rice into thick gruel 죽을 걸게 쑤다

soup
[suːp]

n. 국

soup makings 국거리

bread
[bred]

n. 빵

a loaf[slice] of bread 식빵 한 덩어리[조각]

egg
[eg]

n. 달걀, 계란

break an egg 달걀을 깨다

boiled egg
[bɔild eg]

n. 삶은 달걀

a soft-boiled egg 반숙한 달걀

fried egg
[fraid eg]

n. 계란프라이

a folded fried egg 알송편

eggroll
[egroul]

n. 계란말이

Egg roll cookies 에그롤쿠키

kimchi
[kímtʃiː]

n. 김치

sliced radish kimchi
[slaisd rǽdiʃ kímtʃi]

n. 깍두기

watery plain kimchi
[wɔ́ːtəri plein kímtʃi]

n. 물김치

pot stew
[pɑt stjuː]

n. 찌개

bean-paste pot stew
[biːn peist pɑt stjuː]

n. 된장찌개

fish pot stew
[fiʃ pɑt stjuː]

n. 생선찌개

kimchi stew *n.* 김치찌개
[kímtʃi stjuː]

bean curd *n.* 두부(=tofu)
[biːn kəːrd]

beef-rib soup *n.* 갈비탕
[biːf rib suːp]

loach soup *n.* 추어탕
[loutʃ suːp]

dog-meat soup *n.* 보신탕
[dɔ(ː)g miːt suːp]

steamed short ribs *n.* 갈비찜
[stiːmd ʃɔːrt ribs]

roast meat *n.* 불고기
[roust miːt]

(handmade) cut noodles *n.* 칼국수
[kʌt núːdls]

cold noodles *n.* 냉면
[kould núːdls]

noodle *n.* 국수
[núːdl]
make noodles 국수를 밀다

rice-cake soup *n.* 떡국
[rais keik suːp]

flat cake
[flæt keik]

n. 부침개

curry and rice
[kɔ́:ri ænd rais]

n. 카레라이스

curry and rice premixed 미리 섞인 카레라이스

spaghetti
[spəgéti]

n. 스파게티

seafood spaghetti 해물 스파게티

pizza
[pí:tsə]

n. 피자

a slice of pizza 피자 한조각

sandwich
[sǽndwitʃ]

n. 샌드위치

ham sandwiches 햄샌드위치

salad
[sǽləd]

n. 샐러드

a fruit salad 과일 샐러드

hamburger
[hǽmbə̀:rgər]

n. 햄버거

a hamburger roll 햄버거 롤

barbecue
[bá:rbikjù:]

n. 바비큐

barbecue sauce 바비큐[숯불구이]용 소스

noodles with bean sauce
[nú:dls wið bi:n sɔ:s]

n. 자장면

sweet-and-sour pork
[swi:t ænd sáuər pɔ:rk]

n. 탕수육

dumpling
[dʌ́mpliŋ]

n. 만두

a steamed dumpling 찐만두

steak
[steik]

n. 스테이크

Hamburg steak 햄버그스테이크

pork cutlet
[pɔːrk kʌ́tlit]

n. 돈까스

frozen pork cutlet 냉동 돈까스

beef cutlet
[biːf kʌ́tlit]

n. 비후까스

■ 디저트와 과자류

dessert
[dizə́ːrt]

n. 디저트

a dessert fork 디저트 포크

sweets
[swiːts]

n. 과자류

have a weakness for sweets
단것을 무척 좋아하다

sweet red-bean soup
[swiːt red biːn suːp]

n. 단팥죽

gum
[gʌm]

n. 껌

chew gum 껌을 씹다

candy
[kǽndi]

n. 사탕

be fond of candy 사탕을 좋아하다

cake
[keik]

n. 케이크

a birthday cake 생일케이크

hot cake
[hɑt keik]

n. 핫케이크

have a hot cake for dessert
디저트로 핫케이크를 먹다

hot-dog
[hɑt dɔ(:)g]

n. 핫도그

a hot-dog stand 핫도그 판매대

ice cream
[ais kri:m]

n. 아이스크림

an ice cream cone 아이스크림콘

sherbet
[ʃə́:rbit]

n. 셔벗

red-bean sherbet 팥빙수

cookie
[kúki]

n. 쿠키

chocolate-chip cookies 초콜릿칩 쿠키

biscuit
[bískit]

n. 비스킷

ginger biscuits 생강이 든 비스킷

doughnut
[dóunʌt]

n. 도넛

coffee and doughnuts 도넛과 커피

pudding
[púdiŋ]

n. 푸딩

custard pudding 커스터드 푸딩

chocolate
[tʃɔ́:kəlit]

n. 초콜릿

bitter chocolate 맛이 쓴 초콜릿

dried persimmon
[draid pə:rsímən]

n. 곶감

Cinnamon Punch with Dried Persimmon 수정과

■ 음료

soft drink
[sɔ(:)ft driŋk]

n. 청량음료

be on a soft drink diet
청량음료 마시는 양을 제한하고 있다

ice
[ais]

n. 얼음

ice tongs 얼음 집게

water
[wɔ́:tər]

n. 물

cold water 냉수

tea
[ti:]

n. 차

barley tea 보리차 / ginseng tea 인삼차

milk
[milk]

n. 우유

a milk diet 우유식

coffee
[kɔ́:fi]

n. 커피

order four coffees 커피 4잔을 주문하다

juice
[dʒu:s]

n. 주스, 즙

fruit juice 과즙

coke
[kouk]

n. 콜라

a Diet Coke 다이어트 콜라

soda
[sóudə]

n. 탄산음료, 소다수

a Scotch and soda 스카치 소다

■ 주류

thirsty
[θə́ːrsti]

a. 목마른
feel thirty 목마르다

drink
[driŋk]

v. 마시다
drink beer 맥주를 마시다

pour
[pɔːr]

v. 따르다, 붓다
pour a person some soju
…에게 소주를 따라주다

fill
[fil]

v. 채우다
fill a glass with water 컵에 물을 채우다

beverage
[bévəridʒ]

n. 마실 것, 음료
alcoholic beverages 알코올음료

alcohol
[ǽlkəhɔ̀(ː)l]

n. 알코올, 술
drink alcohol 술을 마시다

liquor
[líkər]

n. 술, 독주
the liquor traffic 주류 판매

beer
[biər]

n. 맥주
draft beer 생맥주 / bottled beer 병맥주
soju 소주

raw rice wine
[rɔː rais wain]

n. 막걸리
brew rice wine 막걸리를 익히다

refined rice wine
[rifáind rais wain]

n. 청주

special grade refined rice wine 특급청주

champagne
[ʃæmpéin]

n. 샴페인

dose champagne with sugar
샴페인에 설탕을 섞다

brandy
[brǽndi]

n. 브랜디

brandy and water 물 탄 브랜디

wine
[wain]

n. 포도주, 와인

sound wine 질이 좋은 포도주

whisky
[hwíski]

n. 위스키

sheer whisky 물 타지 않은 위스키

cocktail
[káktèil]

n. 칵테일

a cocktail circuit 칵테일파티

gin
[ʤin]

n. 진

gin and tonic 진 토닉

vodka
[vádkə]

n. 보드카

a vodka and lime 라임을 띄운 보드카 한잔

spirit
[spírit]

n. 화주, 독한 술

spirit and water 물을 탄 화주

brew
[bru:]

v. 양조하다

this year's brew 올해 양조된 술

distill
[distíl]

v. 증류하다

distilled water 증류수

accompaniment
[əkʌ́mpənimənt]

n. 안주

accompaniment to a drink 술 안주

toast
[toust]

v. 건배(하다)

toast a person's health
아무의 건강을 위해 건배하다

■ 식재료

meat
[miːt]

n. 고기

chilled meat 냉장육

pork
[pɔːrk]

n. 돼지고기

ribs of pork 돼지 갈비

beef
[biːf]

n. 쇠고기

the imported beef 수입 쇠고기

mutton
[mʌ́tn]

n. 양고기

mutton tallow 양기름

chicken
[tʃíkin]

n. 닭고기

chicken soup 닭고기 수프

egg
[eg]

n. 계란

a raw egg 날계란

butter
[bʌ́təːr]

n. 버터

spread toast with butter
토스토에 버터를 바르다

cheese
[tʃiːz]

n. 치즈

green cheese 생치즈

bacon
[béikən]

n. 베이컨

a rasher of bacon (얇게 썬) 베이컨 한 조각

sausage
[sɔ́ːsidʒ]

n. 소시지

ham sausage 햄 소시지

vegetable
[védʒətəbəl]

n. 야채

grow vegetables 채소를 재배하다

salad
[sǽləd]

n. 샐러드

a tomato salad 토마토 샐러드

fruit
[fruːt]

n. 과일

fruit juice 과일 주스

fish
[fiʃ]

n. 생선

a saltwater fish 바닷물고기

ham
[hæm]

n. 햄

ham and eggs (아침 식사의) 햄 에그

canned food
[kænd fuːd]

n. 통조림

openers for canned food 통조림따개

flour
[flauə*r*]

n. 밀가루

two cups of flour 밀가루 2컵

jam
[dʒæm]

n. 잼

bread and jam 잼을 바른 빵

honey
[hʌ́ni]

n. 꿀

(as) sweet as honey 꿀처럼 단

starch syrup
[stɑːrtʃ sírəp]

n. 물엿

starch syrup candy 엿

■ 조미료

spices
[spais]

n. 조미료, 양념

flavor food with spices 음식을 양념으로 맛내다

sesame
[sésəmi]

n. 깨

black sesame 검은 깨

vinegar
[vínigə*r*]

n. 식초

pickle in vinegar 식초에 담그다

pepper
[pépə*r*]

n. 후추

sprinkle pepper 후추를 치다

sugar
[ʃúgə*r*]

n. 설탕

a lump of sugar 각설탕 하나

salt
[sɔːlt]

n. 소금

preserve in salt 소금에 절이다

soybean paste
[sɔ́ibìːn peist]

n. 된장

boil in soybean paste 된장을 넣고 끓이다

soy sauce
[sɔi sɔːs]

n. 간장

put soy sauce 간장을 넣다

hot pepper paste
[hɑt pépər peist]

n. 고추장

barley hot pepper paste 찰보리 고추장

oil
[ɔil]

n. 기름

vegetable oil 식물성 기름

sesame oil
[sésəmi ɔil]

n. 참기름

extract some[the] sesame oil 참기름을 짜다

garlic
[gáːrlik]

n. 마늘

garlic bread 마늘빵

ginger
[ʤínʤər]

n. 생강

ginger tea 생강차

hot pepper
[hɑt pépər]

n. 고추

hot pepper powder 고춧가루

powdered red[hot] pepper
[páudərd red pépər]

n. 고춧가루

finely powdered red[hot] pepper 가는 고춧가루

shredded red pepper
[ʃredid red pépər]

n. 실고추

*seasoned red-pepper sauce 다대기

mustard
[mʌ́stəːrd]

n. 겨자

mustard seed 겨자씨

sauce
[sɔːs]

n. 소스

tomato sauce 토마토 소스

ketchup
[kétʃəp]

n. 케첩

a bottle of tomato ketchup 토마토케첩 한 병

mayonnaise
[mèiənéiz]

n. 마요네즈

dress with mayonnaise 마요네즈를 치다

dressing
[drésiŋ]

n. 드레싱

salad dressing 샐러드드레싱

potato powder
[pətéitou páudər]

n. 감자가루

powder sweet potato 분질 고구마

■ 조리법

recipe
[résəpìː]

n. 조리법

a recipe for a cake 케이크 만드는 법

cooking
[kúkiŋ]

n. 요리

home cooking 가정 요리

roast
[roust]

v. (오븐에) 굽다

roast the beans brown 콩을 노릇노릇 볶다

broil
[brɔil]

v. (불에) 굽다

broil a steak 스테이크를 굽다

grill
[gril]

v. (석쇠에) 굽다

a hot grill of oysters and bacon
갓 구운 굴과 베이컨 요리

fry
[frai]

v. (기름에) 튀기다

fry fish 생선을 튀기다

saute
[soutéi]

n. 소테(기름에 살짝 튀기다)

pork saute 돼지고기 소테

rare
[rɛəːr]

a. 설익은

rare roast beef 설익은 로스트비프

medium
[míːdiəm]

n. 중간정도로 익은

have one's steak medium
스테이크를 미디움으로 해달라고 하다

well-done
[wel dʌn]

n. 바짝 구운

prefer one's steak well done
바짝 구운 스테이크를 더 좋아하다

boil
[bɔil]

v. 삶다

boil an egg soft 계란을 반숙하다

steam
[stiːm]

v. 찌다

steamed pudding 찐 푸딩

bake
[beik]

v. (빵, 과자 등을) 굽다

bake cake in an oven 케이크를 오븐에서 굽다

toast
[toust]

v. 노르스름하게 굽다

toast bread 토스트를 굽다

cut [kʌt]	*v.* 자르다 cut a joint of meat 고깃덩이를 썰다
slice [slais]	*v.* 얇게 썰다 slice an apple 사과를 얇게 썰다
chop [tʃɑp]	*v.* 잘게 썰다 chop up a cabbage 양배추를 잘게 썰다
dice [dais]	*v.* 깍둑썰다 dice carrots 당근을 깍두기 꼴로 썰다
mince [mins]	*v.* (고기 등을) 저미다 minced lamb 다진 양고기
grind [graind]	*v.* 갈다, 빻다 grind coffee beans 커피콩을 갈다
grate [greit]	*v.* 비비다, 갈다 grate a carrot 당근을 갈다
peel [piːl]	*v.* 껍질을 벗기다 peel an orange 귤의 껍질을 벗기다
squeeze [skwiːz]	*v.* 바짝 짜다 squeeze a lemon dry 레몬즙을 모조리 짜내다
mix [miks]	*v.* 섞다, 혼합하다 mix flour and salt 밀가루와 소금을 섞다
blend [blend]	*v.* 섞다 blend red with white 빨강에다 흰색을 섞다

season [síːz-ən]	*v.* 맛내다, 양념하다 season a dish with salt 요리에 간을 맞추다
freeze [friːz]	*v.* 냉동하다 freeze meat 고기를 냉동하다
defrost [diːfrɔ́ːst]	*v.* 해동하다 defrost frozen food 냉동식품을 해동하다

■ 맛을 나타내는 형용사

taste [teist]	*n.* 맛 sweet to the taste 맛이 단
appetite [ǽpitàit]	*n.* 식욕, 입맛 loss of appetite 식욕부진
delicious [dilíʃəs]	*a.* 맛있는 a delicious dinner 맛있는 정찬
tasteless [téistlis]	*a.* 맛없는 tasteless dishes 맛없는 요리
flat [flæt]	*a.* 싱거운 The dishes taste flat. 음식이 싱겁다
salty [sɔ́ːlti]	*a.* 짠 be too salty 간이 짜다
bitter [bítər]	*a.* 쓴 a bitter medicine 쓴 약

hot
[hɑt]

a. 매운
hot curry 매운 카레 요리

sweet
[swiːt]

a. 단, 달콤한
sweet stuff 단것(과자류)

sour
[sáuəːr]

a. 신
a sour apple 신[덜 익은] 사과

sweet and sour
[swiːt ænd sáuəːr]

a. 새콤달콤한
Chinese sweet and sour pork
중국식 새콤달콤한 탕수육

astringent
[əstríndʒənt]

a. 떫은
astringent persimmons 떫은 감

greasy
[gríːsi]

a. 느끼한
greasy food 느끼한 음식

fishy
[fíʃi]

a. 비린내 나는
smell fishy 비린내가 나다

■ 기타

cigarette
[sìgərét]

n. 담배
a pack of cigarettes 담배 한 갑

smoking
[smóukiŋ]

n. 흡연
a smoking room 흡연실

ashtray
[ǽʃtrèi]

n. 재떨이

draw an ashtray near 재떨이를 끌어 당기다

match
[mætʃ]

n. 성냥

a box of matches 성냥 한 갑

lighter
[láitəːr]

n. 라이터

light a cigarette with a lighter
라이터로 담뱃불을 붙이다

cigarette butt
[sìgərét bʌt]

n. 담배꽁초

grind a cigarette butt under one's foot
담배꽁초를 발로 비비다

napkin
[nǽpkin]

n. 냅킨

a paper napkin 종이 냅킨

04 주거(住)

■ 주거 전반

residence
[rézid-əns]
n. 주거
a summer residence 여름 별장

house
[haus]
n. 집, 주택
a two-storied house 2층집

apartment
[əpáːrtmənt]
n. 아파트
an apartment-application deposit
주택청약예금

home
[houm]
n. 집, 가정
at home 집에서

dormitory
[dɔ́ːrmətɔ̀ːri]
n. 기숙사
live in a dormitory 기숙사 생활을 하다

company house
[kʌ́mpəni haus]
n. 사택
live in a company house 사택에서 살다

underground
[ʌ́ndərgràund]
n. 지하
an underground parking lot 지하 주차장

move [muːv]	*v.* 이사	move into a new house 새 집으로 이사하다
lease [liːs]	*n.* 임대	put (out) to lease 임대하다
rent [rent]	*n.* 집세	pay low rent 낮은 집세를 내다
real estate [ríːəl istéit]	*n.* 부동산	deal in real estate 부동산을 매매하다
real estate agency [ríːəl istéit éidʒənsi]	*n.* 부동산 중개소	real estate agency and rental 부동산중개 및 임대업
light and heat expenses [lait ænd hiːt ikspénsis]	*n.* 광열비	
public utility charges [pʌ́blik juːtíləti tʃɑːrdʒis]	*n.* 공공요금	curb the hikes of public utility charges 공공요금 인상을 억제하다
house owner [haus óunər]	*n.* 집 주인	a land and house owner 토지 및 가옥 소유자
house for rent [haus fɔːr rent]	*n.* 셋집	hunt for a house for rent 셋집을 구하러 돌아다니다
lodging [ládʒiŋ]	*n.* 하숙	live in lodgings 하숙 생활을 하다

build
[bild]

v. 짓다, 건축하다

build a house 집을 짓다

own
[oun]

v. 소유하다

own a duplex house 2세대 주택을 소유하다

remodel
[ri:mádl]

v. 개축하다, 개조하다

remodel a kitchen 부엌을 개조하다

interior
[intíəriər]

n. 실내, 내부

an interior decorator 실내 장식가

■ 주거의 구조

room
[ru:m]

n. 방

tidy up the room 방을 정돈하다

garret
[gǽrət]

n. 다락방

a poor man living in a garret
다락방에 사는 가난한 남자

study
[stʌ́di]

n. 서재

be confined in one's study
서재에 틀어박혀 있다

living room
[líviŋ ru:m]

n. 거실

dust the living room 거실의 먼지를 털다

bedroom
[bédru:m]

n. 침실

a charmingly decorated bedroom
아기자기하게 꾸민 침실

bathroom
[bǽθrù(ː)m]

n. 욕실, 화장실

go to the bathroom 화장실에 가다

bathtub
[bǽθtʌ̀b]

n. 욕조

refill a bathtub 욕조의 물을 갈다

washstand
[wáʃstænd]

n. 세면대

washstand tops 세면대 탑

kitchen
[kítʃin]

n. 부엌

prepare a meal in the kitchen
부엌에서 식사를 준비하다

sink
[siŋk]

n. 싱크대

wash the dishes in the sink
싱크대에서 설거지하다

garage
[gərάːʒ]

n. 차고

put a car in the garage 차고에 차를 넣다

doorbell
[dɔ́ːrbèl]

n. 초인종

ring the doorbell 초인종을 누르다

entrance
[éntrəns]

n. 입구, 현관

the main entrance to the building
그 건물의 정문

exit
[égzit]

n. 출구

an emergency exit 비상구

corridor
[kɔ́:ridər]

n. 복도

wipe the corridor with mop
복도를 걸레로 훔치다

balcony
[bǽlkəni]

n. 발코니

go out on the balcony 발코니로 나가다

floor
[flɔ:r]

n. 마루, 바닥

spill coffee on the floor 바닥에 커피를 엎지르다

window
[wíndou]

n. 창문

open the window 창문을 열다

door
[dɔ:r]

n. 문

close the door 문을 닫다

stair
[stɛə:r]

n. 계단

down stairs 아래층에서

story
[stɔ́:ri]

n. 층

a building of three stories 3층 건물

spacious
[spéiʃəs]

a. 넓은, 널따란

a very spacious kitchen 아주 넓은 부엌

basement
[béismənt]

n. 지하실

convert the basement into the spare bedroom 지하실을 여분의 침실로 개조하다

ceiling
[síːliŋ]

n. 천장

from floor to ceiling 바닥에서 천장까지

roof
[ruːf]
n. 지붕
a bird's nest on the roof 지붕 위의 새집

chimney
[tʃímni]
n. 굴뚝
sweep a chimney 굴뚝을 쑤시다

pillar
[pílər]
n. 기둥
a pillar of fire 불기둥

wall
[wɔːl]
n. 담, 벽
paint a wall 벽에 페인트를 칠하다

fence
[fens]
n. 울타리
put up a fence 울타리를 치다

yard
[jɑːrd]
n. 마당
a front yard 앞마당

garden
[gáːrdn]
n. 정원, 뜰
botanical gardens 식물원

faucet
[fɔ́ːsit]
n. 수도꼭지
turn on the faucet 수도꼭지를 틀다

drain
[drein]
n. 배수구, 하수시설
disinfect the drains 하수시설을 소독하다

gas
[gæs]
n. 가스
natural gas 천연가스

electricity
[ilèktrísəti]
n. 전기
static electricity 정전기

■ 가구와 세간

furniture
[fə́:rnitʃə:r]

n. 가구
a set of furniture 가구 한 벌

chair
[tʃɛər]

n. 의자
an easy chair 안락의자

desk
[desk]

n. 책상
an office desk 사무실 책상

bookshelf
[búkʃèlf]

n. 책꽂이
a built-in bookshelf 붙박이 책장

drawer
[drɔ́:ər]

n. 서랍
a cash drawer 현금 보관용 서랍

table
[téibəl]

n. 탁자
a dining table 식탁

tablecloth
[téibəlklɔ̀(:)θ]

n. 식탁보
a vinyl tablecloth 비닐 식탁보

clock
[klɑk]

n. 벽시계
an electric clock 전자시계

mirror
[mírər]

n. 거울
look in a mirror 거울을 보다

carpet
[ká:rpit]

n. 카펫
lay[put down] a carpet 카펫을 깔다

curtain
[kə́ːrtən]

n. 커튼

furl a curtain 커튼을 올리다

couch
[kautʃ]

n. 긴 의자

a studio couch 침대 겸용 의자

sofa
[sóufə]

n. 소파

sit on a sofa 소파에 앉다

cushion
[kúʃən]

n. 방석

sit on a cushion 방석에 앉다

vase
[veis]

n. 꽃병

put a rose in a vase 꽃병에 장미 한송이를 꽂다

calendar
[kǽləndər]

n. 달력

a desk calendar 탁상용 달력

key
[kiː]

n. 열쇠

a master key (여러 자물쇠에 맞는) 곁쇠, 마스터 키

shelf
[ʃelf]

n. 선반

a wall shelf 벽에 붙인 선반

mattress
[mǽtris]

n. 매트리스

make a bed 요를 깔다

blanket
[blǽŋkit]

n 담요

fold a blanket double 담요를 두 겹으로 접다

sheet
[ʃiːt]

n. 커버, 홑이불

ruffled sheets 구겨진 홑이불

cradle
[kréidl]

n. 요람

rock a cradle 요람을 흔들다

dresser
[drésər]

n. 화장대

a solid pine dresser
통소나무로 만든 화장대

closet
[klázit]

n. 벽장, 골방

set in closets 붙박이 장

chandelier
[ʃæ̀ndəlíər]

n. 샹들리에

the glitter of chandelier
샹들리에의 반짝거림

rug
[rʌg]

n. 깔개

a rug in front of the fire 난로 앞에 있는 깔개

cabinet
[kǽbənit]

n. 장

a bedroom cabinet 침실장

pillow
[pílou]

n. 베게

a high pillow 높은 베게

■ 가전제품

television
[téləvìʒ-ən]

n. 텔레비전

two television sets 2대의 텔레비전

stove
[stouv]

n. 난로

put a pan on the stove
스토브 위에 냄비를 올려놓다

radio
[réidiòu]

n. 라디오

listen to the radio 라디오를 듣다

camera
[kǽmərə]

n. 카메라

load a camera 카메라에 필름을 넣다

stereo
[stériòu]

n. 오디오

a car stereo 자동차 스테레오

personal computer
[pə́ːrsənəl kəmpjúːtər]

n. 개인용 컴퓨터 (=PC)

desktop personal computer 데스크톱

sewing machine
[sóuiŋ məʃíːn]

n. 재봉틀

a treadle sewing machine 발재봉틀

iron
[áiərn]

n. 다리미

a steam-iron 증기다리미

humidifier
[hjuːmídəfàiər]

n. 가습기

fill the humidifier with water 가습기에 물을 채우다

washing machine
[wáʃiŋ məʃíːn]

n. 세탁기

turn on a washing machine 세탁기를 돌리다

vacuum cleaner
[vǽkjuəm klíːnər]

n. 진공청소기

clean the room with vacuum cleaner 진공청소기로 방을 청소하다

dishwasher
[diʃ wɑ̀ʃər]

n. 식기 세척기

dishwasher detergent 식기 세척기 세제

outlet
[áutlet]

n. 콘센트

insert a plug in a wall outlet
콘센트에 플러그를 꽂다

photocopier
[fóutoukùpiə]

n. 복사기

a paper jam in the photocopier
복사기에서의 종이 걸림

calculator
[kǽlkjəlèitər]

n. 전자계산기

a pocket calculator 포켓용 계산기

facsimile / fax
[fæksíməli]/[fæks]

n. 팩시밀리, 팩스

send a letter by facsimile
팩스로 편지를 보내다

air conditioner
[ɛər kəndíʃənər]

n. 에어컨

an air conditioned building
냉방장치를 한 건물

electric razor
[iléktrik réizɔːr]

n. 전기면도기

use an electric razor 전기면도기를 사용하다

coffee maker
[kɔ́ːfi méikəːr]

n. 커피메이커

use coffee maker 커피메이커를 이용하다

fix
[fiks]

v. 고치다, 수선하다 (=repair)

fix a leaky faucet 새는 수도꼭지를 고치다

remote control
[rimóut kəntróul]

n. 리모컨

click the remote control 리모컨을 누르다

toaster
[tóustəːr]

n. 토스터기

a pop-up toaster 자동 토스터

oven
[ʌ́vən]

n. 오븐

take the bread out of the oven
오븐에서 빵을 꺼내다

CD player
[síːdíːpléiər]

n. CD플레이어

buy a new CD player 새 CD 플레이어를 사다

tape
[teip]

v. 녹화하다, 녹음하다

tape the baseball game 농구경기를 녹화하다

heater
[híːtər]

n. 난방장치

a gas heater 가스히터

electric fan
[iléktrik fæn]

n. 선풍기

the breeze from electric fan 선풍기의 바람

light
[lait]

n. 전등, 조명

put on the light 조명을 켜다

lamp
[læmp]

n. 램프

a spirit lamp 알코올램프

switch
[switʃ]

n. 스위치

an on-off switch 점멸(點滅) 스위치

■ 부엌용품

bowl
[boul]

n. 그릇

a bowl of soup 수프 한 그릇

dish
[diʃ]

n. 접시, 요리

a meat dish 고기 접시

plate
[pleit]

n. 접시

sandwiches on a plate 접시 위의 샌드위치

chopstick
[tʃápstìk]

n. 젓가락

a pair of chopsticks 젓가락 한 벌

spoon
[spuːn]

n. 숟가락

eat soup with a spoon 숟가락으로 수프를 먹다

fork
[fɔːrk]

n. 포크

eat with a knife and fork 나이프와 포크로 먹다

cup
[kʌp]

n. 컵, 잔

a cup of coffee 커피 한 잔

glass
[glæs]

n. 유리컵

a glass of milk 우유 한 컵

saucer
[sɔ́ːsəːr]

n. 받침 접시

a cup and saucer 컵과 컵받침

thermos
[θə́ːrməs]

n. 보온병

a thermos filled with soup
수프를 가득 담은 보온병

grater
[gréitər]

n. 강판

grate carrot with a grater 강판에 당근을 갈다

eggbeater
[eǵbì:tər]

n. 거품기

beat eggs with an eggbeater
거품기로 달걀을 거품내다

sieve
[siv]

n. 체로 치다

sieve flour 밀가루를 체로 치다

measuring cup
[méʒəriŋ kʌp]

n. 계량컵

use a measuring cup to add sugar
계량컵을 사용하여 설탕을 넣다

scale
[skeil]

n. 저울

weigh the flour on a scale
저울로 밀가루를 재다

oven
[ʌ́vən]

n. 오븐

bake a cake in the oven 오븐에 케이크를 굽다

stove
[stouv]

n. 스토브, 가스렌지

put a pan on the stove
스토브 위에 냄비를 올려 놓다

pot
[pɑt]

n. 냄비

cook stew in a pot 냄비에 찌개를 만들다

frying pan
[fraiŋ pæn]

n. 프라이팬

fry eggs in a frying pan
프라이 팬으로 계란을 후라이 하다

turner
[tə́:rnə:r]

n. 뒤집게

turn bacon and eggs with a turner
뒤집게로 베이컨과 계란을 뒤집다

knife
[naif]

n. 식칼

sharpen a knife 칼을 갈다

tablecloth
[téib-əklɔ̀(:)θ]

n. 식탁보

a check tablecloth 체크무늬 식탁보

tray
[trei]

n. 쟁반

a tea-tray 차 쟁반

kettle
[kétl]

n. 주전자

put a kettle of water on the stove
물을 담은 주전자를 난로에 얹다

dishwasher
[díʃwàʃər]

n. 설거지용 세제

do the dishes with a dishwasher
식기세제로 설거지하다

dishcloth
[díʃ[klɔ̀(:)θ]

n. 행주

wipe with a dishcloth 행주질하다

apron
[éiprən]

n. 앞치마

wear an apron 앞치마를 두르고 있다

cutting board
[kʌ́tiŋ bɔ:rd]

n. 도마

slice ham on a cutting board
도마에서 햄을 자르다

scoop
[skuːp]

n. 주걱

rice scoop 밥 주걱

ladle
[léidl]

n. 국자

pour soup with a ladle 국자로 수프를 뜨다

sink
[siŋk]

n. 개수대

a sink unit 싱크대

ventilation fan
[vèntəléiʃən fæn]

n. 환풍기

switch on the ventilation fan 환풍기를 켜다

freezer
[fríːzəːr]

n. 냉동고

a home freezer 가정용 냉동고

refrigerator
[rifrídʒərèitəːr]

n. 냉장고

put in a refrigerator 냉장고에 넣다

toaster
[tóustəːr]

n. 토스터기

toast bread in the toaster
토스터기에 빵을 굽다

microwave oven
[máikrouwèiv ʌ́vən]

n. 전자레인지

put frozen meat in the microwave oven
전자레인지에 냉동육을 넣다

blender
[bléndər]

n. 믹서

mix eggs and milk in a blender
믹서로 계란과 우유를 혼합하다

rice cooker
[rais kúkər]

n. 밥솥

electric rice cooker 전기밥솥

■ 기타 가사용품

housework
[háuswə̀ːrk]

n. 가사, 집안일
do housework 집안일을 하다

broom
[bru(ː)m]

n. 비, 빗자루
sweep with a broom 비로 쓸다

dustpan
[dʌ́stpæ̀n]

n. 쓰레받기
sweep into a dustpan 쓰레받기에 쓸어 담다

bucket
[bʌ́kit]

n. 양동이
empty a bucket 양동이를 비우다

duster
[dʌ́stər]

n 걸레
wipe with a wet duster 물걸레로 닦다

mop
[map]

n. 마포걸레, 대걸레
mop the floor 마루를 대걸레로 닦다

detergent
[ditə́ːrdʒənt]

n. 세제
a neutral detergent 중성세제

toilet paper
[tɔ́ilit péipər]

n. 화장지
a toilet roll 두루마리 화장지

garbage can
[gáːrbidʒ kæn]

n. 쓰레기통
throw garbage into a garbage can
쓰레기를 쓰레기통에 버리다

brush
[brʌʃ]

n. 솔
brush off dust 먼지를 솔로 털다

basin
[béisən]

n. 대야

a hand basin 세숫대야

laundry
[lɔ́:ndri]

n. 세탁, 세탁물

do the laundry 세탁하다

clothespin
[klouðpin]

n. 빨래집게

clip up on clothespin 빨래집게로 집다

cleaning
[klí:niŋ]

n. 청소

general cleaning 대청소

dust
[dʌst]

n. 먼지

lay dust 먼지를 가라앉히다

waste
[weist]

n. 쓰레기

food waste 음식 쓰레기

mosquito repellent
[məskí:tou ripélənt]

n. 모기향

burn mosquito repellent incense
모기향을 피우다

mold
[mould]

n. 곰팡이

green mold 푸른곰팡이

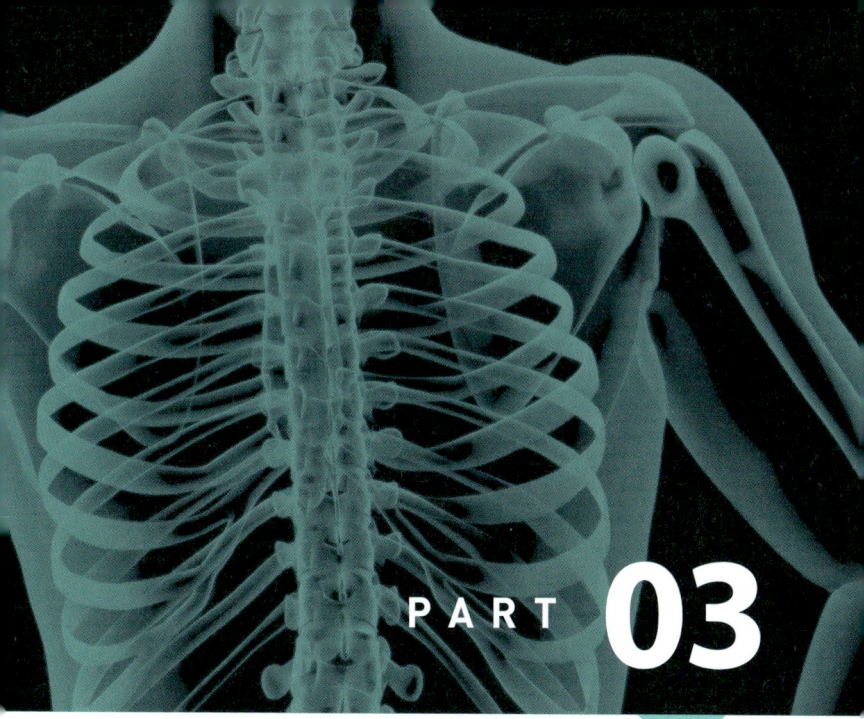

PART 03

인체와 건강

01 인체

■ 인체 전반

body
[bádi]

n. 육체
build up one's body 몸을 만들다[단련하다]

spirit
[spírit]

n. 정신
the world of spirit 정신세계

power
[páuər]

n 힘, 정력
full of energy 정력이 넘쳐

vigor
[vígər]

n. 기운, 활기
lose one's vigor 활기를 잃다

life
[laif]

n. 생명, 목숨
the origin of life 생명의 기원
a long life 장수

health
[helθ]

n. 건강
health care at the change of season
환절기의 건강관리

■ 인체의 명칭

head
[hed]

n. 머리
from head to foot 온몸, 전신

hair
[hɛər]

n. 머리카락
long hair 긴 머리

brain
[brein]

n. 뇌
have a good brain 머리가 좋다
brain death 뇌사

forehead
[fɔ́ːrhèd]

n. 이마
a high[wide] forehead 넓은 이마

face
[feis]

n. 얼굴
a sad face 슬픈 얼굴

temple
[témpəl]

n. 관자놀이
The temples throb with pain.
관자놀이가 쑤시고 아프다

dimple
[dímpəl]

n. 보조개
Her face dimples with a smile.
그녀는 웃으면 보조개가 진다

pimple
[pímpl]

n. 여드름
teenage pimples 십대 여드름

birthmark
[bə́ːrθmàːrk]

n. 모반, 점
a person with a birthmark 점박이

wrinkle
[ríŋkəl]

n. 주름
fine wrinkles 잔주름

discoloration
[diskʌləréiʃən]

n. 기미
have discoloration on the face
얼굴에 기미가 끼다

freckle
[frékl]

n. 주근깨
a freckled face 주근깨가 있는 얼굴

eye
[ai]

n. 눈
the naked eye 육안

pupil
[pjú:pəl]

n. 눈동자, 동공
the pupil of the eye 눈의 검은자위

eyesight
[aisàit]

n. 시력
have good eyesight 시력이 좋다

eyebrow
[aibràu]

n. 눈썹
bushy eyebrows 짙은 눈썹

eyelid
[ailìd]

n. 눈꺼풀
the upper eyelid 윗 눈꺼풀

double eyelid
[dʌ́bəl ailìd]

n. 쌍꺼풀
have double eyelid surgery done
쌍꺼풀수술을 하다

single eyelid
[síŋɡəl ailìd]

n. 홑꺼풀
She has single eyelids.
그녀는 쌍꺼풀이 없어요.

eyelashes
[aíl`æ`ʃis]

n. 속눈썹

by an eyelash 근소한 차이로

ear
[iər]

n. 귀

a keen ear 예민한 청력

cheek
[tʃi:k]

n. 볼(뺨)

chubby cheeks 통통한 볼

nose
[nouz]

n. 코

the bridge of the nose 콧대

nostril
[nástril]

n. 콧구멍

flared nostrils 벌름거리는 콧구멍

mouth
[mauθ]

n. 입

with one mouth 이구동성으로

tongue
[tʌŋ]

n. 혀

a coated tongue 설태(舌苔)

lip
[lip]

n. 입술

the upper lip 윗 입술

tooth
[tu:θ]

n. 이(치아)

brush one's tooth 이를 닦다

wisdom tooth
[wízdəm tu:θ]

n. 사랑니

cut a wisdom tooth 사랑니가 나다

canine tooth
[kéinain tu:θ]

n. 송곳니, 견치

canine tooth luxation 견치 탈구

snaggletooth
[snǽgəltùːθ]

n. 덧니

cut a snaggletooth 덧니가 나다

milk tooth
[milk tuːθ]

n. 젖니

mandible milk tooth 하악 유치

false[artificial] tooth
[fɔːls(ὰːrtəfíʃəl) tuːθ]

n. 의치

have a false tooth put in 의치를 해 넣다

gum
[gum]

n. 잇몸

an ulcerated gum 뭉크러진 잇몸

throat
[θrout]

n. 목구멍

a sore throat 인후염

esophagus
[isáfəgəs]

n. 식도

cancer of the esophagus 식도암

jaw
[dʒɔː]

n. 턱

punch on the jaw 턱에 펀치를 먹이다

chin
[tʃin]

n. 아래턱

a double chin 이중 턱

beard
[biərd]

n. 턱수염

a full beard 텁수룩한 턱수염

whisker
[hwískəːr]

n. 구레나룻

have a shaggy growth of whiskers
구레나룻이 텁수룩하게 나다

sideburns
[saidbə́ːrnz]

n. 짧은 구레나룻

grow sideburns 구레나룻을 기르다

mustache
[mʌ́stæʃ]

n. 콧수염

grow a mustache 콧수염을 기르다

neck
[nek]

n. 목

have a stiff neck 목이 뻣뻣하다

arm
[ɑːrm]

n. 팔

arm in arm 서로 팔을 끼고

elbow
[élbou]

n. 팔꿈치

an elbow joint 팔꿈치의 관절

wrist
[rist]

n. 손목

favor a sore wrist 아픈 손목을 돌보다

hand
[hænd]

n. 손

the right hand 오른손

fist
[fist]

n. 주먹

shake one's fist (화를 드러내며) 주먹을 쥐고 떨다

palm
[pɑːm]

n. 손바닥

sweaty palms 땀이 밴 손바닥

finger
[fíŋɡər]

n. 손가락

not lift a finger 손가락 하나 까딱하지 않다

thumb
[θʌm]

n. 엄지손가락

bite one's thumbs 초조하여 엄지손가락을 깨물다

index finger
[índeks fíŋɡər]

n. 집게손가락(인지)

rub one's thumb and index finger together 엄지 손가락과 인지를 포개어 비비다

middle finger
[mídl fíŋɡər]

n. 가운뎃손가락(중지)

cut one's middle finger 가운데 손가락을 베다

ring finger
[riŋ fíŋɡər]

n. 약손가락(무명지)

a ring on one's finger 손가락에 낀 반지

little finger
[lítl fíŋɡər]

n. 새끼손가락

turn a man round her little finger 남자를 마음대로 구슬리다

nail
[neil]

n. 손톱, 발톱

fingernail 손톱 / toenail 발톱

shoulder
[ʃóuldə:r]

n. 어깨

a person with broad shoulders 딱 벌어진 어깨를 가진 사람

side
[said]

n. 옆구리

the left side 왼편 옆구리

chest
[tʃest]

n. 가슴

chest trouble 폐병

breast
[brest]

n. 젖가슴

a pigeon breast 새가슴

nipple
[nípəl]

n. 젖꼭지

jogging nipple 조깅 유두 염증(셔츠에 쓸려서 생김)

navel [néivəl]	*n.* 배꼽 a deep[sunken] navel 움푹 들어간 배꼽
womb [wu:m]	*n.* 자궁 cancer of the womb 자궁암
waist [weist]	*n.* 허리 waist measurements 허리 치수
back [bæk]	*n.* 등 a rounded back 새우 등
rib [rib]	*n.* 갈비뼈, 늑골 a rib injury 늑골의 손상
buttocks [bʌ́təks]	*n.* 엉덩이 the left buttock 왼쪽 엉덩이
anus [éinəs]	*n.* 항문 artificial anus 인공항문
bowel movement [báuəl mú:vmənt]	*n.* 배변 have a bowel movement 변을 보다
leg [leg]	*n.* 다리 an artificial leg 의족
thigh [θai]	*n.* 넓적다리, 허벅지 the thigh-bone 대퇴골
lap [læp]	*n.* 무릎(앉았을 때 허리에서 무릎마디까지) rest one's head on lap 무릎베개하다

knee [niː]	*n.* 무릎 a knee-length skirt 무릎까지 오는 스커트
shin [ʃin]	*n.* 정강이 get kicked on the shin 정강이를 차이다
joint [dʒɔint]	*n.* 관절 knee joint 무릎관절
calf [kæf]	*n.* 종아리, 장딴지 get whipped on the calf 종아리를 맞다
ankle [ǽŋkl]	*n.* 발목 sprain the ankle 발목을 삐다
foot [fut]	*n.* 발 stand on one foot 한 발로 서다.
heel [hiːl]	*n.* 발뒤꿈치 out at (the) heel(s) 신발 뒤축이 닳아서
toe [tou]	*n.* 발가락 open-toed sandals 발가락 부분이 트인 샌들
big toe [big tou]	*n.* 엄지발가락 a big toe side rising part 엄지발가락측 입상부
second toe [sékənd tou]	*n.* 둘째발가락 second toe transfer 척골신경압박
third toe [θəːrd tou]	*n.* 셋째발가락 *toe out 밭장다리로 걷다

fourth toe
[fɔːrθ tou]

n. 넷째발가락

*toe the line 방침에 따르다

little toe
[lítl tou]

n. 새끼발가락

curl the little toe 새끼발가락을 구부리다

organ
[ɔ́ːrgən]

n. 장기, 기관

an organ transplant 장기 이식

heart
[hɑːrt]

n. 심장

the right[left] heart 우[좌]심실

liver
[lívər]

n. 간장

a liver complaint 간장병

lung
[lʌŋ]

n. 폐, 허파

lung power 폐활량

bronchus
[bráŋkəs]

n. 기관지

bronchus camera 기관지카메라

stomach
[stʌ́mək]

n. 배, 위

on an empty stomach 배가 고플 때에

bowel
[báuəl]

n. 창자

have a bowel trouble 장이 나쁘다

intestines
[intéstinz]

n. 장

have weak intestines 장이 나쁘다

small intestine
[smɔːl intéstin]

n. 소장

small intestine organ 소장 기관

large intestine [lɑːrdʒ intéstin]	*n.* 대장	large intestine cell 대장 세포
pancreas [pǽŋkriəs]	*n.* 췌장	pancreatitis 췌장염
spleen [spliːn]	*n.* 비장	a ruptured spleen 파열된 비장
bladder [blǽdər]	*n.* 방광	a bladder stone 방광 결석
kidney [kídni]	*n.* 신장	put a patient on a kidney machine 인공 신장을 환자에게 이식하다
spine [spain]	*n.* 척추	a spine-chilling horror story 등골이 오싹한 공포소설
flesh [fleʃ]	*n.* 살	proud flesh (상처가 아물면서 나오는) 새살
blood [blʌd]	*n.* 피, 혈액	loss of blood 출혈
bone [boun]	*n.* 뼈	cheek bones 광대뼈
muscle [mʌ́səl]	*n.* 근육	the calf muscle 종아리 근육

neuron
[njúərɑn]

n. 신경

a sensory (nerve) neuron 지각 신경 (=nerve)

cell
[sel]

n. 세포

stem cell 줄기세포

skin
[skin]

n. 피부

a skin disease 피부병

tendon
[téndən]

n. 힘줄

strain a tendon 힘줄을 접질리다

blood vessel
[blʌd vésəl]

n. 혈관

a capillary blood vessel 모세 혈관

arteries
[áːrtəriz]

n. 동맥

the main artery 대동맥

vein
[vein]

n. 정맥

the median vein 중정맥

02 건강

■ 생리적 현상

breath
[breθ]
n. 호흡, 숨
be short of breath 숨이 차다

sigh
[sai]
n. 한숨 *v.* 한숨 쉬다
give a sigh of relief 안도의 한숨을 쉬다

cough
[kɔ(:)f]
n. 기침
a dry cough 마른기침

sneeze
[sni:z]
n. 재채기 *v.* 재채기 하다
fetch a sneeze 재채기 하다

yawn
[jɔ:n]
n. 하품 *v.* 하품하다
with a yawn 하품을 하면서

heat
[hi:t]
n. 열, 뜨거움
in the heat of the day 한낮에

sweat
[swet]
n. 땀 *v.* 땀나다
break out in a cold sweat 식은땀이 나다

grime
[graim]

n. 때

a garment greasy with grime 때에 결은 옷

tear
[tiə:r]

n. 눈물

shed tears 눈물을 흘리다

snivel
[snívəl]

n. 콧물 *v.* 콧물을 흘리다

stop snivelling 코를 훌쩍이지 마라

saliva
[səláivə]

n. 침

spit saliva 침을 뱉다

wind
[wind]

n. 방귀 (=gas)

break wind 방귀를 뀌다

feces
[fí:si:z]

n. 똥, 대변

examine feces 대변 검사를 하다

urine
[júərin]

n. 오줌, 소변

pass (one's) urine 오줌 누다

hiccup
[híkʌp]

n. 딸꾹질 *v.* 딸꾹질 하다

have the hiccups 딸꾹질을 하다.

burp
[bə:rp]

n. 트림 *v.* 트림시키다

burp a baby 아기를 트림시키다

stretch
[stretʃ]

n. 기지개 *v.* 기지개를 켜다

with a yawn and a stretch
하품하며 기지개를 켜서

sleep [sliːp]	*v.* 잠자다 sleep well 잘 자다
nap [næp]	*n.* 낮잠 *v.* 낮잠 자다 take a nap 낮잠 자다
gooseflesh [guːsflèʃ]	*n.* 소름 *v.* 소름 돋다 be gooseflesh all over 온몸에 소름이 끼치다

■ 체력

physical [fízikəl]	*a.* 육체의, 신체의 physical strength 체력
weight [weit]	*n.* 몸무게, 체중 gain[lose] weight 체중이 늘다[줄다]
height [hait]	*n.* 신장 in height 높이[키]는
blood pressure [blʌd préʃər]	*n.* 혈압 bring down the blood pressure 혈압을 낮추다
normal blood pressure [nɔ́ːrməl blʌd préʃər]	*n.* 정상 혈압 *high[low] blood pressure 고[저]혈압
pulse [pʌls]	*n.* 맥박 a normal[rapid] pulse 정상적[빠른] 맥박

(body) temperature *n.* 체온
[témpərətʃuə:r]

take one's temperature 체온을 재다

eyesight
[áisàit]

n. 시력

a person with good[poor] eyesight
시력이 좋은[나쁜] 사람

hearing
[híəriŋ]

n. 청력

have a keen sense of hearing 청력이 좋다

voice
[vɔis]

n. 목소리

a sweet[beautiful] voice
달콤한[아름다운] 목소리

normal
[nɔ́:rməl]

a. 정상적인

normal mentality 정상적인 심리 상태

abnormal
[æbnɔ́:rməl]

a. 비정상적인

abnormal behavior 비정상적인 행위

03 질병

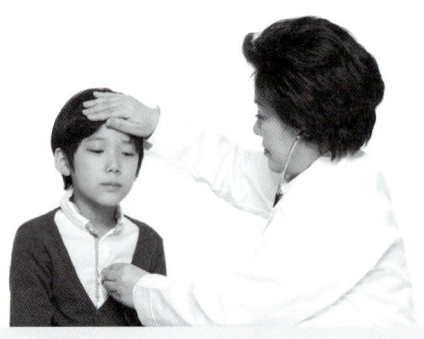

■ 병과 증상

symptom
[símptəm]
n. 증상
a subjective symptom 자각 증상

disease
[dizíːz]
n. 질병
a family disease 유전병

illness
[ílnis]
n. 병
serious illnesses 심각한 병

sickness
[síknis]
n. 병, 아픔
altitude sickness 고공병

ill
[il]
a. 아픈 (=sick)
be taken ill 병이 나다

acute
[əkjúːt]
a. 급성의
acute pneumonia 급성 폐렴

chronic
[kránik]
a. 만성의
chronic bronchitis 만성 기관지염

relapse
[rilǽps]

n. 악화, 재발

have a relapse 병이 도지다

cold
[kould]

n. 감기

be in bed with a cold 감기로 누워 있다

flu
[fluː]

n. 유행성 감기, 독감

catch (the) flu 유행성 감기에 걸리다.

fatigue
[fətíːg]

n. 피로, 피곤

suffer from fatigue 몸살이 나다

virus
[váiərəs]

n. 바이러스

the virus of scarlet fever 성홍열 바이러스

hangover
[hǽŋòuvər]

n. 숙취

have a hangover 숙취를 느끼다

fever
[fíːvər]

n. 열

a high[slight] fever 고열[미열]

scar
[skɑːr]

n. 상처

emotional scars 마음의 상처

vomit
[vámit]

v. 구토(하다)

die vomiting blood 피를 토하고 죽다

diarrhea
[dàiəríːə]

n. 설사

have diarrhea 설사를 하다.

nausea
[nɔ́ːziə]

n. 매스꺼움

feel nausea 속이 메스꺼워지다

dizziness
[dízinis]

n. 현기증
be subject to dizziness 어지럼을 타다

fracture
[frǽktʃəːr]

n. 골절
suffer a fracture 골절[접골]하다

break
[breik]

v. 부러뜨리다
break one's neck 목이 부러지다

headache
[hédèik]

n. 두통
have a bad headache 머리가 몹시 아프다

blood pressure
[blʌd préʃər]

n. 혈압
high[low] blood pressure 고혈압[저혈압]

burn
[bəːrn]

n. 화상
suffer a burn 화상을 입다

diabetes
[dàiəbíːtis]

n. 당뇨병
have diabetes 당뇨병을 앓다

heart disease
[hɑːrt dizíːz]

n. 심장병
be liable to heart disease
심장병에 걸리기 쉽다

heart attack
[hɑːrt ətǽk]

n. 심장발작
have a heart attack 심장마비를 일으키다

stroke
[strouk]

n. 뇌졸중
have a stroke 뇌졸중에 걸리다

dementia
[diménʃiə]

n. 치매

senile dementia 노인성 치매

hardening of the arteries
[háːrdniŋ ɑv ði áːrtəriz]

n. 동맥경화(증)

myocardial infarction
[màiəkáːrdiəl infáːrkʃən]

n. 심근경색

die of myocardial infarction
심근경색으로 사망하다

cardiac failure
[káːrdiæk féiljər]

n. 심부전(心不全)

acute cardiac failure 급성 심부전

leukemia
[luːkíːmiə]

n. 백혈병

have leukemia 백혈병을 앓고 있다

anemia
[əníːmiə]

n. 빈혈

have an attack of anemia 빈혈을 일으키다

osteoporosis
[àstioupəróusis]

n. 골다공증

have osteoporosis 골다공증에 걸리다

cataract
[kǽtərækt]

n. 백내장

a senile cataract 노인성 백내장

glaucoma
[glɔːkóumə]

n. 녹내장

closed-angle glaucoma
협각 녹내증(狹角綠內症)

dermatitis
[də̀ːrmətáitis]

n. 피부염

atopic dermatitis 아토피성 피부염

epilepsy
[épəlèpsi]

n. 간질

a fit of epilepsy 간질 발작

pneumonia
[njumóunjə]

n. 폐렴

acute pneumonia 급성 폐렴

tuberculosis
[tjubə̀ːrkjəlóusis]

n. 결핵

develop symptoms of tuberculosis 결핵의 증상을 나타내다

AIDS
[eidz]

n. 후천성 면역 결핍증 (=acquired immuno-deficiency syndrome)

a person (living) with AIDS 에이즈 환자

cancer
[kǽnsər]
lung cancer 폐암

n. 암

a cancer of the stomach 위암

tumor
[tjúːməːr]

n. 종양

a benign[malignant] tumor 양[악]성 종양

ulcer
[ʌ́lsər]

n. 궤양

a gastric ulcer 위궤양

asthma
[ǽzmə]

n. 천식

a severe asthma attack 심한 천식 발작

chicken pox
[tʃíkin pɑks]

n. 수두

a chicken pox vaccine 수두백신

measles
[míːzəlz]

n. 홍역

catch (the) measles 홍역에 걸리다

stomach trouble
[stʌ́mək trʌ́bəbl]

n. 배탈

suffer from a stomach trouble 배탈이 나다

constipation
[kɑ̀nstəpéiʃə]

n. 변비

suffer from constipation 변비로 고생하다

hemorrhoids
[hémərɔ̀idz]

n. 치질

external[internal] hemorrhoids 수[암]치질

period pains
[píəriəd peins]

n. 생리통

suffer from period pain 생리통으로 고생하다

food poisoning
[fuːd pɔ́izəniŋ]

n. 식중독

be stricken by food poisoning
식중독에 걸리다

indigestion
[ìndidʒéstʃən]

n. 소화불량

have an attack of indigestion
소화 불량에 걸리다

insomnia
[insámniə]

n. 불면증

suffer (from) insomnia 불면증이 되다

feigned illness
[feind ilnis]

n. 꾀병

be absent from school with a feigned illness 꾀병 부려서 학교를 쉬다

pregnancy
[prégnənsi]

n. 임신

extrauterine pregnancy 자궁외 임신

delivery
[dilívəri]

n. 출산

the expected date of delivery 출산 예정일

swoon [swuːn]	*n.* 실신, 기절 be in[fall into] a swoon 기절해 있다[하다]
comatose [kóumətòus]	*n.* 혼수상태 fall into a coma 혼수 상태에 빠지다
(human) vegetable [(hjúːmən) védʒətəbəl]	*n.* 식물인간 keep alive at a vegetable level 식물인간으로 살아가다
brain death [brein de]	*n.* 뇌사 brain-dead people 뇌사자
athlete's foot [ǽθliːts fut]	*n.* 무좀 have athlete's foot 무좀에 걸리다
allergy [ǽlərdʒi]	*n.* 알레르기 an allergy to pollen 꽃가루 알레르기
rash [ræʃ]	*n.* 발진, 뾰루지 a nettle-rash 두드러기
obesity [oubíːsəti]	*n.* 비만증 the main cause of obesity 비만의 주요 원인
morning sickness [mɔ́ːrniŋ síknis]	*n.* 입덧 suffer from morning sickness 입덧나다
chill [tʃil]	*n.* 오한 catch a chill 오한이 들다

bruise
[bruːz]

n. 멍

get a bruise 멍들다

cut
[kʌt]

v. 절개하다

cut out the affected part 환부를 절개하다

sprain
[sprein]

v. 삐다, 접질리다

sprain one's ankle 발목을 삐다

wound
[wuːnd]

n. 부상, 상처

heal a wound 상처를 치료하다

injury
[índʒəri]

n. 상처

an injury to the head 머리의 상처

bleeding
[blíːdiŋ]

n. 출혈

stop bleeding 출혈을 멎게 하다

overwork
[òuvərwɔ́ːrk]

n. 과로

stress caused by overwork
과로로 인한 스트레스

stress
[stres]

n. 스트레스, 압박

suffer from stress 스트레스를 받다

cavity
[kǽvəti]

n. 썩은 이빨, 충치

get a cavity in a back tooth
어금니 하나가 썩었다

aftereffect
[ǽftərifèkt]

n. 후유증

suffer from after-effects 후유증을 앓다

transplant
[trænsplǽnt]

n. 이식 *v.* 이식하다

a heart transplant 심장 이식

pain
[pein]

n. 통증

stomach pains 복통

feel
[fi:l]

v. 느끼다

feel pain 고통을 느끼다

ache
[eik]

n. 아픔, 쑤심

aches and pains 아픔, 고통

itch
[itʃ]

n. 가려움

have the itch 옴에 걸리다

sore
[sɔːr]

a. 아픈

a sore foot 구두에 닿아서 까진 발

toothache
[tú:θèik]

n. 치통

have a toothache 치통을 앓다

backache
[bǽkèik]

n. 요통

have a backache 요통이 있다

■ 의료

medical
[médikəl]

a. 의료의/의학의

have a medical checkup 건강진단을 받다

examination
[igzæ̀mənéiʃən]

n. 검사, 진찰

take a physical examination 건강진단을 받다

sanitation
[sæ̀nətéiʃ-ən]

n. 위생

an inspector of sanitation 위생 검사관

immunity
[imjúːnəti]

n. 면역

give a person immunity to a disease
에게 병에 대한 면역성을 주다

germ
[ʤəːrm]

n. 세균

influenza germs 인플루엔자 병원균

diagnosis
[dàiəgnóusis]

n. 진단

erroneous diagnosis 오진

treatment
[tríːtmənt]

n. 치료

a new treatment for cancer
암의 새로운 치료법

temperature
[témp-ərətʃuəːr]

n. 체온

run a temperature 열이 나다

thermometer
[θəːrmámitəːr]

n. 온도계

a clinical thermometer 체온계

nutrition
[njuːtríʃ-ən]

n. 영양

inadequate nutrition 불충분한 영양

recover
[rikʌ́vəːr]

v. 회복하다

recover consciousness 의식을 회복하다

care
[kɛər]

n. 간호, 돌봄

in doctor's care 의사의 치료를 받고 있는

relieve
[rilíːv]

v. 완화하다

drugs to relieve the pain
통증을 덜어주는 약물들

medical checkup
[médikəl tʃekʌ́p]

n. 건강진단

undergo a medical checkup
건강 진단을 받다

blood
[blʌd]

n. 피

blood test 피검사

therapy
[θérəpi]

n. 치료, 요법

physical therapy 물리치료

operation
[ὰpəréiʃən]

n. 수술

a liver transplant operation 간 이식수술

shot / injection
[ʃɑt]/[indʒékʃən]

n. 주사

(an) intramuscular injection 근육 주사

blood type
[blʌd taip]

n. 혈액형

a rare blood type 드문 혈액형

sling
[sliŋ]

n. 어깨에 맨 붕대

have one's arm in a sling
팔에 멜빵 붕대를 하고 있다

cast
[kæst]

n. 깁스

ware a (plaster) cast 깁스를 하다

disinfection
[dìsinfékʃən]

n. 소독

steam disinfection 증기 소독

anesthesia
[æ̀nəsθíːʒə]

n. 마취

local[general]anesthesia 국소[전신] 마취

X-rays
[eks rei]

n. 엑스레이

a chest X-ray 흉부 엑스레이 사진

prescription
[priskrípʃən]

n. 처방전

make up a prescription 처방전대로 조제하다

vaccination
[væ̀ksənéiʃən]

n. 예방접종

a vaccination scar 우두자국

needle
[níːdl]

n. 침, 바늘

pinprick with a needle 바늘로 콕 찌르다

acupuncture
[ǽkjupʌ̀ŋktʃər]

n. 침술

be treated with acupuncture 침을 맞다

blood transfusion
[blʌd trænsfjúːʒ-ən]

n. 수혈

give a blood transfusion 수혈하다

blood donation
[blʌd dounéiʃən]

n. 헌혈

donate[give] blood 헌혈하다

microscope
[máikrəskòup]

n. 현미경

see under a microscope 현미경으로 보다

■ 병원

hospital
[háspitl]

n. 종합병원

go to the hospital 입원하다

clinic
[klínik]

n. 개인(전문)병원

a pain clinic 통증 (전문) 치료소

patient
[péiʃənt]

n. 환자

examine a patient 환자를 진찰하다

doctor
[dáktər]

n. 의사

see a doctor 의사에게 진찰받다

physician
[fizíʃən]

n. 의사, 내과의사

a skilled physician 용한 의사

surgeon
[sə́:rdʒən]

n. 외과의사

plastic surgeon 성형외과 의사

dentist
[déntist]

n. 치과의사

go to (see) the dentist 치과에 가다

internal medicine
[intə́:rn médəs-ən]

n. 내과

internal medicine doctor 내과의사

surgery
[sə́:rdʒəri]

n. 외과

oral surgery 구강외과

pediatrics
[pì:diǽtriks]

n. 소아과

a pediatrics ward 소아과 병동

ophthalmology
[àfθælmálədʒi]

n. 안과

ophthalmology resident 안과 레지던트

dermatology
[də̀:rmətálədʒi]

n. 피부과

dermatology patient 피부병 환자

plastic surgery
[plǽstik sɔ́ːrdʒəri]

n. 성형외과

have plastic surgery 성형수술을 받다

urology
[juərálədʒi]

n. 비뇨기과

International Society of Urology
국제 비뇨기 학회(ISU)

obstetrics and gynecology
[əbstétriks ænd gàinikálədʒ]

n. 산부인과

obstetrics and gynecology hospital
산부인과 전문병원

orthopedics
[ɔ̀ːrθoupíːdiks]

n. 정형외과

orthopedics inpatient 정형외과 입원환자

radiology
[rèidiálədʒ]

n. 방사선과

radiology resident 방사선학 전공의

neurology
[njuərálədʒi]

n. 신경과

department of neurology 신경과

neuropsychiatry
[njùərousaikáiətri]

n. 신경정신과

department of neuropsychiatry 신경정신과

dental clinic
[déntl klínik]

n. 치과

dental clinic drill 치과 드릴

Oriental medicine clinic
[ɔ̀ːriéntl médəs-ən klínik]

n. 한의원

go to the Oriental medicine clinic
한의원에 가다

oriental medicine doctor
[ɔ̀ːriéntl médəs-ən dáktə]

n. 한의사

*take Chinese medicine 한약을 복용하다

nurse
[nəːrs]

n. 간호사

call a nurse 간호사를 부르다

hospital gown
[háspitl gaun]

n. 환자복

wear a hospital gown 환자복을 입다

ward
[wɔːrd]

n. 병실

an isolation ward 격리 병동 병실, 병동

ambulance
[ǽmbjuləns]

n. 구급차

call (for) an ambulance 구급차를 부르다

emergency room
[imə́ːrdʒənsi ruːm]

n. 응급실

be rushed to the emergency room
응급실에 실려가다

delivery room
[dilívəri ruːm]

n. 분만실

Delivery room management
분만장 치료

wheelchair
[hwíːltʃɛ̀əːr]

n. 휠체어

sit in one's wheelchair 휠체어를 타고 있다

■ 약품

drug
[drʌg]

n. 약

drug addict 마약 중독

medicine
[médəs-ən]

n. 내복약

a medicine for a cold 감기약

pharmacy
[fáːrməsi]

n. 약국

go to the pharmacy 약국에 가다

pharmacist
[fáːrməsist]

n. 약사

wait for the pharmacist to make up her prescription
약사가 처방전을 작성해 주기를 기다리다

liquid medicine
[líkwid médəs-ən]

n. 물약

liquid medicine for children 어린이용 물약

powder
[páudər]

n. 가루약

digestive powder 분말 소화제

tablet
[tǽblit]

n. 정제

a vitamin tablet 비타민 정제

pill
[pil]

n. 알약

sleeping pills 수면제

ointment
[ɔ́intmənt]

n. 연고

apply ointment 연고를 바르다

capsule
[kǽpsəl]

n. 캡슐

rectal capsule 직장 투여 캡슐

eyelotion
[ailóuʃən]

n. 안약

apply eyelotion 안약을 넣다

drip
[drip]

n. 점적약

an intravenous drip (링거 등의) 정맥내 점적

vitamin
[váitəmin]

n. 비타민

be rich in vitamin 비타민이 많다

side effect
[said ifékt]

n. 부작용

the possible side effects of the drug
그 약의 가능한 부작용

plaster
[plǽstər]

n. 반창고

stick a plaster 반창고를 붙이다

bandage
[bǽndidʒ]

n. 붕대

wear a bandage 붕대를 감다

fever reducer
[fíːvər ridjúːsər]

n. 해열제

take a fever reducer 해열제를 복용하다

antibiotic
[æ̀ntibaiátik]

n. 항생물질

a tolerance to antibiotics
항생 물질에 대한 내성

painkiller
[péinkìlə]

n. 진통제

painkiller for a migraine 편두통용의 진통제

nutrient
[njúːtriənt]

n. 영양제

protein nutrients 단백질을 포함한 영양소

sedative
[sédətiv]

n. 진정제

give a person a sedative …에게 진정제를 주다

sleeping drug
[slíːpiŋ drʌg]

n. 수면제

take a large dose of a sleeping drug
다량의 수면제를 먹다

digestive medicine
[didʒéstiv médəs-ən]

n. 소화제

take a digestive medicine 소화제를 먹다

vaccine
[væksí(:)n]

n. 백신

influenza vaccine 인플루엔자 백신

laxative
[læksətiv]

n. 완하제, 관장약

take a laxative 하제를 먹다

gargle
[gá:rgəl]

v. 양치질 하다

gargle a sore throat 아픈 목구멍을 양치질하다

dose
[dous]

n. 복용량

take three doses a day 약을 하루에 세 번 먹다

PART 04

가족과 인간관계

01 가족

■ 가족관계

ancestor
[ǽnsestər]

n. 조상, 선조
ancestor worship 조상 숭배

relative
[rélətiv]

n. 친척, 일가
a near relative 가까운 친척

home
[houm]

n. 가정
a sweet home 단란한 가정

family
[fǽməli]

n. 가족, 식구
support a family 가족을 부양하다

grandparents
[grǽndpɛ̀ərənts]

n. 조부모
my grandparents on my father's side
아버지 쪽의 조부모

grandfather
[grǽndfɑ̀:ðər]

n. 할아버지
my maternal grandfather 나의 외할아버지

grandmother
[grǽndmʌ̀ðər]

n. 할머니
my paterna grandmother 나의 친할머니

grandchild
[grǽndtʃàild]

n. 손자 손녀

get a grandchild 손자를 보다

grandson
[grǽndsʌn]

n. 손자

give a present to one's grandson
손자에게 선물을 주다

granddaughter
[grǽnddɔ̀:tər]

n. 손녀

be proud of one's granddaughter
손녀를 자랑스러워하다

parents
[pɛ́ərənts]

n. 양친, 부모

a biological parent 친부모

mother
[mʌ́ðəːr]

n. 어머니

become a mother 어머니가 되다

father
[fɑ́:ðər]

n. 아버지

have a look of one's father
아버지의 모습을 닮다

stepfather
[stepfɑ́:ðər]

n. 의붓아버지

a cruel stepfather 잔인한 의붓 아버지

stepmother
[stepmʌ́ðəːr]

n. 의붓어머니

new stepmother 새어머니

stepchild
[steptʃàild]

n. 의붓자식

stepdaughter 의붓딸

wife
[waif]

n. 부인

one's former wife 전처

husband
[hʌ́zbənd]

n. 남편

a devoted husband 애처가

son
[sʌn]

n. 아들

an only son 외아들

daughter
[dɔ́ːtər]

n. 딸

an only daughter 외동딸

siblings
[síblinz]

n. 형제자매

squabbles between siblings
형제[동기] 간의 싸움

brother
[brʌ́ðər]

n. 남자 형제

make a blood brother compact
형제의 의를 맺다

sister
[sístəːr]

n. 여자 형제

twin sister 쌍둥이 자매

uncle
[ʌ́ŋkəl]

n. 삼촌(숙부), 아저씨

call on my uncle 나의 삼촌을 방문하다

aunt
[ænt]

n. 숙모(고모, 이모)

his maternal aunt 그의 숙모

cousin
[kʌ́zn]

n. 사촌

a letter from my cousin 내 사촌한테 온 편지

nephew
[néfjuː]

n. 남자조카

a wife's nephew 처조카

niece
[niːs]

n. 여자조카

adopt one's niece as a daughter
조카를 양녀로 들이다

daughter-in-law
[dɔ́ːtər in lɔ̀ː]

n. 며느리

be cruel to one's daughter-in-law
며느리를 들볶다

son-in-law
[sʌ́n in lɔ̀ː]

n. 사위

the oldest son-in-law 맏사위

father-in-law
[fɑ́ːðər in lɔ̀ː]

n. 시아버지

a good father-in-law 좋은 시아버지

mother-in-law
[mʌ́ðər in lɔ̀ː]

n. 시어머니

daughter-in-law and mother-in-law conflicts 고부간의 갈등

sister-in-law
[sístər in lɔ̀ː]

n. 시누이, 올케

have a sister-in-law 시누이가 한명 있다

brother-in-law
[brʌ́ðər in lɔ̀ː]

n. 시동생, 처남

the youngest brother-in-law 막내 시동생

02 인간관계

■ 인생과 결혼

human life
[hjúːmən laif]

n. 인생
diverse aspects of human life
인생의 여러 양상

birth
[bəːrθ]

n. 출생, 탄생
resister one's birth 출생신고를 하다

name
[neim]

n. 성명, 이름
leave a name behind 후세에 이름을 남기다

birthday
[bə́ːrθdèi]

n. 생일
on my birthday 내 생일에

life
[laif]

n. 삶, 생활
struggle for life 삶의 투쟁

lifetime
[láiftàim]

n. 일생, 평생, 생애
once in a lifetime 평생에 단 한 번

love
[lʌv]

n. 사랑 *v.* 사랑하다
first love 첫사랑

lover
[lʌ́vər]

n. 애인

act like lovers 연인 커플처럼 행동하다

engagement
[engéidʒmənt]

n. 약혼

an engagement of a young couple
젊은 남녀의 약혼

*fiancee 약혼자(남자), fiance 약혼녀(여자)

marriage
[mǽridʒ]

n. 결혼

arranged marriage 중매결혼
love marriage 연애결혼

one-sided love
[wʌn sáidi lʌv]

n. 짝사랑

That's a one-sided love! 그건 짝사랑이군요!

kiss
[kis]

n. 입맞춤

kiss on the lips 입술에 키스하다

ring
[riŋ]

n. 반지

wedding ring 결혼반지

wedding ceremony
[wédiŋ sérəmòuni]

n. 결혼식

have a wedding ceremony 결혼식을 올리다

honeymoon
[hʌ́nimùːn]

n. 신혼여행

a honeymoon resort 신혼 여행지

bridegroom
[bráidgrù(ː)m]

n. 신랑

bride and groom 신랑신부

bride
[braid]

n. 신부

stand up with the bride 신부의 들러리를 서다

single
[síŋ-əl]

a. 미혼의

a single person 미혼자

married
[mǽrid]

a. 기혼의

a married man 유부남

divorce
[divɔ́ːrs]

n. 이혼 *v.* 이혼하다

a divorce suit 이혼소송

meeting
[míːtiŋ]

n. 만남

an casual meeting 우연한 만남

parting
[páːrtiŋ]

n. 이별

tears at parting 이별의 눈물

funeral
[fjúːn-ərəl]

n. 장례식

attend a funeral 장례식에 참석하다

burial
[bériəl]

n. 매장

the burial at sea 수장(水葬)

grave
[greiv]

n. 무덤, 묘

worship at a grave 묘에 참배하다

tombstone
[túːmstòun]

n. 묘비

a marble tombstone 대리석묘비

cremation
[kriméiʃən]

n. 화장

electric cremation 전기 화장

deceased
[disíːst]

n. 고인

the deceased father 죽은 아버지

death
[deθ]

n. 죽음, 사망

a painless death 고통 없는 죽음

fate
[feit]

n. 운명

by an irony of fate 운명의 장난으로

friend
[frend]

n. 친구, 벗

a real friend 참다운 친구

neighborhood
[néibərhùd]

n. 근처, 이웃

in my neighborhood 우리집 가까이에

neighbor
[néibər]

n. 이웃사람

a next-door neighbor 옆집 사람

age
[eidʒ]

n. 나이

same age 동갑

kid
[kid]

n. 꼬마, 어린이

have lots of kids 아이가 많다

boy
[bɔi]

n. 소년, 사내 아이

have a babt boy 사내 아이를 낳다

girl
[gəːrl]

n. 소녀

a girl's school 여학교

youth
[juːθ]

n. 청년, 젊은이

a youth of twenty 20세의 청년

adult
[ədʎlt]

n. 성인, 어른

an adult disease 성인병

elder
[éldər]

n. 노인, 연장자

be respectful to one's elder 어른을 공경하다

guy
[gai]

n. 놈, 녀석

a bad guy 나쁜 녀석

guarantor
[gǽrəntɔ́ːr]

n. 보증인

a financial guarantor 재정 보증인

guardian
[gáːrdiən]

n. 보호자, 후견인

a guardian angel 수호천사

man
[mæn]

n. 남자

behave like a man 남자답게 행동하다

woman
[wúmən]

n. 여자

woman's wit 여자의 지혜

03 교제와 사교

■ 이성과의 교제

relationship
[riléiʃ-ənʃip]

n. 관계
a father-son relationship 부자관계

associate
[əsóuʃièit]

v. 교제하다
associate with good people
선량한 사람들과 사귀다

together
[təgéðə:r]

ad. 함께
go out together 함께 외출하다

alone
[əlóun]

a. 혼자서
home alone 나홀로 집에

reputation
[rèpjətéiʃ-ən]

n. 평판
a man of good reputation 평판이 좋은 사람

love
[lʌv]

n. 사랑 *v.* 사랑하다
Platonic love 플라토닉 러브(정신적인 사랑)

trust
[trʌst]

n. 신뢰 *v.* 신뢰하다
put trust in others 남을 신뢰하다

respect
[rispékt]

n. 존경 *v.* 존경하다

a mark of respect 존경의 표시

rely
[rilái]

v. 의존하다

rely on one's father for his help
아버지의 도움에 의지하다

praise
[preiz]

n. 칭찬

speak words of praise 찬사를 보내다

obey
[oubéi]

v. 복종하다

obey the law 법률을 준수하다

follow
[fálou]

v. 따르다

follow the instructions 지시를 따르다

excuse
[ikskjúːz]

v. 용서하다

excuse a fault 잘못을 용서하다

hate
[heit]

v. 싫어하다

her hated rival 그녀가 증오하는 라이벌

despise
[dispáiz]

v. 경멸하다

despise somebody's meanness
누구의 비열함을 경멸하다

insult
[ínsʌlt]

v. 모욕하다

insult a man by calling him a simpleton
바보라고 불러 남을 모욕하다.

envy
[énvi]

v. 부러워하다

I envy you. 네가 부러워.

rumor
[rúːməːr]

n. 소문

a groundless rumor 근거 없는 풍문

apology
[əpálədʒi]

n. 사과

a letter of apology 사과편지

attitude
[ǽtitjùːd]

n. 태도

an attitude of arrogance 거만한 태도

purpose
[pə́ːrpəs]

n. 목적

for that purpose 그런 목적으로

opportunity
[ὰpərtjúːnəti]

n. 기회

have an opportunity 기회를 갖다

miss
[mis]

v. 그리워하다

I miss you. 보고 싶다

propose
[prəpóuz]

n. 청혼 *v.* 청혼하다

propose marriage to a person
남에게 청혼하다

dump
[dʌmp]

v. 차버리다

She dumped me once.
그녀는 전에 나를 차버렸다.

favor
[féivər]

n. 호의, 은혜

return the favor 은혜를 갚다

scar
[skɑːr]

n. 상처

emotional scars 마음의 상처

charm
[tʃɑːrm]

n. 매력

feminine charms 여성미

popularity
[pàpjəlǽrəti]

n. 인기

enjoy popularity 인기를 끌다

memories
[méməriz]

n. 추억

memories of childhood 유년 시절의 추억

■ 트러블

trouble
[trʌ́b-əl]

n. 곤란

in trouble 곤란한 처지에 있다

problem
[prɑ́bləm]

n. 문제

solve a problem 문제를 풀다

matter
[mǽtəːr]

n. 문제, 일, 사건

a trivial matter 사소한 일

situation
[sìtʃuéiʃ-ən]

n. 상황, 입장

an embarrassing situation 난처한 처지

reason
[ríːz-ən]

n. 이유, 까닭

for some reason or other 그 어떤 이유로

result
[rizʌ́lt]

n. 결과

meet with good results 좋은 결과를 얻다

fight
[fait]

n. 싸움 *v.* 싸우다

pick a fight (…에게) 싸움을 걸다

hit
[hit]

v. 때리다

hit a person in the face 남의 얼굴을 때리다

slap
[slæp]

n. 찰싹 때리다

slap a person's face …의 뺨을 찰싹 때리다

pinch
[pintʃ]

v. 꼬집다

give a sharp pinch 세게 꼬집다

kick
[kik]

v. 발고 차다

kick a person in the shin …의 정강이를 차다

quarrel
[kwɔ́ːrəl]

n. 말다툼 *v.* 말다툼하다

lover's quarrel 연인들의 다툼

argue
[áːrgjuː]

v. 논의하다, 논쟁하다

argue for the right to strike
파업할 권리를 위해 논쟁하다

accuse
[əkjúːz]

v. 고발하다, 비난하다

accuse a person of stealing
…을 절도죄로 고발하다

blame
[bleim]

v. 나무라다, 책망하다

blame (a person) for his fault
…의 잘못을 나무라다

apology
[əpálədʒi]

n. 사과

make an apology 사과하다

■ 방문·초대

greet
[griːt]

v. 맞이하다, 환영하다
greet the New Year 새해를 맞다

greeting
[gríːtiŋ]

n. 인사
a greetings card 인사 카드

introduce
[ìntrədjúːs]

v. 소개하다, 도입하다
introduce a girl to society
소녀를 처음으로 사교계에 등장시키다

invite
[inváit]

v. 초대하다, 초청하다
invite a friend to dinner 친구를 식사에 초대하다

invitation
[ìnvətéiʃən]

n. 초대
an invitation ticket 초대권

visit
[vízit]

n. 방문 *v.* 방문하다
visit a friend 친구를 찾아가다

welcome
[wélkəm]

n. 환영 *v.* 환영하다
Welcome home! 집에 오신 것을 환영합니다

relationship
[riléiʃ-ənʃip]

n. 관계
a father-son relationship 부자관계

colleague
[káliːg]

n. 동료 (=coworker)
a former colleague 이전의 동료

manners
[mǽnəːrs]

n. 예의
learn manners 예의 범절을 배우다

activity
[æktívəti]

n. 활동

outdoor activities 야외활동

participation
[pɑːrtìsəpéiʃən]

n. 참가

a participation show
【라디오TV】 시청자 참가 프로

business card
[bízniskɑːrd]

n. 명함

exchange cards 명함을 주고받다

meeting
[míːtiŋ]

n. 모임

attend a meeting 모임에 참석하다.

guide
[gaid]

n. 안내 *v.* 안내하다

a guided tour 가이드가 동행하는 (관광)여행

shake hands
[ʃeik hændz]

v. 악수하다

shake on something
~에 대해 합의의 악수를 나누다[합의를 보다]

host
[houst]

n. 주인

act as host 주인 노릇을 하다.

guest
[gest]

n. 손님

a house guest 집에서 묵어가는 손님

meet
[miːt]

v. 만나다

meet a person in the face ~와 우연히 만나다

appointment
[əpɔ́intmənt]

n. 약속

a visit by appointment 미리 약속된 방문

party
[páːrti]

n. 파티

give a party 파티를 열다

ceremony
[sérəmòuni]

n. 의식

hold a graduation ceremony
졸업식을 거행하다

anniversary
[æ̀nəvə́ːrsəri]

n. 기념일

celebrate a wedding anniversary
결혼기념일을 축하하다

congratulate
[kəngrǽtʃəlèit]

v. 축하하다 (=celebrate)

congratulate on …을 축하하다

gift
[gift]

n. 선물 (=present)

a birthday gift 생일 선물

accept
[æksépt]

v. 받아들이다

accept an apology 사과를 받아들이다

decline
[dikláin]

v. 거절하다

decline a gift with thanks
선물을 정중히 사절하다

polite
[pəláit]

a. 정중한

a polite refusal 정중한 거절

rude
[ruːd]

a. 무례한

a rude reply 무례한 대답

PART 05

사회

01 사회

■ 사회 일반

society
[səsáiəti]

n. 사회
human society 인간 사회

activity
[æktívəti]

n. 활동
social activities 사회 활동

attendance
[əténdəns]

n. 참석
a large attendance 다수의 참석자

request
[rikwést]

n. 부탁
a personal request 개인적 부탁

help
[help]

n. 도움
ask a person for help 도움을 청하다

solution
[səlúːʃ-ən]

n. 해결
a problem capable of solution
해결 가능한 문제

■ 복지

welfare
[wélfɛə:r]

n. 복지
social welfare 사회복지

social security
[sóuʃ-əl sikjú-əriti]

n. 사회보장
a social security system 사회보장 제도

disabled
[diséibəld]

a. 장애를 가진
disabled parking 장애자용 주차장

Human Rights
[hjú:mən raits]

n. 인권
UN Commission on Human Rights
유엔 인권 위원회

annuity
[ənjú:əti]

n. 연금
a life annuity 종신 연금

pension
[pénʃən]

n. 연금
live on one's pension 연금으로 생활하다

insurance
[inʃúərəns]

n. 보험
buy insurance 보험에 가입하다

premium
[prí:miəm]

n. 보험료
pay a hefty premium 많은 보험료를 지불하다

medical insurance
[médik-əl inʃúərəns]

n. 의료보험
a medical insurance card 의료보험증

day-care-center
[dei kɛər séntər]

n. 탁아소

leave a child at the day-care-center
탁아소에 아이를 맡기다

volunteer
[vàləntíər]

n. 자원봉사자

recruit volunteers 자원봉사자를 모집하다

hospice
[háspis]

n. 호스피스

a hospice for the terminally ill
말기 환자들을 위한 호스피스

fitness
[fítnis]

n. 건강(상태), 몸매 가꾸기

a fitness test 체력 테스트

healthcare
[helθkèər]

n. 건강관리

a healthcare center 건강관리 센터

physical strength
[fízikəl streŋkθ]

n. 체력

the physical strength measurement
체력장(章)

metabolism
[mətǽbəlìzəm]

n. 신진대사

have a high metabolism 신진대사가 활발하다

prevention
[privénʃən]

n. 예방

disease prevention 질병의 예방

exercise
[éksərsàiz]

n. 운동

gymnastic exercises 체조, 체육

training
[tréiniŋ]

n. 훈련, 교육

professional training 직업 교육

jogging
[dʒágiŋ]

n. 조깅, 달리기

take up jogging 조깅을 계속하다

tough
[tʌf]

a. 튼튼한, 강인한

a tough athlete 강인한 운동선수

overweight
[óuvərwèit]

n. 중량초과

an overweight child 과다체중인 아이

■ 범죄와 사건

crime
[kraim]

n. 범죄

a capital crime (사형에 처할 만한) 중죄

incident
[ínsədənt]

n. 사건

a surprising incident 놀라운 사건

bribe
[braib]

n. 뇌물

accept a bribe 뇌물을 받다

doubt
[daut]

n. 의심

a growing doubt 더해가는 의심

investigation
[invèstəgéiʃən]

n. 수사

a criminal investigation 범죄 수사

police
[pəlíːs]

n. 경찰

police station 경찰서

punishment
[pʌ́niʃmənt]

n. 처벌

receive punishment 처벌을 받다

rule
[ruːl]

n. 규칙

the basic rules 기본 규칙

norm
[nɔːrm]

n. 규범, 표준

a sound social norm 건전한 사회 규범

speeding
[spíːdiŋ]

n. 속도위반

a $50 fine for speeding
속도위반에 대한 50불의 벌금

housebreaking
[hausbrèikiŋ]

n. 가택침입

the charge of housebreaking 주거침입죄

protection
[prətékʃən]

n. 보호

for the protection of lives and property
생명과 재산의 보호를 위하여

guard
[gɑːrd]

n. 경비, 수위

stand guard 보초 서다, 감시하다

danger
[déindʒər]

n. 위험

in (the) face of danger 위험을 무릅쓰고

violence
[váiələns]

n. 폭력

TV violence TV 폭력

theft
[θeft]

n. 절도

commit a theft 도둑질을 하다

criminal
[krímənl]

a. 범죄의

have a criminal record 전과가 있다

culprit
[kʌ́lprit]

n. 범인

shelter a culprit 죄인을 두둔하다

suspect
[səspékt]

n. 용의자

a murder suspect 살인 용의자

robber
[rάbə:r]

n. (노상) 강도

a robber band 강도의 일당

burglar
[bə́:rgləər]

n. (주거침입) 강도

an armed burglar 흉기를 든 강도

shoplift
[ʃɑplìft]

n. (가게) 좀도둑

the previous conviction for shoplifting
가게 좀도둑질의 전과

steal
[sti:l]

v. 훔치다

steal the money from the safe
금고에서 돈을 훔치다

rob
[rɑb]

v. 강탈하다

rob a bank 은행을 털다

riot
[ráiət]

n. 폭동

cause a riot 폭동을 일으키다

murder
[mə́:rdə:r]

n. 살인, 모살

an attempted murder 살인 미수

kill
[kil]

v. 죽이다

kill a person by poison 남을 독살하다

suicide [súːəsàid]	*n.* 자살	commit suicide 자살하다
assassinate [əsǽsənèit]	*v.* 암살하다	plan to assassinate life 암살을 기도하다
missing [mísiŋ]	*a.* 행방불명의	a missing child 미아
abuse [əbjúːz]	*n.* 학대, 혹사	child abuse 아동학대
detective [ditéktiv]	*n.* 형사, 탐정	a private detective 사설 탐정
arrest [ərést]	*v.* 체포하다	arrest a person for murder 남을 살인 혐의로 체포하다
witness [wítnis]	*n.* 목격자	an witness account of a crime 범죄에 대한 증인의 설명
thief [θiːf]	*n.* 도둑	a car thief 차량 절도범
pickpocket [pikpàki]	*n.* 소매치기	tail after a pickpocket 소매치기를 뒤쫓다
arson [áːrsn]	*n.* 방화	an arson attack on a school 한 학교에 대한 방화

fraud
[frɔːd]

n. 사기

a real estate fraud 부동산 사기

kidnap
[kídnæp]

v. 유괴하다

a kidnap victim 유괴의 희생자들

rape
[reip]

n. 강간

a partial rape 강간 미수

ransom
[rǽnsəm]

n. 몸값

a king's ransom 왕의 몸값; 큰 돈

hostage
[hάstidʒ]

n. 인질

hold a person (as a) hostage
남을 볼모로 잡아 두다

chase
[tʃeis]

n. 추적 *v.* 추적하다

chase a thief 도둑을 뒤쫓다

evidence
[évidəns]

n. 증거

reliable evidence 확실한 증거

fingerprint
[fíŋɡərprìnt]

n. 지문

take the prisoner's fingerprints
죄수의 지문을 찍다

clue
[kluː]

n. 단서, 실마리

with this clue to go upon 이것을 실마리로

drug
[drʌɡ]

n. 마약

a drug addict 마약 중독

pistol
[pístl]

n. 권총

a pistol shot 권총 발사

handcuffs
[hǽndkʌ̀fz]

n. 수갑

be led away in handcuffs
수갑이 채워져 끌려가다

prison
[prízn]

n. 감옥, 교도소

a juvenile prison 소년원

jail
[dʒeil]

n. 구치소

police jail 경찰서 유치장 / break jail 탈옥하다

release
[rilíːs]

v. 석방하다

release a person from slavery
남을 노예의 신분에서 해방시키다

■ 종교

faith
[feiθ]

n. 신앙, 믿음

have faith in God 하느님을 믿다

religion
[rilídʒ-ən]

n. 종교

believe in a religion 어떤 종교를 믿다

God
[gɑd]

n. 신, 하느님

believe in God 하느님(의 존재)을 믿다

evil
[íːvəl]

n. 악

evil spirits 악령

ghost
[goust]
n. 도깨비, 귀신
look like a ghost 유령처럼 보이다

devil
[dévl]
n. 악마, 마귀
the devil of greed 탐욕의 화신

sin
[sin]
n. 죄
commit a sin 죄를 범하다

heaven
[hévən]
n. 천국
the kingdom of heavens 천국, 하늘 나라

hell
[hel]
n. 지옥
Go to hell! 뒈져버려!

believer
[bilíːvəːr]
n. 신자
a believer in Christianity 크리스트교 신자

Bible
[báibəl]
n. 성경
a leather-bound bible 가죽장정이 된 성서

baptism
[bǽptizəm]
n. 세례
accept baptism 세례를 받다

Christianity
[krìstʃiǽnəti]
n. 기독교
convert to Christianity 기독교로 개종시키다

Christian
[krístʃən]
n. 기독교도
a christian faith 그리스도교 신앙

Catholic
[kǽθəlik]
n. 카톨릭 교도
Catholic doctrines 카톨릭 교리

Protestan
[prátəstənt]

n. 신교도(프로테스탄트)

the Protestant interest 신교파

Mass
[mæs]

n. 미사

go to mass 미사에 참례하다

service
[sə́ːrvis]

n. 예배

attend (divine) service 예배에 참석하다

cathedral
[kəθíːdrəl]

n. 성당

a cathedral city 대성당이 있는 도시

church
[tʃəːrtʃ]

n. 교회

the Presbyterian Church 장로교회

shrine
[ʃrain]

n. 신사, 사당

a shrine of art 예술의 전당

temple
[témp-əl]

n. 신전, 절

a historic temple 유서 깊은 절

meditation
[mèdətéiʃən]

n. 명상

be buried in meditation 명상에 잠기다

Buddhism
[búːdizəm]

n. 불교

Buddhist art 불교 미술

Buddhist
[búːdist]

n. 불교도

a devout Buddhist 독실한 불교신자

Buddha
[búːdə]

n. 부처

an image of Buddha 불상

shaman [ʃáːmən]	*n.* 주술사, 무당 one's regular shaman 단골무당
religious [rilídʒəs]	*a.* 종교적인 a religious book 종교 서적
theology [θiːálədʒi]	*n.* 신학 a theology student 신학교 학생
cardinal [káːrdənl]	*n.* 추기경 cardinal vicar 【가톨릭】 주교 대리
bishop [bíʃəp]	*n.* 주교 the metropolitan bishop 수도 대주교
Confucianism [kənfjúːʃənìzəm]	*n.* 유교 preach Confucianism 공자의 도를 펴다
Hinduism [híndùːìzəm]	*n.* 힌두교 malaysian hinduism 말레이시아 힌두교
Muslim / Islam [mʌ́zləm]/[íslɑːm]	*n.* 이슬람교도 a Muslim[an Islamic] country 이슬람 국가
Judaism [dʒúːdìːzəm]	*n.* 유대교 Orthodox Judaism 정통파 유대교
Resurrection [rèzərékʃ-ən]	*n.* 부활 the resurrection of hope 희망의 부활
holy [hóuli]	*a.* 신성한 the Holy Bible 성서

hymn
[him]

n. 찬송가, 성가

a gospel hymn 복음 찬미가

cross
[krɔːs]

n. 십자가

the penalty of the cross
십자가(에 못박히는) 형벌

angel
[éindʒəl]

n. 천사

an evil angel 악마

paradise
[pǽrədàis]

n. 낙원

an earthly paradise 지상의 낙원

pray
[prei]

n. 기도 *v.* 기도하다

pray God's forgiveness 신의 용서를 빌다

preach
[priːtʃ]

n. 설교 *v.* 설교하다

preach the gospel 복음을 전도하다

oath
[ouθ]

n. 서약, 선서

an official oath 취임 선서

predict
[pridíkt]

v. 예언하다

predict a good harvest 풍작을 예언하다

believe
[bilíːv]

v. 믿다

believe in God 신을 믿다

bless
[bles]

v. 축복하다

God bless you! 그대에게 신의 축복이 있기를!

02 사고와 재해

■ 사고

accident [ǽksidənt]
n. 사고
traffic accidents 교통사고

disaster [dizǽstər]
n. 재해
natural disasters 천재(天災)

emergency [imə́ːrdʒənsi]
n. 비상(사태)
an emergency bell 비상 벨

collide [kəláid]
v. 충돌하다
The car collided against the wall.
차가 담에 부딪쳤다.

sink [siŋk]
v. 가라앉다, 침몰하다
sink to the bottom of the sea
해저에 가라앉다

deviation [dìːviéiʃən]
n. 탈선
a deviation from the rules 규칙이탈

explosion [iksplóuʒən]
n. 폭발
gas explosion 가스 폭발

damage
[dǽmidʒ]

n. 손해

claim damages 손해 배상금을 요구하다

hit
[hit]

v. 때리다, 치다

hit the target 표적을 맞히다

strike
[straik]

v. 공격하다

strike the fort 요새를 공격하다

bump
[bʌmp]

v. 추돌하다

bump against each other 충돌하다

scrape
[skreip]

v. 스치다, 스치기

a scrape on the car door
자동차 문 위의 긁힌 자국

drunk driving
[drʌ́ŋk draiviŋ]

n. 음주운전

be killed in a drunk driving accident
음주운전사고로 사망하다

violate
[váiəlèit]

v. 위반하다

violate a law 법률을 어기다

negligence
[néglidʒəns]

n. 과실, 부주의

gross negligence 중(重)과실

burn
[bəːrn]

v. 불타다, 불태우다

burn down 불타 무너지다

fire engine
[faiər éndʒən]

n. 소방차

a fire engine carrying 8 fighters
소방사 8명을 태운 소방차

ambulance
[ǽmbjuləns]

n. 구급차

call (for) an ambulance 구급차를 부르다

drown
[draun]

v. 익사하다, 익사시키다

a drowned body 익사체

lifeguard
[láifgàːrd]

n. 해난구조대원

ask a lifeguard for help
해난구조원에게 도움을 청하다

rescue
[réskjuː]

v. 구출하다, 구조하다

rescue a child from drowning
물에 빠진 아이를 구조하다

survive
[sərváiv]

v. 생존하다

survive an earthquake 지진에서 살아남다

injured
[índʒərd]

a. 부상당한

injured legs 다친 두 다리

victim
[víktim]

n. 희생자

victims of the storm 그 폭풍의 희생자

casualty
[kǽʒuəlti]

n. 사상자

heavy casualties 많은 사상자

explode
[iksplóud]

v. 폭발하다

gun powder explodes 화약이 터지다

identify
[aidéntəfài]

v. 신원을 확인하다

identify a body 시체를 확인하다

happen
[hǽpən]

v. (일이) 일어나다, 우연히 ~하다

Accidents will happen
<속담> 사고란 일어나게 마련

danger
[déindʒər]

n. 위험

risk danger 위험을 무릅쓰다

dangerous
[déindʒərəs]

a. 위험한

a dangerous man 위험 인물

safe
[sief]

a. 안전한

a safe place 안전한 장소

contact
[kántækt]

n. 연락 *v.* 연락하다

make contact with the lost ship
조난선과 연락이 닿다

fire station
[faiər stéiʃ-ən]

n. 소방서

report a fire to the fire station
소방서에 화재신고를 하다

fire
[faiər]

n. 화재

fire prevention 화재 예방

■ 재해

disaster
[dizǽstər]

n. 재해

human disaster 인재 /natural disaster 천재

earthquake
[ə́ːrθkwèik]

n. 지진

a strong earthquake 강진 (aftershock = 여진)

eruption
[irʌ́pʃən]

n. 폭발, 분화

a volcano in violent eruption
심하게 분화하고 있는 화산

fire
[faiər]

n. 화재, 불

a forest fire 산불

storm
[stɔːrm]

n. 폭풍

the calm before a storm 폭풍 전의 고요

typhoon
[taifúːn]

n. 태풍

the center of a typhoon 태풍의 중심

tornado
[tɔːrnéidou]

n. 폭풍(토네이도)

houses destroyed by the tornado
폭풍으로 파괴된 집

hurricane
[hə́ːrəkèin]

n. 허리케인

the path of a hurricane 허리케인의 진로

flood
[flʌd]

n. 홍수, 범람

a flood causing severe damage
심각한 피해를 입힌 홍수

landslide
[lǽndslàid]

n. 산사태

The rain caused a landslide.
비가 와서 산사태가 났다

rockfall
[rɑfkɔːl]

n. 낙석

be killed by the rockfall 낙석에 맞아 죽다

collapse
[kəlǽps]

v. 붕괴하다

a roof collapses with a thud
지붕이 쾅하고 내려 앉다

evacuate
[ivǽkjuèit]

v. 대피시키다

evacuate the wounded 부상병을 후송하다

lightning
[láitniŋ]

n. 번개

be struck by lightning 번개에 맞다

thunder
[θʌ́ndəːr]

n. 천둥

a thunder of applause 우레같은 박수

tide wave
[taid weiv]

n. 해일

a tide wave driven by an earthquake
지진으로 인한 해일(=tsunami)

cold wave
[kould weiv]

n. 한파

A cold wave swept the country.
한파가 전국을 엄습했다.

drought
[draut]

n. 가뭄

a serious drought 심한 가뭄

crash
[kræʃ]

n. 추락, 충돌

be killed in an airplane crash
비행기추락으로 죽다

shelter
[ʃéltəːr]

n. 피난처, 쉼터

a bus shelter 버스 대기소

prevention
[privénʃən]

n. 예방

fire[accident] prevention 화재[사고] 예방

refuge
[réfju:dʒ]

n. 피난

take refuge from a storm
폭풍우로부터 피난하다

tsunami
[tsu:nɑ:mi]

n. 쓰나미

potential tsunami fault 잠재적 쓰나미 단층

PART 06

정보와 교통

01 정보통신과 미디어

■ 전화

communication
[kəmjùːnəkéiʃən]

n. 통신
a means of communication 통신수단

telephone
[téləfòun]

n. 전화
make a telephone call 전화를 걸다

cellular phone
[séljələr foun]

n. 휴대전화
carry a cellular phone
휴대전화를 가지고 다니다

toll-free number
[toul friːnʌ́mbəːr]

n. 수신자부담번호
dial the toll-free number
수신자부담번호로 걸다

dial tone
[dáiəl toun]

n. 발신음
listen for the dial tone 발신음을 듣다

call
[kɔːl]

v. 전화하다
call back 다시 전화하다

hold on
[hould ɑn]

v. (끊지않고)기다리다
hold on and wait 전화를 끊지않고 기다리다

hang up
[hæŋ ʌp]

v. 끊다

hang up the phone 전화를 끊다

connect
[kənékt]

v. 접속하다, 연결하다

get connected to the customer service
고객서비스센터에 연결되다

message
[mésidʒ]

n. 전갈, 메시지

leave a message 메시지를 남기다

receiver
[risíːvəːr]

n. 수화기

pick up the receiver 수화기를 들다

pay phone
[pei téləfòun]

n. 공중전화

pay phone booth 공중전화박스

text message
[tekst mésidʒ]

n. 문자 메시지

send a text message 문자메시지를 보내다

dial
[dáiəl]

v. 다이얼을 돌리다 *n.* 다이얼

turn a dial 다이얼을 돌리다

crank call
[kræŋk kɔːl]

n. 장난전화

make a crank call 장난 전화하다

cross
[krɔːs]

n. 혼선

be crossed 혼선되다

telephone directory
[téləfòun diréktəri]

n. 전화번호부

put one´s name in the telephone directory 전화번호부에 이름을 올리다

directory assistance [diréktəri əsístəns]	*n.* 전화번호 안내	directory assistance call 전화번호문의 전화
international telephone call [ìntərnǽʃənəl téləfòun kɔ:l]	*n.* 국제전화	international telephone call services 국제전화서비스업
domestic call [douméstik kɔ:l]	*n.* 국내전화	*national mobile telephone 국내 휴대전화
long-distance call [lɔ:ŋ dístəns kɔ:l]	*n.* 장거리전화	make a long-distance call 시외전화를 걸다
trunk call [trʌŋk kɔ:l]	*n.* 시외전화	long trunk call 장거리 통화
local call [lóukəl kɔ:l]	*n.* 시내전화	free local call 무료 시내전화
collect call [kəlékt kɔ:l]	*n.* 수신자부담 전화	to make a collect call 수신자 요금 부담으로 전화를 걸다
answering machine [ǽnsəriŋ məʃí:n]	*n.* 자동응답전화기	leave a message on the answering machine 자동응답기에 메시지를 남기다
videophone [vídioufòun]	*n.* 화상전화	internet videophone 인터넷 비디오폰
extension number [iksténʃən nʌ́mbə:r]	*n.* 내선번호	direct extension number 직통 내선번호

■ 우편

post [poust]
n. 우편
post office 우체국

letter [létəːr]
n. 편지
letter paper 편지지

envelope [énvəlòp]
n. 봉투
address an envelope 봉투에 주소를 쓰다

stamp [stæmp]
n. 우표
a commemorative stamp 기념 우표

postcard [póustkàːrd]
n. 엽서
a picture postcard 그림엽서

postage [póustidʒ]
n. 우편요금
pay the postage 우편요금을 지불하다

money order [mʌ́ni ɔ́ːrdər]
n. 우편환
a telegraphic money order 전신환

postmark [póustmàːrk]
v. 소인을 찍다
postmark a postcard 엽서에 소인을 찍다

zip code [zip koud]
n. 우편번호
search by ZIP code 우편번호를 찾다

mailbox [méilbàks]
n. 우체통
mail a letter at a mailbox
편지를 우체통에 넣다

window
[wíndou]

n. 창구

a cashier's window 출납 창구

address
[ədrés]

n. 주소

an address book 주소록

registered
[rédʒəstəːrd]

a. 등기의

registered letter 등기우편

send
[send]

v. 보내다

send a package 소포를 부치다

telegram
[téləgræ̀m]

n. 전보

an urgent telegram 지급 전보

parcel
[páːrsəl]

n. 소포

wrap up a parcel 소포를 꾸리다

scale
[skeil]

n. 저울

a pair of scales 천칭

home-delivery service
[houm dilívəri səːrvis]

n. 택배

send a parcel by home-delivery service
짐을 택배로 보내다

notice
[nóutis]

n. 통지

receive notice 통지를 받다

enclose
[enklóuz]

v. 동봉하다

enclose a return envelope
반신용 봉투를 동봉하다

airmail
[ɛərmèil]

n. 항공우편

send a letter (by) airmail
편지를 항공 우편으로 보내다
*sea mail 배편, surface mail 우편(육상우편)

junk mail
[dʒʌŋk mèil]

n. 광고 우편물

receive a junk mail 광고우편물을 받다

sender
[séndər]

n. 발신인, 발송인

return to the sender 발송자에게 반송하다
(receiver = 수취인)

answer
[ǽnsər]

n. 회답, 답장

in answer[reply] 회답으로

■ 매스미디어

media
[míːdiə]

n. 매체

the mass media 대중매체

magazine
[mæ̀gəzíːn]

n. 잡지

women's magazines 여성 잡지

journalist
[dʒɔ́ːrnəlist]

n. 언론인, 기자

a free-lance journalist 프리랜서의 저널리스트

publish
[pʌ́bliʃ]

v. 출판하다

publish a new edition 신판을 내다

interview
[íntərvjùː]

n. 회견, 인터뷰

a job interview 면접

reporter
[ripɔ́:rtɚːr]

n. 기자

a financial reporter 경제 기자

anchor
[ǽŋkər]

n. 방송앵커

an anchor woman 앵커우먼

sponsor
[spánsəːr]

v. 스폰서(가 되다)

sponsor a television program
텔레비전 프로그램의 스폰서가 되다

producer
[prədjúːsər]

n. 프로듀서(PD),제작자

an independent producer 독립 제작사

journalism
[dʒɔ́:rnəlìzəm]

n. 언론계

a career in journalism 신문 잡지 업에서의 경력

broadcast
[brɔ́:dkæ̀st]

n. 방송

a broadcast program 방송 프로

station
[stéiʃ-ən]

n. 방송국

television station TV방송국
radio station 라디오방송국

documentary
[dàkjəméntəri]

n. 다큐멘터리, 기록물

a documentary film 기록 영화

news
[njuːz]

n. 뉴스, 소식, 보도

the latest news 최신 뉴스.

drama
[drá:mə]

n. 극, 연극

a historical drama 역사극

rerun
[ríːrÀn]
n. 재상영
show a rerun of an old movie
옛날 영화를 재방송하다

satellite
[sǽtəlàit]
n. 위성
satellite channels 위성방송 채널

cable
[kéibəl]
n. 케이블
cable television 케이블 TV

commercial
[kəmə́ːrʃəl]
n. 방송 광고
do a commercial for Nike
나이키 광고에 출연하다

newspaper
[njúːzpèipəːr]
n. 신문
morning paper 조간신문
evening paper 석간신문

article
[áːrtikl]
n. 기사
a leading article (신문의) 사설

editorial
[èdətɔ́ːriəl]
n. 사설
an editorial writer 논설위원

advertisement
[ædvərtáizmənt]
n. 광고
a newspaper advertisement 신문 광고

press
[pres]
n. 보도기관
a press photographer 신문 사진 기자

news agency
[njuːz éidʒənsi]
n. 통신사
Tass News Agency 타스 통신사

report
[ripɔ́ːrt]

n. 보도, 기사

a newspaper report 신문 보도

coverage
[kʌ́vəridʒ]

n. 취재, 보도

the scope of news coverage activities
취재 활동 범위

audience
[ɔ́ːdiəns]

n. 시청자, 청취자

a TV audience TV 시청자

book
[buk]

n. 서적

books by Hemingway 헤밍웨이의 저작

fiction
[fíkʃən]

n. 소설

science fiction 공상 과학 소설

novel
[nɑ́v-əl]

n. (장편) 소설

the modern novel 현대 소설 문학

dictionary
[díkʃənèri]

n. 사전, 사서

a biographical dictionary 인명 사전

encyclopedia
[ensàikloupíːdiə]

n. 백과사전

an encyclopedia of music 음악 백과사전

author
[ɔ́ːθər]

n. 저자

an anonymous author 무명[익명] 작가

contribute
[kəntríbjuːt]

v. 기고하다

contribute to a magazine 잡지에 기고하다

edit
[édit]

v. 편집하다

finish editing the Annual Report
연례 보고서 편집을 마치다

manuscript
[mǽnjəskrìpt]

n. 원고

submit a manuscript to a publisher
출판사에 원고를 제출하다

deadline
[dédlàin]

n. (원고) 마감시간

meet a deadline for submitting a report
정해진 기한에 리포트를 제출하다

printing
[príntiŋ]

n. 인쇄

a first printing of 5000 copies 초판 5천부

■ 컴퓨터와 인터넷

computer
[kəmpjúːtər]

n. 컴퓨터

operate a computer 컴퓨터를 조작하다

desktop
[désktɑp]

n. 탁상용 컴퓨터

save a file on the desktop
데스크톱에 파일을 보관하다

laptop
[lǽptɑ̀]

n. 노트북

carry a laptop computer
노트북컴퓨터를 가지고 다니다

display
[displéi]

n. 화면표시기

a computer display 컴퓨터용 화면표시기

mouse
[maus]

n. 마우스

click a mouse 마우스를 누르다

click
[klik]

v. 클릭하다, 누르다

click no 아니오를 클릭하다

boot
[buːt]

v. 시동시키다, 띄우다

boot a computer 컴퓨터를 가동시키다

storage
[stɔ́ːridʒ]

n. 기억[저장]장치

computerized storage systems
컴퓨터 저장 시스템

hardware
[háːrdwèər]

n. 하드웨어

a hardware manufacturer 하드웨어 제조기업

software
[sɔ́ːftwèəːr]

n. 소프트웨어

download software 소프트웨어를 내려 받다

operating system
[ápərèitiŋ sístəm]

n. 운영체계

upgrade the operating system
운영체계를 업그레이드시키다

upgrade
[ʌ́pgrèid]

v. 업그레이드하다

upgrade one's computer
컴퓨터를 업그레이드하다

data
[déitər]

n. 자료

data storage 데이터 저장

database
[déitəbèis]

n. 데이터베이스

database industry 데이터베이스 산업

input
[ínpùt]

n. 입력

an input device 입력장치

output
[áutpùt]

n. 출력

control the data output 데이터 출력을 제어하다

printout
[príntàut]

n. 프린트 출력

file the printouts 프린트출력물을 철해두다

save
[seiv]

v. 저장하다

save the file 파일을 저장하다

file
[fail]

n. 기록철, 파일

copy a file 파일을 복사하다

analyze
[ǽnəlàiz]

v. 분석하다

analyze the results 결과를 분석하다

information
[ìnfərméiʃən]

n. 정보

pick up useful information 유익한 정보를 얻다

network
[nétwə̀:rk]

n. 통신망

a local area network 지역 네트워크

computer graphics
[kəmpjú:tər grǽfiks]

n. 컴퓨터 그래픽

a computer graphics specialist
컴퓨터 그래픽의 전문가

internet
[íntərnèt]

n. 인터넷

have access to the internet
인터넷에 접근하다

keyboard
[kíːbɔ̀ːrd]

n. 키보드, 자판

punch the keyboard 키보드를 치다

program
[próugræm]

n. 프로그램

run a test program 테스트 프로그램을 운용하다

search engine
[səːrtʃ éndʒən]

n. 검색엔진

use multiple search engines
여러개의 검색엔진을 사용하다

e-commerce
[iː kámərs]

n. 전자상거래

a pioneer in e-commerce
전자상거래의 선구자

home page
[houm peidʒ]

n. 홈페이지

set up a home page 홈페이지를 개설하다

messenger
[mésəndʒər]

n. 전달자, 메신저

instant messenger 인테넷상의 즉석대화

email
[íːmèil]

n. 전자우편

send an email 전자우편을 보내다

print
[print]

n. 인쇄 *v.* 인쇄하다

colour prints 칼라 인쇄

delete
[dilíːt]

n. 삭제 *v.* 삭제하다

delete some system files
시스템 파일들을 삭제하다

copy
[kápi]

n. 복사 *v.* 복사하다

a copy of a letter 편지의 사본

paste
[peist]

v. 붙이다

paste posters onto the wall
포스트를 벽에 붙이다

Identification(ID)
[aidèntəfikéiʃən]

n. 신원확인, 아이디

the Identification of a drowned body
익사체의 신원 확인

password
[pǽswə̀ːrd]

n. 비밀번호

give the password 암호를 대다

transmit
[trænsmít]

v. 전송하다

transmit an information 정보를 전송하다

download
[dáunlòud]

v. 다운로드(하다)

download a file 파일을 내려 받다

online
[ánlain]

a. 온라인의

an online ticket booking system
온라인 예매 시스템

offline
[ɔ́ːflàin]

a. 오프라인의

offline message 오프라인 메시지

virus
[váiərəs]

n. 바이러스

computer virus 컴퓨터 바이러스

hacker
[hǽkər]

n. 컴퓨터 침입자

identify the hacker 해커의 신원을 밝히다

02 교통과 건설

■ 도로 교통

traffic
[trǽfik]

n. 교통

a line of traffic 차량 행렬

transport
[trænspɔ́:rt]

n. 운송

the transport of mail by air
우편물의 항공 수송

baggage
[bǽgidʒ]

n. 수하물

carry two pieces of baggage
수하물을 2개 가지고 있다

elevator
[éləvèitər]

n. 승강기

a freight elevator 화물용 엘리베이터

escalator
[éskəlèitər]

n. 에스컬레이터

get on the escalator 에스컬레이터를 타다

car
[kɑ:r]

n. 자동차

a sleeping-car 침대차

transportation
[trænspə:rtéiʃ-ne-ən]

n. 운송, 교통

public transportation 공공 운송 체계

bus
[bʌs]

n. 버스

sightseeing bus 관광버스

subway
[sʌ́bwèi]

n. 지하철

travel by subway 지하철로 이동하다

airplane
[ɛ́ərplèin]

n. 비행기

by airplane 비행기로

truck
[trʌk]

n. 트럭

a dump truck 덤프트럭

jeep
[dʒi:p]

n. 지프

climb in(to) a jeep 지프차에 타다

ferry
[féri]

n. 배, 연락선

take the ferry 연락선을 타다.

helicopter
[hélikὰptər]

n. 헬리콥터

a helicopter pilot 헬리콥터 조종사

train
[trein]

n. 기차

an express train 급행열차

bicycle, bike
[báisikəl / baik]

n. 자전거

a duplex bicycle 2인승 자전거

motorcycle
[móutəːrsàikl]

n. 오토바이

motorcycle gangs 오토바이 폭주족

taxi
[tǽksi]

n. 택시

call a taxi 택시를 전화로 부르다

drive [draiv]	*v.* 운전하다	drive a car 차를 운전하다
get on [get ɔ:n]	*v.* 타다	get on a bus 버스를 타다
get off [get ɔ:f,]	*v.* 내리다	get off an airplane 비행기에서 내리다
ticket [tíkit]	*n.* 표	ticket window 매표구
fare [fɛər]	*n.* 요금	a bus fare 버스요금
expressway [ikspréswèi]	*n.* 고속도로	Gyongbu Expressway 경부 고속도로
toll gate [toul geit]	*n.* 요금소	collect tolls at a toll gate 요금소에서 요금을 모으다
railroad [réilròud]	*n.* 철도	underground railroad 지하 철도
driver's license [dráivər's láisəns]	*n.* 운전면허	renewal of a driver's license 운전 면허의 갱신
steering wheel [stí-əriŋ hwi:l]	*n.* 핸들	a lockable steering-wheel 잠글 수 있는 핸들

horn
[hɔːrn]

n. 경적

sound a car horn 경적을 울리다

accelerator
[æksélərèitər]

n. 가속장치

step on the accelerator 액셀러레이터를 밟다

brake
[breik]

n. 제동장치, 브레이크

with the brakes off 브레이크를 걸지 않고

tire
[taiər]

n. 바퀴

a spare tire 스페어 타이어

trunk
[trʌŋk]

n. 트렁크

stow clothes (away) in a trunk
트렁크 안에 옷을 집어넣다

road
[roud]

n. 도로, 길

road junctions 도로 교차점

street
[striːt]

n. 거리, 가로

a main street 큰 거리

avenue
[ǽvənjùː]

n. 대로

walk down avenue 큰 길을 걸어가다

way
[wei]

n. 길

lose one's way 길을 잃다

alley
[ǽli]

n. 좁은 길, 샛길

a back alley 뒷골목

seat belt
[siːt belt]

n. 안전벨트

Fasten your seat-belts! 안전벨트를 매라!

commuter
[kəmjúːtər]

n. 통근자

a commuter train 통근열차

passenger
[pǽsəndʒər]

n. 승객

a passenger boat 여객선

parking
[páːrkiŋ]

n. 주차

illegal parking 불법주차

gas station
[gæs stéiʃ-ən]

n. 주유소

fill up at a gas station 주유소에서 가득 주유하다

crossing
[krɔ́ːsiŋ]

n. 건널목

railroad crossing 철도 건널목

intersection
[ìntərsékʃən]

n. 교차점

at an intersection 교차점에서

traffic light
[trǽfik lait]

n. 신호등

stop at a traffic light 신호등에서 멈추다

traffic sign
[trǽfik sain]

n. 교통표지

miss the traffic sign 교통표지판을 놓치다

crosswalk
[krɔːswɔ́ːk]

n. 횡단보도

cross the street at a crosswalk
도로를 횡단보도에서 건너다

sidewalk
[sáidwɔ̀ːk]

n. 인도, 보도

walk a dog along the sidewalk
개를 인도에서 산책시키다

lane
[lein]

n. 차선

exclusive bus lanes 버스 전용차선

curve
[kəːrv]

n. 곡선, 커브

a sharp curve in the road 도로의 급커브

detour
[díːtuər]

n. 우회로

make a detour 우회하다

distance
[dístəns]

n. 거리

within walking distance 차로 갈 수 있는 거리

speed limit
[spiːd limit]

n. 제한속도

exceed the speed limit 제한 속도를 초과하다

speeding
[spíːdiŋ]

n. 속도위반

a speeding ticket 속도 위반 딱지

traffic law
[trǽfik lɔː]

n. 교통법규

violate traffic law 교통법규를 위반하다

traffic jam
[trǽfik dʒæm]

n. 교통체증

be stuck in a traffic jam
교통체증으로 꼼짝못하다

fine
[fain]

n. 벌금

a parking fine 주차 위반 벌금
be fined 벌금을 내다

pedestrian
[pədéstriən]

n. 보행자

a pedestrian walkway 보행자용 보도

shortcut
[ʃɔːrtkʌt]

n. 지름길

take a shortcut 지름길로 가다

■ 열차

railroad
[réilròud]

n. 철도

buy a railroad ticket 철도 표를 사다

subway
[sʌ́bwèi]

n. 지하철

a subway station 지하철 역

train
[trein]

n. 기차

miss the train 기차를 놓치다

station
[stéiʃ-ən]

n. 역

a freight station 화물역

terminal
[tə́ːrmən-əl]

n. 종점

the terminal station 종착역

platform
[plǽtfɔːrm]

n. 승강장

see off a person on the platform
플랫폼에서 남을 전송하다

crossing
[krɔ́ːsiŋ]

n. 건널목

railroad crossing 철도 건널목

derail
[diréi]

v. 탈선하다

get derailed 탈선하다

passenger
[pǽsəndʒər]

n. 승객

a passenger train 여객 열차

baggage
[bǽgidʒ]

n. 화물

a baggage tag 수화물의 꼬리표

crowded
[kráudid]

a. 혼잡한

crowded trains 만원 열차

empty
[émpti]

a. 빈

an empty seat 빈자리

one-way
[wʌn wei]

a. 편도의

a one-way ticket 편도 승차권

round-trip
[raund trip]

a. 왕복의

a round-trip ticket 왕복 승차권

transfer
[trænsfə́ːr]

v. 갈아타다

transfer from a bus to a train
버스에서 기차로 갈아타다

timetable
[táimtèibl]

n. 시각표

a train timetable 기차 시간표

transport
[trænspɔ́ːrt]

n. 운송 *v.* 운송하다

rail transport 철도 수송선

deliver
[dilívər]

v. 배달하다

deliver a package 소포를 배달하다

ship
[ʃip]

v. 수송(발송)하다

ship goods by rail 상품을 철도편으로 부치다

■ 항공

aviation
[èiviéiʃən]

n. 항공

civil aviation 민간 항공

aircraft
[ɛ́ərkræ̀ft]

n. 항공기

a passenger aircraft 여객기

jumbo jet
[dʒʌ́mbou dʒet]

n. 점보기(초대형여객기)

a jumbo jet disaster 점보기 사고

airline
[ɛ́ərlàin]

n. 항공로

scheme (out) a new airline
새로운 항공 노선을 계획하다

airport
[ɛ́ərpɔ̀ːrt]

n. 공항

Gimpo Airport 김포공항

control tower
[kəntróul táuəːr]

n. 관제탑

work in a control tower 관제탑에서 근무하다

airplane
[ɛ́ərplèin]

n. 비행기

by airplane 비행기로

flight
[flait]

n. 비행, 편

a direct flight 직항편

departure
[dipá:rtʃər]

n. 출발

time of departure 출발 시간

arrival
[əráivəl]

n. 도착

safe arrival 안착

delay
[diléi]

n. 연착 *v.* 연착되다

unexpected delays 예기치 않은 연착

boarding pass
[bɔ́:rdiŋ pæs]

n. 탑승권

show a boarding pass 탑승권을 보여주다

confirm
[kənfɔ́:rm]

v. (예약을) 확인하다

confirm one's reservation 예약을 확인하다.

take off
[teik ɔ:f]

v. 이륙하다

take off smoothly 부드럽게 이륙하다

land
[lænd]

v. 착륙하다

land an airplane in an airport
비행기를 공항에 착륙시키다

pilot
[páilət]

n. 조종사

a test pilot 테스트 파일럿

flight attendant
[flait əténdənt]

n. 객실승무원 (=flight crew)

ask a flight attendance for a glass of water 객실 승무원에게 물 한잔 달라고 하다

fly
[flai]

v. 비행하다

fly to Hong Kong 비행기로 홍콩에 가다

■ 선박

voyage
[vɔ́idʒ]

n. 항해

a transatlantic voyage 대서양 횡단 항해

sail
[seil]

v. 항해하다

sail in a steamer 기선으로 여행하다

ship
[ʃip]

n. 큰배

a merchant ship 상선

boat
[bout]

n. 작은배

a boat for hire 빌려주는 보트

ferry
[féri]

n. 페리, 연락선

suspend ferry service 페리 운행을 중단하다

cruise
[kruːz]

v. 순항하다

cruise along the shore 연안을 순항하다

tanker
[tǽŋkəːr]

n. 유조선

an oil tanker 유조선

port
[pɔːrt]

n. 항

a free port 자유항

harbor
[háːrbər]

n. 항구

a natural harbor 천연의 항구

breakwater
[bréikwɔ̀:tər]

n. 방파제

build a breakwater 방파제를 쌓다

lighthouse
[láithàus]

n. 등대

a lighthouse keeper 등대지기

anchor
[ǽŋkər]

n. 닻

weigh anchor 닻을 올리다

pirate
[páiərət]

n. 해적

clear the sea of pirates 해적을 퇴치하다

captain
[kǽptin]

n. 선장

In the mutiny the captain was killed
선상 반란으로 선장이 살해되었다

mate
[meit]

n. 항해사

the chief mate 1등 항해사

engineer
[èndʒəníər]

n. 기관사

a first engineer 1등 기관사

03 지리

■ 세계의 대륙과 지역

continent [kάntənənt]
n. 대륙
the Continent of Asia 아시아 대륙

Asia [éiʒə]
n. 아시아

Europe [júərəp]
n. 유럽

Africa [ǽfrikə]
n. 아프리카

Oceania [òuʃiǽniə]
n. 오세아니아

North America [nɔːrθ əmérikə]
n. 북아메리카
North America nebula 북아메리카 성운

South America [sauθ əmérikə]
n. 남아메리카
on a visit to South America
남아메리카 방문 중에

Alaska [əlǽskə]
n. 알래스카
Alaska Range 알래스카 산맥

Middle East
[mídl iːst]

n. 중동

an acute situation in the Middle East
중동의 급박한 정세

Central Asia
[séntrəl éiʒə]

n. 중앙아시아

music of the Central Asia 중앙아시아의 음악

Siberia
[saibíəriə]

n. 시베리아

the cold in Siberia 시베리아의 추위

Pacific (Ocean)
[pəsífik]

n. 태평양

the Pacific coast 태평양 연안

Atlantic (Ocean)
[ətlǽntik]

n. 대서양

the atlantic islands 대서양 제도

Indian Ocean
[índiən óuʃən]

n. 인도양

British indian Ocean Territory
영국령 인도양 식민지

Hawaiian Islands
[həwáiən áiləndz]

n. 하와이 제도

Mediterranean
[mèdətəréiniən]

n. 지중해

Mediterranean climate 지중해성 기후

North Pole
[nɔːrθ poul]

n. 북극

the geographical North Pole 북극점

South Pole
[sauθ poul]

n. 남극

fail to make it to the South Pole
남극 정복에 실패하다

■ 세계의 여러 나라

Japan [dʒəpǽn]   *n.* 일본

Korea [kərí:ə]   *n.* 한국

North Korea [nɔ:rθ kərí:ə]   *n.* 북한

China [tʃáinə]   *n.* 중국

Taiwan [táiwá:n]   *n.* 대만

Mongolia [mɑŋgóuliə]   *n.* 몽골

Vietnam [vjètná:m]   *n.* 베트남

Thailand [táilænd]   *n.* 태국

India [índiə]   *n.* 인도

Pakistan [pà:kistá:n]   *n.* 파키스탄

Singapore [síŋgəpɔ̀:r]   *n.* 싱가포르

Indonesia [ìndouní:ʒə]   *n.* 인도네시아

the Philippines
[ðə fíləpìːn]
n. 필리핀

America [əmérikə]
n. 미국

Mexico [méksikòu]
n. 멕시코

Ecuador [ékwədɔ̀ːr]
n. 에콰도르

Uruguay [júərəgwài]
n. 우루과이

Brazil [brəzíl]
n. 브라질

Argentina
[ὰːrdʒəntíːnə]
n. 아르헨티나

chile [tʃíli]
n. 칠레

Australia [ɔːstréiljə]
n. 오스트레일리아

New Zealand
[njuːzíːlənd]
n. 뉴질랜드

Canada [kǽnədə]
n. 캐나다

England [íŋglənd]
n. 영국

France [fræns]
n. 프랑스

Germany [dʒə́ːrməni]	n. 독일
Switzerland [swítsərlənd]	n. 스위스
Austria [ɔ́ːstriə]	n. 오스트리아
Poland [póulənd]	n. 폴란드
Hungary [hʌ́ŋɡəri]	n. 헝가리
the Netherlands [ðə nédəːrləndz]	n. 네덜란드
Italy [ítəli]	n. 이탈리아
vatican [vǽtikən]	n. 바티칸
Spain [spein]	n. 스페인
Portugal [pɔ́ːrtʃəɡəl]	n. 포르투갈
Sweden [swíːdn]	n. 스웨덴
Norway [nɔ́ːrwei]	n. 노르웨이
Russia [rʌ́ʃə]	n. 러시아

Greece [griːs]   *n.* 그리스

Yugoslavia [jùːgousláːviə]   *n.* 유고슬라비아

Ukraine [juːkréin]   *n.* 우크라이나

Israel [ízriəl]   *n.* 이스라엘

Egypt [íːdʒipt]   *n.* 이집트

Turkey [tə́ːrki]   *n.* 터키

Kuwait [kuwéit]   *n.* 쿠웨이트

Saudi Arabia [sáudi əréibiə]   *n.* 사우디아라비아

Yemen [jémən]   *n.* 예멘

Iran [irǽn]   *n.* 이란

Iraq [iráːk]   *n.* 이라크

Afghanistan [æfgǽnəstæ̀n]   *n.* 아프가니스탄

Ethiopia [ìːθióupiə]   *n.* 에티오피아

Kenya [kénjə]	*n.* 케냐
South Africa [sauθ ǽfrikə]	*n.* 남아프리카공화국
Morocco [mərákou]	*n.* 모로코
Algeria [ældʒíəriə]	*n.* 알제리
Hawaii [həwáiiː]	*n.* 하와이

■ 세계의 여러 나라 사람

American [əmérikən]	*n.* 미국인
Japanese [dʒæ̀pəníːz]	*n.* 일본인
Korean [kəríːən]	*n.* 한국인
Chinese [tʃainíːz]	*n.* 중국인
English [íŋgliʃ]	*n.* 영국인
German [ʤə́ːrmən]	*n.* 독일인
Italian [itǽljən]	*n.* 이태리인

Swiss [swis]	*n.* 스위스인
Canadian [kənéidiən]	*n.* 캐나다인
Russian [rʌ́ʃ-ən]	*n.* 러시아인
Greek [griːk]	*n.* 그리스인
Dutch [dʌtʃ]	*n.* 네덜란드인
Mexican [méksikən]	*n.* 멕시코인
Thai [tai]	*n.* 태국인
French [frentʃ]	*n.* 프랑스인
Filipino [filəpíːnou]	*n.* 필리핀인
Turkish [tə́ːrkiʃ]	*n.* 터키인
Australian [ɔːstréiljən]	*n.* 호주인(=Aussie)
New Zealander [njuːzíːləndər]	*n.* 뉴질랜드인(=Kiwi)
Spaniard [spǽnjərd]	*n.* 스페인사람

Pakistani [pàːkistáːni]   *n.* 파키스탄인

Singaporean
[síŋgəpɔ̀ːriən]   *n.* 싱가포르인

Indonesian
[ìndouníːʒən]   *n.* 인도네시아인

Swede [swiːd]   *n.* 스웨덴인

PART 07

자연과
과학

01 자연과 자연현상

■ 자연 전반

nature
[néitʃər]

n. 자연
preserve[destroy] nature
자연을 보호[파괴]하다

continent
[kántənənt]

n. 대륙
the New Continent 신대륙

mountain
[máunt-ən]

n. 산
climb a mountain 등산하다

mountain range
[máunt-ən reindʒ]

n. 산맥
the Taebaek mountain range 태백산맥

valley
[væli]

n. 골짜기(계곡)
a mountain valley 산골짜기

hill
[hil]

n. 언덕
go up a hill 언덕을 오르다

slope
[sloup]

n. 비탈, 경사지
steep slope 가파른 경사

ocean
[óuʃən]

n. 대양

the Pacific Ocean 태평양

sea
[siː]

n. 바다

across the sea(s) 바다를 건너, 해외로

river
[rívəːr]

n. 강

The Hudson River 허드슨 강

pond
[pɑnd]

n. 연못

a duck pond 오리 연못

lake
[leik]

n. 호수

Lake Victoria 빅토리아 호수

spring
[spriŋ]

n. 샘

spring water 샘물

well
[wel]

n. 우물

dig a well 우물을 파다

peninsula
[pinínsələ]

n. 반도

the Iberian peninsula 이베리아 반도

gulf
[gʌlf]

n. 만

the Gulf of Mexico 멕시코만

coast
[koust]

n. 해안, 연안

on the Pacific coast 태평양 연안에서

beach
[biːtʃ]

n. 해변

on a sandy beach 모래 해변에서

wave [weiv]	*n.* 파도	a breaking wave 부서지는 파도
tide [taid]	*n.* 조류, 조수	ebb[or low] tide 썰물, 간조
current [kə́:rənt]	*n.* 해류, 기류	a tidal current 조류
(water)fall [wɔ́:tə*r*fɔ̀:l]	*n.* 폭포	Niagara Falls 나이아가라 폭포
rock [rɑk]	*n.* 바위	a giant rock 거대한 바위
stone [stoun]	*n.* 돌	a house built of stone 석조 주택
pebble [pébəl]	*n.* 자갈	toy with a pebble 공기돌을 가지고 손장난하다
sand [sænd]	*n.* 모래, 사막	a grain of sand 한 알의 모래
land [lænd]	*n.* 땅, 나라	by land 육로로
field [fi:ld]	*n.* 밭	a corn field 옥수수밭
farm [fɑ:*r*m]	*n.* 농장	a fruit farm 과수원

soil [sɔil]	*n.* 흙, 토양	soil conditioner 토양 개량제
mud [mʌd]	*n.* 진흙	a mud hut 흙집
flatland [flǽtlænd]	*n.* 평지	a vast flatland 넓은 평지
jungle [dʒʌ́ŋgl]	*n.* 정글(밀림지대)	the king of the jungle 밀림의 왕
village [vílidʒ]	*n.* 마을	a fishing village 어촌
island [áilənd]	*n.* 섬	a desert island 무인도
sky [skai]	*n.* 하늘	a blue sky 푸른 하늘
air [ɛər]	*n.* 공기	the night air 밤공기
ozone layer [óuzoun léiəːr]	*n.* 오존층	the hole in the ozone layer 오존층에 난 구멍
bush [buʃ]	*n.* 수풀	a clump of bushes 관목 숲
forest [fɔ́(ː)rist]	*n.* 숲	cut down a forest 삼림의 수목을 벌채하다

creature
[kríːtʃər]

n. 생물

dumb creatures 동물

latitude
[lǽtətjùːd]

n. 위도

in latitude 40°N 북위 40도에

longitude
[lándʒətjùːd]

n. 경도

20 degrees 15 minutes of east longitude 동경 20도 15분

North Pole
[nɔːrθ poul]

n. 북극

walk to the North Pole 북극까지 걸어가다

South Pole
[sauθ poul]

n. 남극

an ozone hole over the South Pole 남극 상공의 오존 구멍

equator
[ikwéitər]

n. 적도

right on the equator 적도 직하의[에서]

desert
[dézərt]

n. 사막

the Sahara Desert 사하라사막

oasis
[ouéisis]

n. 오아시스

an oasis in the desert 사막의 오아시스

volcano
[vɑlkéinou]

n. 화산

an active volcano 활화산

glacier
[gléiʃər]

n. 빙하

an alpine glacier 고산성 빙하

iceberg
[aisbə:rg]

n. 빙산

the tip of the iceberg 빙산의 일각

swamp
[swɑmp]

n. 늪

the rot and waste of a swamp
부패한 불모의 소택지

marsh
[mɑ:rʃ]

n. 초지, 늪

cattle grazing the marshes
초지에서 풀을 뜯는 소들

sunlight
[sʌ́nlàit]

n. 햇살

ray of sunlight 한 줄기의 햇빛

ultraviolet rays
[ʌ̀ltrəváiəlit reiz]

n. 자외선

absorb ultraviolet rays 자외선을 흡수하다

horizon
[həráizən]

n. 수평선, 지평선

beyond the horizon 수평선 너머로

light
[lait]

n. 빛

in light 빛을 받고, 비치어

darkness
[dá:rknis]

n. 어둠

in the darkness 어둠속에서

earthquake
[ə́:rθkwèik]

n. 지진

feel an earthquake 지진을 느끼다

sunrise
[sʌ́nràiz]

n. 일출

before the sunrise 해뜨기 전에

sunset
[sÁnsèt]

n. 일몰

after sunset 일몰 후에

■ 날씨

weather
[wéðə:r]

n. 날씨

good weather for a walk 산책에 좋은 날씨

tropical
[trápik-əl]

a. 열대의

tropical diseases 열대병

temperate
[témp-ərit]

a. 온대의

temperate regions 온대 지방

frigid
[frídʒid]

a. 극한의, 한대의

a frigid day 몹시 추운 날

rain
[rein]

n. 비

a drizzling rain 이슬비

snow
[snou]

n. 눈

the snows of Mount Everest
에베레스트 산의 눈

wind
[wind]

n. 바람

a breath of wind 산들바람

sky
[skai]

n. 하늘

a blue sky 푸른 하늘

fair
[fɛər]
a. 청명한
fair weather 갠 날씨

cloudy
[kláudi]
a. 흐린
a cloudy sky 흐린 하늘

season
[síːz-ən]
n. 계절
the four seasons 사계절

cloud
[klaud]
n. 구름
a dark cloud 먹구름

fog
[fɔ(ː)g]
n. 안개
a dense fog 짙은 안개

frost
[frɔːst]
n. 서리
a heavy frost 된서리

shower
[ʃáuəːr]
n. 소나기
be caught in a shower 소나기를 만나다

downpour
[daunpɔ́ːr]
n. 폭우
be caught in a torrential downpour
억수 같은 호우를 만나다

hail
[heil]
n. 싸락눈, 우박
a piece of hail 한 알의 우박

climate
[kláimit]
n. 기후
a mild climate 온대성 기후

typhoon
[taifúːn]

n. 태풍

be in the path of a typhoon
태풍의 진로 안에 들다

storm
[stɔːrm]

n. 폭풍우

a storm of rain 폭우

thunder
[θʌ́ndəːr]

n. 천둥

a crash of thunder 천둥의 굉음

snowstorm
[snoustɔ́ːrm]

n. 눈보라

The snowstorm hit. 눈보라가 휘몰아쳤다

lightning
[láitniŋ]

n. 번개

a flash of lightning 번갯불

weather forecast
[wéðəːr fɔ́ːrkæ̀st]

n. 일기예보

according to the weather forecast
일기예보에 의하면

pressure
[préʃər]

n. 기압

air pressure 공기압

temperature
[témp-ərətʃuəːr]

n. 기온

a rise in temperature 기온의 상승

Fahrenheit
[fǽrənhàit]

n. 화씨

110 degrees Fahrenheit[=110°F]
화씨 110도

Celsius
[sélsiəs]

n. 섭씨

a thermometer with a Celsius scale
섭씨 눈금의 온도계

below zero
[bilóu zí-ərou]

n. 영하

fall to 10 degrees below zero
영하16도로 내려가다

above zero
[əbʌ́v zí-ərou]

n. 영상

ten degrees above zero 영상 10도

equator
[ikwéitər]

n. 적도

an equatorial climate 적도 기후

rainy season
[réini síːz-ən]

n. 장마

a long rainy season 긴 장마

humid
[hjúːmid]

a. 습기 찬, 눅눅한

a humid climate 눅눅한 기후

rainbow
[réinbòu]

n. 무지개

all the colors of the rainbow 갖가지 빛깔

blow
[blou]

v. (바람이) 불다

The storm blew up. 폭풍이 불었다

freeze
[friːz]

v. 얼다

Water freezes at 32°F.
물은 화씨 32도에서 언다.

drizzle
[drízl]

v. 이슬비가 내리다

It drizzles. 이슬비가 내리고 있다.

warm [wɔːrm]
a. 따뜻한
a warm room 따뜻한 방

wet [wet]
a. 젖은
a wet breeze 습한 바람

humidity [huːmídəti]
n. 습기, 습도
75 per cent humidity 75%의 습도

dry [drai]
a. 건조한
a dry spell 건기, 가뭄

east [iːst]
n. 동쪽
the east coast 동해안

west [west]
n. 서쪽
the west wind 서풍

south [sauθ]
n. 남쪽
a southeasterly wind 남동풍

north [nɔːrθ]
n. 북쪽
a northwesterly wind; a northwester 북서풍

■ 시간의 변화

dawn [dɔːn]
n. 새벽
at dawn 새벽녘에

sunrise
[sʌ́nràiz]

n. 일출, 해돋이

at sunrise 해 뜰 무렵에

morning
[mɔ́ːrniŋ]

n. 아침

in the morning 아침에

daytime
[deitaim]

n. 낮

in the daytime 낮에

noon
[nuːn]

n. 한낮, 정오

at noon 정오에

evening
[íːvniŋ]

n. 저녁

in the evening 저녁에

sunset
[sʌ́nset]

n. 일몰, 해넘이

at sunset 해질녘에

night
[nait]

n. 밤

late at night 밤 늦게

midnight
[mídnàit]

n. 한밤중

at midnight 한밤중에

eve
[iːv]

n. 전날, 전날 밤

Christmas Eve 크리스마스이브

02 과학

■ 테크놀로지

technology
[teknálədʒi]
n. 과학기술
new computer technologies
새로운 컴퓨터 기술

invention
[invénʃən]
n. 발명
the scientific inventions of the 20th century 20 세기의 과학 발명품

high-tech
[hai tek]
n. 첨단기술
the high-tech industry 하이테크 산업

develop
[divéləp]
v. 개발하다, 발전시키다
develop natural resources
천연자원을 개발하다

cell
[sel]
n. 세포
the nucleus of a cell 세포핵

nuclear power plant
[njúːkliəːr páuər plænt]
n. 원자력발전소
a nuclear power plant accident
원자력 발전소 사고

patent
[pǽtənt]

n. 특허

take out a patent for an invention
발명 특허를 받다

laser
[léizəːr]

n. 레이저

laser printer 레이저 프린터

genetics
[dʒinétiks]

n. 유전학

an expert on genetics 유전학의 전문가

gene
[dʒiːn]

n. 유전자

a dominant[recessive] gene
우성[열성] 유진자

clone
[kloun]

n. 복제생물, 클론

cloned sheep Dolly 복제양 돌리

metal
[métl]

n. 금속

a metal pipe 금속 파이프

■ 우주와 천체

space
[speis]

n. 우주

travel through space 우주여행을 하다.

celestial body
[səléstʃəl bádi]

n. 천체

an image of a celestial body 천체의 형상

galaxy
[gǽləksi]

n. 은하, 은하수 (=Milky Way)

bright stars in a galaxy
은하에서 밝게 빛나는 별

star
[stɑːr]

n. 별

a shooting[falling] star 유성(流星), 별똥별

moon
[muːn]

n. 달

a full moon 만월(보름달)

satellite
[sǽt-əlàit]

n. (인공)위성

a communications satellite 통신위성

telescope
[téləskòup]

n. 망원경

an astronomical telescope 천체 망원경

observation
[àbzərvéiʃən]

n. 관측

make a meteorological observation
기상을 관측하다

space shuttle
[speis ʃʌ́tl]

n. 우주 왕복선

space shuttle at takeoff 발사 단계의 우주왕복

space station
[speis stéiʃ-ən]

n. 우주정거장

International Space Station 국제우주정거장

astronaut
[ǽstrənɔ̀ːt]

n. 우주 비행사

a space shuttle astronaut 우주왕복선 비행사

spacecraft
[spéiskræ̀ft]

n. 우주선

spacecraft orbiting the earth
지구 궤도를 도는 우주선

space exploration
[spéis èksplǝréiʃǝn]

n. 우주탐사

a space exploration program[project]
우주탐사계획

rocket
[rákit]

n. 로켓

launch a rocket 로켓을 쏴 올리다

unidentified flying object
[Ànaidéntəfàid fláiiŋ ábdʒikt]

n. 미확인 비행 물체 (=UFO)

a UFO sighting 미확인 비행 물체의 목격

orbit
[ɔ́ːrbit]

n. 궤도

a space station in orbit round the moon
달 궤도내의 우주 정거장

gravity
[grǽvəti]

n. 중력

zero gravity 무중력 상태

Solar system
[sóuləːr sístəm]

n. 태양계

origin of the solar system 태양계의 기원

planet
[plǽnət]

n. 행성

the major planets 대행성

Jupiter
[dʒúːpətər]

n. 목성

the satellites of Jupiter 목성의 위성들

Mars
[maːrz]

n. 화성

mars attacks 화성 침공

Saturn
[sǽtəːrn]

n. 토성

Saturn's rings 토성의 고리

Venus
[víːnəs]

n. 금성

the mount of Venus
비너스의 언덕, (손금의) 금성구(金星丘)

Mercury
[mə́:rkjəri]

n. 수성

The closest planet to the Sun is Mercury. 태양에서 가장 가까운 행성은 수성이다.

Sun
[sʌn]

n. 태양

a bright sun 밝은 태양

Earth
[ə:rθ]

n. 지구

the earth's orbit round the sun
태양주위의 지구 궤도

North Star
[nɔ:rθ stɑ::r]

n. 북극성

*Polaris 북극성

eclipse
[iklíps]

n. 일식

a lunar[solar] eclipse 월식[일식]

comet
[kámit]

n. 혜성

the tail of a comet 혜성의 꼬리

meteor
[mí:tiər]

n. 유성, 별똥별

a meteor shower 쏟아져 내리는 유성

alien
[éiljən]

n. 외계인

aliens from outer space 우주로부터 온 외계인

solar
[sóulə:r]

a. 태양의

the solar calendar 양력

lunar
[lú:nər]

a. 달의

the lunar calendar 음력

03 환경과 에너지

■ 환경문제

environment [inváiərənmənt]
n. 환경
live in a polluted environment
오염된 환경에서 살다

ecology [i:káládʒi]
n. 생태학, 환경보존
ecology movement 환경 보호 운동

ecosystem [í:kousìstəm]
n. 생태계
equilibrium of ecosystem 생태계의 평형

destroy [distrói]
v. 파괴하다
destroy a town 도시를 파괴하다

harm [hɑːrm]
n. 해(악), 손해
do more harm than good 백해무익하다

resource [ríːsɔːrs]
n. 자원
natural resources 천연자원

recycling [riːsáik-əliŋ]
n. 재활용 *v.* 재활용하다
envelopes made from recycled paper
재생지로 만든 봉투

disposal [dispóuzəl]	*n.* 처리, 폐기 sewage disposal systems 오물처리 시스템	
conservation [kànsəːrvéiʃən]	*n.* 보호, 보존 (the) conservation of wildlife 야생 생물 보호	
regulate [régjəlèit]	*v.* 규제하다 regulate the traffic 교통을 단속하다	
prevent [privént]	*v.* 방지하다, 예방하다 prevent waste 낭비를 막다	
eliminate [ilímənèit]	*v.* 제거하다 eliminate smudges 얼룩을 빼다	
wildlife [wáildlàif]	*n.* 야생동물 a wildlife sanctuary 야생동물 보호지역	
extinct [ikstíŋkt]	*a.* 절멸한, 사멸한 an extinct species 멸종된 종	
pollution [pəlúːʃən]	*n.* 오염, 공해 environmental pollution 환경 오염	
contaminate [kəntǽmənèit]	*v.* 오염시키다 contaminate a river 강물을 더럽히다	
chemical [kémikəl]	*a.* 화학의 chemical action 화학 작용	
toxic [táksik]	*a.* 독성의, 유독한 a toxic drug 독약	

greenhouse effect
[gri:nhàus ifékt]

n. 온실효과

curb the greenhouse effect
온실효과를 억제하다

---

global warming
[glóubəl wɔ́ːrmiŋ]

n. 지구온난화

indications of global warming
지구온난화의 징후들

---

contain
[kəntéin]

v. 함유하다

face cream containing natural plant extracts 자연식물 추출물을 함유한 화장크림

---

dioxin
[dàiáksin]

n. 다이옥신

a common source of dioxin 다이옥신의 발생원

---

radioactive
[rèidiouǽktiv]

a. 방사능의

radioactive contamination 방사능 오염

---

carbon dioxide
[káːrbən daiáksaid]

n. 이산화탄소

emit carbon dioxide 이산화탄소를 배출하다

---

emission
[imíʃən]

n. 방출, 방사

thermionic emission 열이온 방사

---

waste
[weist]

n. 폐기물

industrial waste 산업 폐기물

---

trash
[træʃ]

n. 쓰레기

throw trash out 쓰레기를 내버리다

---

ozone
[óuzoun]

n. 오존

destruction of the ozone rayer 오존층의 파괴

04 생물

■ 동물

animal
[ǽnəməl]

n. 동물
a carnivorous animal 육식 동물동물

beast
[biːst]

n. 짐승
a beast of prey 맹수, 육식 동물

livestock
[láivstɑk]

n. 가축
livestock farming 목축(업), 축산.

young
[jʌŋ]

n. 새끼
the young of the eel 뱀장어 새끼

mother
[mʌ́ðəːr]

n. 어미
a mother dog 어미 개

female
[fíːmeil]

n. 암컷
a female cat 암코양이

male
[meil]

n. 수컷
a male dog 수캐

tail
[teil]

n. 꼬리

lift its tail 꼬리를 치다

wing
[wiŋ]

n. 날개

spread its wings 날개를 펴다

mammal
[mǽm-əl]

n. 포유동물

higher mammals 고등 포유동물

pet
[pet]

n. 애완동물

a pet shop 애완동물 가게

dog
[dɔ(:)g]

n. 개

guard dogs 맹인안내견

cat
[kæt]

n. 고양이

a he-cat 수고양이

rabbit
[rǽbit]

n. 토끼

rabbit warren 토끼장

pig
[pig]

n. 돼지

roast pig 통째로 구운 돼지.

horse
[hɔːrs]

n. 말

wild horses 야생마

cow
[kau]

n. 암소, 젖소

milk a cow 소의 젖을 짜다

cattle
[kǽtl]

n. 축우, 소

raise cattle 소를 키우다

mouse
[maus]

n. 생쥐
a house mouse 집쥐

rat
[ræt]

n. 쥐
like a drowned rat 흠뻑 젖어, 몹시 낙담하여

lamb
[læm]

n. 새끼 양
a flock of lambs 한 떼의 어린양

sheep
[ʃi:]

n. 양
raise[keep] sheep 양을 치다

goat
[gout]

n. 염소
goat's cheese 염소 치즈

donkey
[dáŋki]

n. 당나귀
stubborn as a donkey 당나귀처럼 고집센

zebra
[zí:brə]

n. 얼룩말
zebra stripes 얼룩말의 띠

elephant
[éləfənt]

n. 코끼리
a herd of elephant 코끼리 떼

monkey
[máŋki]

n. 원숭이
the Year of the Monkey 원숭이 해

deer
[diər]

n. 사슴
run like a deer 재빠르게 달리다

bear
[bɛər]

n. 곰
the polar bear 흰곰, 북극곰

camel
[kǽməl]

n. 낙타

a camel-hair coat 낙타털 코트

tiger
[táigəːr]

n. 호랑이

work like a tiger 맹렬히 일하다

lion
[láiən]

n. 사자

brave as a lion 사자같이 용맹스러운

giraffe
[dʒərǽf]

n. 기린

Giraffes have long necks. 기린은 목이 길다

reptile
[réptil]

n. 파충류

the reptilian age 파충류 시대

lizard
[lízərd]

n. 도마뱀

a lizard with a poisonous bite
독이를 가진 도마뱀

alligator
[ǽligèitər]

n. 악어

alligator handbag 악어 핸드백

fox
[fɑks]

n. 여우

a fox in his lair 굴에 있는 여우

wolf
[wulf]

n. 늑대

a pack of wolves 한 패의 늑대들

snake
[sneik]

n. 뱀

a poisonous snake 독사

■ 조류

bird
[bəːrd]

n. 새

a flock of birds 한 떼의 새

cage
[keidʒ]

n. 새장(우리)

a caged bird 새장의 새

nest
[nest]

n. 둥지, 보금자리

an ants' nest 개미집

tail
[teil]

n. 꼬리

a bushy tail 털이 북슬북슬한 꼬리

wing
[wiŋ]

n. 날개

untried wings 아직 날아본 일이 없는 날개

hatch
[hætʃ]

v. 알을 깨다, 부화하다

hatch chickens artificially
인공적으로 병아리를 부화시키다

duck
[dʌk]

n. 오리

a mandarin duck 원앙새

chicken
[tʃíkin]

n. 닭

free-range chickens 놓아 기른 닭

hen
[hen]

n. 암탉

Hens lay eggs. 닭은 알을 낳다.

chick
[tʃik]

n. 병아리

a hen with her chicks 병아리들을 거느린 암탉

goose [guːs]	*n.* 거위 A goose squawks. 거위가 꽥꽥 울다.
wild goose [waild guːs]	*n.* 기러기 A wild goose is honking. 기러기가 끼루룩거리다
sparrow [spǽrou]	*n.* 참새 house sparrow (보통의) 참새
swallow [swálou]	*n.* 제비 Swallows were twittering. 제비가 지지배배 울고 있었다.
pigeon [pídʒən]	*n.* 비둘기 a homing pigeon 제 집으로 돌아오는 비둘기
hawk [hɔːk]	*n.* 매 hawk- billed 매부리 같은
eagle [íːgəl]	*n.* 독수리 eagles hunting their prey 먹이를 사냥하는 독수리
crow [krou]	*n.* 까마귀 a white crow 아주 드문 것, 진기한 것
magpie [mǽgpài]	*n.* 까치 magpie lark 까치종다리
pheasant [féz∂nt]	*n.* 꿩 roast pheasant 꿩 구이

skylark
[skáilà:rk]

n. 종달새

skylarks warbling in the sky
하늘에서 지저귀는 종달새들

owl
[aul]

n. 올빼미

hear the hoot of an owl
올빼미가 부엉부엉 하는 소리를 듣다

migrant bird
[máigrənt bə:rd]

n 철새

migrant sea birds 바다 철새

parrot
[pǽrət]

n. 앵무새

play the parrot 남의 흉내를 내다

crane
[krein]

n. 두루미(학)

a hooded crane 흑 두루미

swan
[swɑn]

n. 백조

the Swan of Avon 에이번의 백조
(Shakespeare의 별칭)

peacock
[píːkɑ̀k]

n. 공작

proud as a peacock 공작처럼 뽐내는

ostrich
[ɔ́(:)stritʃ]

n. 타조

a plume of ostrich feathers 타조 털의 깃털

■ 곤충

insect
[ínsekt]

n. 곤충

insect bite 벌레 물린 데

bee
[biː]

n. 꿀벌

queen bee 여왕벌

wasp
[wɑsp]

n. 말벌, 나나니벌

wasp sting 나나니벌의 독침

butterfly
[bʌ́tərflài]

n. 나비

the life cycle of the butterfly
나비의 생활 주기

dragonfly
[drǽgənflài]

n. 잠자리

a red dragonfly 고추잠자리

firefly
[fáiərflài]

n. 반딧불

the glow of a firefly 개똥벌레의 빛

fly
[flai]

n. 파리

a cloud of flies 많은 파리 떼

maggot
[mǽgət]

n. 구더기

be infested with maggots 구더기가 들끓다

mosquito
[məskíːtou]

n. 모기 모기떼

(a column of) swarming mosquitoes
한 무더기의 모기떼

ant
[ænt]

n. 개미

a red ant 불개미

termite
[tə́ːrmait]

n. 흰개미

a termite colony 흰개미 집단

spider
[spáidər]

n. 거미
A spider spins a web. 거미가 거미줄을 치다.

web
[web]

n. 거미줄
a spider's web 거미의 거미집

earthworm
[ə:rθwə̀:rm]

n. 지렁이
An earthworm is wriggling along.
지렁이가 꿈틀거리고 있다.

silkworm
[sílkwə̀:rm]

n. 누에
the silkworm moth 누에나방

grasshopper
[grɑ:shàpər]

n. 메뚜기
Suddenly a grasshopper hopped from the leaf. 갑자기 메뚜기가 잎에서 뛰어올랐다.

flea
[fli:]

n. 벼룩
The flea hopped. 벼룩이 톡 튀었다.

scorpion
[skɔ́:rpiən]

n. 전갈
water scorpion (곤충) 장구애비

beetle
[bí:tl]

n. 딱정벌레, 풍뎅이
stag beetle 사슴벌레

cricket
[kríkit]

n. 귀뚜라미
A cricket chirps. 귀뚜라미가 울다.

ladybug
[leidbʌg]

n. 무당벌레
a ladybug on the leaf 나뭇잎 위의 무당벌레

moth
[mɔ(:)θ]

n. 나방

get the moth (옷이) 좀먹다

caterpillar
[kǽtərpìlər]

n. 유충

A caterpillar turns into a butterfly.
애벌레는 나비가 된다

cocoon
[kəkúːn]

n. 고치, 번데기

reel silk off cocoons 고치에서 실을 잣다

cockroach
[kákròutʃ]

n. 바퀴벌레

exterminate cockroaches
바퀴벌레를 근절하다

snail
[sneil]

n. 달팽이

a snail track 달팽이가 지나간 자국

slug
[slʌg]

n. 민달팽이

the trail of a slug 달팽이의 지나간 자국

■ 어류

fish
[fiʃ]

n. 물고기

resh-water fish 담수어

shrimp
[ʃrimp]

n. 새우

otted shrimps 새우 냄비 요리

squid
[skwid]

n. 오징어

fried squid 튀긴 오징어

octopus [áktəpəs]	*n.* 문어	a boiled octopus 문어 데침
eel [i:l]	*n.* 장어	(as) slippery as an eel (뱀장어처럼) 미끈미끈한
whale [hweil]	*n.* 고래	a sperm whale 향유고래
dolphin [dálfin]	*n.* 돌고래	dolphin oil 돌고래 기름
shark [ʃɑːrk]	*n.* 상어	the great white shark 백상아리
mackerel [mǽk-ərəl]	*n.* 고등어	smoked mackerel 훈제 고등어
sardine [sɑːrdíːn]	*n.* 정어리	canned sardines 정어리 통조림
saury [sɔ́ːri]	*n.* 꽁치	a big catch of saury 꽁치의 풍어
crab [kræb]	*n.* 게	crab meat 게의 살
trout [traut]	*n.* 송어	a piece of smoked trout 훈제 송어 한 조각
salmon [sǽmən]	*n.* 연어	salmon steak 연어 스테이크

tuna
[tjúːnə]

n. 다랑어, 참치

slices of raw tuna 다랑어의 어회

turtle
[tə́ːrtl]

n. 바다거북

turtle-slow barges 거북처럼 느린 거룻배

tortoise
[tɔ́ːrtəs]

n. 민물거북

hare and tortoise 토끼와 거북(의 경주)

frog
[frɔːg]

n. 개구리

an edible frog 식용 개구리

tadpole
[tǽdpòul]

n. 올챙이

A tadpole is transformed into a frog.
올챙이는 개구리가 된다

seaweed
[síːwìːd]

n. 해초, 미역

two bunches of seaweed 미역 두 꼭지(다발)

lobster
[lábstər]

n. 갯가재

catch lobsters in a little stream
개울에서 가재를 잡다

■ 조개류

shellfish
[ʃélfiʃ]

n. 갑각류, 조개

gather shellfish 조개를 줍다

scallop
[skáləp]

n. 가리비

smoked scallop 훈제 가리비 요리

abalone
[æbəlóuni]

n. 전복
abalone porridge 전복죽

oyster
[ɔ́istər]

n. 굴
an oyster harvest 굴 채취

clam
[klæm]

n. 대합조개
open a clam 조개를 바르다

mussel
[mʌ́s-əl]

n. 홍합
mussel soup 홍합탕

05 식물

■ 식물 전반

plant
[plænt]
n. 식물
alpine plants 고산 식물

tree
[tri:]
n. 나무
lemon tree 레몬 나무

flower
[fláuər]
n. 꽃
artificial flowers 조화

leaf
[li:f]
n. 잎
a poppy leaf 양귀비 꽃잎

root
[ru:t]
n. 뿌리
roots of hair 모근

stem
[stem]
n. 줄기
plants with hairy stems 줄기에 털이 많은 식물

branch
[bræntʃ]
n. 가지
a dead branch 죽은 가지

fruit
[fruːt]

n. 과일, 열매

grow fruit 과일을 재배하다

vegetable
[védʒətəbəl]

n. 야채

live on vegetables 채식하다

seed
[siːd]

n. 씨앗

sow seed in the ground 땅에 씨를 뿌리다

skin
[skin]

n. 껍질

the skin of a grape 포도 껍질

bush
[buʃ]

n. 관목, 덤불

trees and bushes 교목과 관목

wood
[wud]

n. 숲

go for a walk in the wood(s)
숲으로 산책하러 가다

grass
[græs]

n. 풀, 잔디

a field of grass 풀밭, 초원

field
[fiːld]

n. 목초지, 풀밭

flowers of the field 들꽃

ivy
[áivi]

n. 담쟁이덩굴

an ivy covered building 담쟁이로 덮인 건물

seedling
[síːdliŋ]

n. 모종, 묘목

tomato seedlings 토마토 묘목

fallen leaves
[fɔ́:lən líːvz]

n. 낙엽

take a walk over the fallen leaves
낙엽을 밟고 산책하다

moss
[mɔ(ː)s]

n. 이끼

moss-covered rocks 이끼가 낀 바위

cotton
[kátn]

n. 목화

pick cotton (from a cotton plant)
목화를 따다

magnolia
[mægnóuliə]

n. 목련

a magnolia blossom 목련꽃

sprout
[spraut]

n. 새싹

new buds sprouting from the trees
나무에서 움트고 있는 새싹들

petal
[pétl]

n. 꽃잎

rose petals 장미 꽃잎

bud
[bʌd]

n. 꽃봉오리

a flower bud 꽃눈

pollen
[pálən]

n. 꽃가루

pollen sack 꽃가루주머니

bulb
[bʌlb]

n. 알뿌리

Lilies grow from bulbs.
백합은 알뿌리에서 성장한다.

vine
[vain]

n. 덩굴

a row of vines 한 줄기로 뻗어나간 덩굴

rose
[rouz]

n. 장미

a wild rose 들장미

cherry blossom
[tʃéri blásəm]

n. 벚꽃

full-blown cherry blossoms 난만한 벚꽃

lily
[líli]

n. 백합

a Madonna lily 흰 백합

sunflower
[sʌ́nflàuər]

n. 해바라기

sunflower oil 해바라기기름

tulip
[tjúːlip]

n. 튜울립

the blooms of tulips 튤립꽃

carnation
[kɑːrnéiʃən]

n. 카네이션

wear a red carnation on the breast
빨간 카네이션을 가슴에 달고 있다

orchid
[ɔ́ːrkid]

n. 난초

a wild orchid 야생란

daffodil
[dǽfədìl]

n. 수선화

a double daffodil 겹꽃 수선화

chrysanthemum
[krisǽnθəməm]

n. 국화

a wild chrysanthemum 들국화

dandelion
[dǽndəlàiən]

n. 민들레

the pappus of a dandelion 민들레의 깃털

bamboo
[bæmbúː]

n. 대나무

bamboo shoots 죽순

thorn
[θɔːrn]

n. 가시

hedges of thorn 가시나무 산울타리

reed
[riːd]

n. 억새

reed shaken with the wind
바람에 흔들리는 갈대

■ 야채

lettuce
[létis]

n. (양)상추

a lettuce and tomato salad
상추와 토마토 샐러드

cabbage
[kǽbidʒ]

n. 양배추

a head of cabbage 양배추 한 통

onion
[ʌ́njən]

n. 양파

onion soup 양파 수프

green onion
[griːn ʌ́njən]

n. 파

green onion bundles 파강회

leek
[liːk]

n. 부추

Korean-leek kimchi 부추김치

carrot [kǽrət]	*n.* 당근 grated carrot 간 당근
cucumber [kjúːkəmbər]	*n.* 오이 cucumber pickles 오이김치
pumpkin [pʌ́mpkin]	*n.* 노란 호박 pumpkin pie 호박 파이
radish [rǽdiʃ]	*n.* 샐러드용 빨간 무 two bunches of radish 무 두 단
garlic [gáːrlik]	*n.* 마늘 a clove of garlic 마늘 한쪽
ginger [dʒíndʒər]	*n.* 생강 crystallized ginger 설탕절임한 생강
green pepper [griːn pépər]	*n.* 피망 peppers stuffed with meat and rice 고기와 쌀을 채운 피망
bean sprout [biːn spraut]	*n.* 콩나물 bean-sprout soup 콩나물국
potato [pətéitou]	*n.* 감자 boiled potatoes 삶은 감자
sweet potato [swiːt pətéitou]	*n.* 고구마 a roast sweet potato 군고구마

tomato
[təméitou]

n. 토마토

tomato ketchup 토마토케첩

bamboo shoot
[bæmbúːʃuːt]

n. 죽순

bamboo shoots after a rain
비온 뒤에 죽순이 나다

spinach
[spínitʃ]

n. 시금치

spinach soup 시금치 수프

broccoli
[brákəli]

n. 브로콜리

forget to buy the broccoli
브로콜리 사는 것을 깜박 잊다

cauliflower
[kɔ́ːləflàuər]

n. 콜리플라워(꽃양배추)

cauliflower cheese
콜리플라워 치즈(콜리플라워에 치즈소스를 얹은 요리)

mushroom
[mʌ́ʃru(ː)m]

n. 송이버섯

a button mushroom 작은 송이버섯

eggplant
[egplǽnt]

n. 가지

barbecued eggplant 가지(산)적

ginseng
[dʒínseŋ]

n. 인삼

ginseng tea 인삼차

celery
[séləri]

n. 샐러리

celery soup 셀러리 수프

asparagus
[əspǽrəgəs]

n. 아스파라거스

a stalk of asparagus 아스파라거스 한 줄기

parsley
[páːrsli]

n. 파슬리

a bunch of parsley 한 다발의 파슬리

lotus root
[lóutəs ruːt]

n. 연근

lotus root extract 연근 추출물

■ 과일

pick
[pik]

v. (과일 등을) 따다, 고르다, 줍다

pick cherries 버찌를 따다

apple
[ǽpl]

n. 사과

peel apples 사과 껍질을 벗기다

tangerine
[tæ̀ndʒ-əríːn]

n. 감귤

a tangerine orchard 감귤농장

peach
[piːtʃ]

n. 복숭아

the fuzz on a peach 복숭아의 잔털

banana
[bənǽnə]

n. 바나나

a hand of bananas 바나나 한 송이

melon
[mélən]

n. 멜론

a slice of melon 멜론 한 조각

orange
[ɔ́(ː)rindʒ]

n. 오렌지

orange peel 오렌지 껍질

strawberry
[strɔ́ːbèri]

n. 딸기

strawberry jam 딸기 잼

watermelon
[wɔ́ːtəːrmèlən]

n. 수박

the rind of a watermelon 수박 껍질

grape
[greip]

n. 포도

a bunch of grapes 포도 한송이

pear
[pɛər]

n. 배

a juicy pear 즙이 많은 배

persimmon
[pəːrsímən]

n. 감

a ripe persimmon 홍시

blueberry
[blúːbèri]

n. 블루베리

bluberry jam 블루베리 잼

kiwi
[kíːwi]

n. 키위

kiwi juice 키위주스

chinese date
[tʃainíːz deit]

n. 대추

stoneless dates 씨 없는 대추

pineapple
[páinæ̀pl]

n. 파인애플

a can of pineapple rings
고리모양으로 자른 파인애플 통조림

cherry
[tʃéri]

n. 버찌

cherry lips 앵두같이 붉은 입술

lime
[laim]

n. 라임

lime juice 라임주스

lemon
[lémən]

n. 레몬

lemon tea 레몬 차

plum
[plʌm]

n. 자두

graft the pear upon the plum
자두나무에 배를 접붙이다

apricot
[éiprəkɑ̀t]

n. 살구

dried apricots 말린 살구

mango
[mǽŋgou]

n. 망고

the sweet flesh of a mango
망고의 달콤한 과육

coconut
[kóukonʌt]

n. 코코넛

coconut oil 코코넛 오일

pomegranate
[páməgræ̀nit]

n. 석류

pomegranate seeds 석류 씨

fig
[pig]

n. 무화과

pulled figs (터키산(産)) 말린 무화과

■ 견과류

walnut
[wɔ́:lnʌ̀t]

n. 호두

crack a walnut 호두를 까다

chestnut
[tʃésnʌ̀t]

n. 밤

roast chestnuts 밤을 굽다

peanut
[píːnʌt]

n. 땅콩

peanut butter 땅콩 버터

pine nut
[pain nʌt]

n. 잣

a gruel made of rice and pine nuts 잣죽

■ 곡물

grain
[grein]

n. 곡물

a field of grain 곡물 밭

rice
[rais]

n. 쌀

boil[cook] rice 밥을 짓다

wheat
[hwiːt]

n. 밀

wheat flour 밀가루

oat
[out]

n. 귀리

oat cakes 귀리 케이크

rye
[rai]

n. 호밀

rye bread 호밀빵

barley
[báːrli]

n. 보리

barley tea 보리차

almond
[áːmənd]

n. 아몬드

almond blossom 아몬드 꽃

corn
[kɔːrn]

n. 옥수수

break corn 옥수수를 따다

sesame [sésəmi]	*n.* 참깨 sesame oil 참기름
bean [biːn]	*n.* 콩 snap beans 깍지가 있는 콩
soy bean [sɔi biːn]	*n.* 대두, 메주콩 soybean paste 된장
redbean [red biːn]	*n.* 팥 cooked rice and red beans 팥밥
unripe bean [ʌnráip biːn]	*n.* 풋콩 *unripe fruit 익지 않은 과일
mungbean [mʌŋ biːn]	*n.* 녹두 a mung-bean pancake 녹두 빈대떡
kidney bean [kídnibiːn]	*n.* 강낭콩 put kidney beans in the rice 밥에 강낭콩을 얹다
pea [piː]	*n.* 완두콩 split peas 껍질을 까서 말린 완두(수프용)
foxtail millet [fákstèil mílit]	*n.* 조 a grain of foxtail millet 조의 낟알
flour [flauər]	*n.* 곡물가루, 밀가루 rye flour 호밀가루

whole wheat
[houl hwiːt]

n. 통밀

wholewheat bread 통밀 빵

adlay
[ǽdlài]

n. 율무

unshelled grains of adlay 율무쌀

glutinous rice
[glúːtənəs rais]

n. 찹쌀

glutinous rice flour 찹쌀가루

buckwheat
[bʌ́khwìːt]

n. 메밀

buckwheat noodles[vermicelli] 메밀국수

brown rice
[braun rais]

n. 현미

germinated brown rice 발아현미

PART 08

교육과
문화

01 교육과 학교

■ 교육

education
[èdʒukéiʃən]

n. 교육
elementary[compulsory] education
초등[의무] 교육

learn
[ləːrn]

v. 배우다
learn English 영어를 배우다

study
[stʌ́di]

n. 공부하다
study physics 물리학 연구를 하다

student
[stjúːd-ənt]

n. 학생
a college[university] student 대학생

literacy
[lítərəsi]

n. 식자(읽고 쓸 줄 앎)
a literacy rate 식자율(識字率)

teacher
[tíːtʃəːr]

n. 선생님
an English teacher 영어 교사

kindergarten
[kíndərgàːrtn]

n. 유치원
a kindergarden teacher 유치원 교사

cram school
[kræm skuːl]

n. 입시학원

go to cram school 입시학원에 다니다

institute
[ínstətjùːt]

n. 연구소

teacher at a research institute
연구소에서 가르치다

lifelong education
[láiflɔ(ː)ŋ èdʒukéiʃən]

n. 평생교육

lifelong education courses 평생교육 과정

teaching method
[tíːtʃiŋ méθəd]

n. 교수법

effective teaching methods 효과적인 교수법

degree
[digríː]

n. 학위

bachelor's degree 학사학위

Master's degree
[mǽstəɾ's digríː]

n. 석사학위

take a Master's degree in English
영어 석사학위를 받다

doctorate
[dáktərit]

n. 박사학위

obtain a doctorate by presenting a thesis 논문을 제출해서 박사 학위를 받다

professor
[prəfésəɾ]

n. 교수

a professor emeritus 명예 교수

tutor
[tjúːtəɾ]

n. 개인교사, 가정교사

a resident tutor 입주 가정 교사

apply
[əplái]

v. 지원하다

apply for a job 구직하다

scholarship
[skálərʃip]

n. 장학금
study on a scholarship 장학금을 받고 공부하다

present
[prézənt]

a. 출석의
be present at the lecture 강의에 출석하다

absent
[ǽbsənt]

a. 결석의
be absent from school 학교에 결석하다

study abroad
[stʌ́di əbrɔ́ːd]

v. 유학하다
study abroad at government expenses 국비로 유학하다

■ 학교

enter
[éntər]

v. 입학, 입학하다
enter a university 대학에 입학하다

elementary
[èləméntəri]

a. 기초의, 초등의
elementary school 초등학교

school
[skuːl]

n. 학교
middle school 중학교 / high school 고등학교

college
[kálidʒ]

n. (전문)대학
go to college 대학에 다니다

university
[jùːnəvə́ːrsəti]

n. 대학교
go to university 대학교에 다니다

01 교육과 학교

grade
[greid]
n. 학년
go up a grade 학년이 올라가다

freshman
[fréʃmən]
n. 대학 1학년
a college freshman 대학 1학년생

sophomore [sáf-əmɔ̀:r]
n. 대학 2학년

junior [dʒú:njər]
n. 3학년, 후배

senior [sí:njər]
n. 4학년, 선배

classmate
[klǽsmèit]
n. 반 친구(급우)
quarrel with a classmate 급우와 말다툼하다

graduate
[grǽdʒuèit]
v. 졸업하다 *n.* 졸업생
graduate from university 대학을 졸업하다
(graduate school = 대학원)

graduation (ceremony)
[grædʒuéiʃən sérəmòuni]
n. 졸업식
hold the graduation 졸업식을 거행하다

dropout
[drɑpàut]
n. 중퇴자
a college drop-out 대학 중퇴자

classroom
[klǽsrù(:)m]
n. 교실
a noisy classroom 시끄러운 교실

library
[láibrèri]
n. 도서관
a circulating library 이동도서관

gym
[ʤim]
n. 체육관
work out in a gym 체육관에서 훈련하다

dormitory
[dɔ́ːrmətɔ̀ːri]
n. 기숙사
live in a dormitory 기숙사 생활을 하다

auditorium
[ɔ̀ːditɔ́ːriəm]
n. 강당
an auditorium with seating accommodation for one thousand 천명의 좌석이 있는 강당

playground
[pléigràund]
n. 운동장, 놀이터
children talking in the playground 운동장에서 이야기하는 아이들

alumnus
[əlʌ́mnəs]
n. 동창생
an alumni association 동창회

entrance exam
[éntrəns igzǽm]
n. 입학시험
college entrance exam 대입시험

bullying
[búliŋ]
n. 괴롭힘, 이지메
a victim of bullying 괴롭힘[왕따]의 희생자

■ 학문

mathematics
[mæ̀θ-əmǽtiks]
n. 수학
higher mathematics 고등수학

history
[hístəri]
n. 역사
do research in history 역사를 연구하다

ethics
[éθiks]

n. 윤리학

practical ethics 실천 윤리학

geography
[ʤiːágrəfi]

n. 지리

human geography 인문지리

literature
[lítərətʃər]

n. 문학

English literature 영문학

economics
[ekənámiks]

n. 경제학

micro economics 미시 경제학

political science
[pəlítikəl sáiəns]

n. 정치학

get a master's degree in political science 정치학 박사학위를 따다

philosophy
[filásəfi]

n. 철학

empirical philosophy 경험철학

psychology
[saikálədʒi]

n. 심리학

child psychology 아동심리학

anthropology
[ænθrəpálədʒi]

n. 인류학

cultural anthropology 문화인류학

archaeology
[àːrkiálədʒi]

n. 고고학

be specialized in archaeology
고고학을 전문으로 하다

science
[sáiəns]

n. 과학

computer science 컴퓨터 과학

engineering
[èndʒəníəriŋ]

n. 공학

electrical engineering 전기공학

chemistry
[kémistri]

n. 화학

organic chemistry 유기화학

biology
[baiálədʒi]

n. 생물

molecular biology 분자생물학

physics
[fíziks]

n. 물리학

the laws of physics 물리학 법칙

genetics
[ʤinétiks]

n. 유전학

microbial genetics 미생물 유전학

medicine
[médəs-ən]

n. 의학

clinical medicine 임상의학

astronomy
[əstránəmi]

n. 천문학

theoretical astronomy 이론천문학

Sociology
[sòusiálədʒi]

n. 사회학

urban sociology 도시 사회학

business administration
[bíznis ædmìnəstréiʃən]

n. 경영학

Master's of Business Administration
경영학 석사학위 (=MBA)

physical education
[fízikəl èdʒukéiʃən]

n. 체육

get the physical education class
체육수업을 받다

fine art
[fain ɑːrt]

n. 미술

applied fine arts 응용미술

music
[mjúːzik]

n. 음악

folk music 민속음악

scholar
[skálər]

n. 학자

history scholar 역사 학자

discovery
[diskʌ́vəri]

n. 발견

a voyage of discovery 발견을 위한 항해

invention
[invénʃən]

n. 발명(품)

exhibit a new invention 신발명품을 전시하다

research
[risə́ːrtʃ]

n. 연구

scientific research 과학적 연구

theory
[θíːəri]

n. 이론

theory and practice 이론과 실제

■ 수업·커리큘럼

teacher
[tíːtʃər]

n. 선생님

class teacher 담임 선생님

attendance
[əténdəns]

n. 출석

take attendance 출석을 체크하다

absence
[ǽbsəns]

n. 결석

a report of absence 결석계

homework
[houmwə*r*k]

n. 숙제

a homework book 숙제장

assignment
[əsáinmənt]

n. 숙제

submit an assignment 숙제를 제출하다

scholarship
[skálə:*r*ʃip]

n. 장학금

win a scholarship to the university
대학 입학 장학금을 받다

quiz
[kwiz]

n. 쪽지 시험

a snap quiz 벼락 시험

lecture
[léktʃə:*r*]

n. 강의

give a lecture 강의하다

thesis
[θí:sis]

n. 논문

a graduation thesis 졸업 논문

textbook
[tékstbùk]

n. 교과서

a grammar textbook 문법 교재

reference book
[réf-ərəns buk]

n. 참고서

choose a reference book 참고서를 고르다

report card
[ripɔ́:*r*t ka:*r*d]

n. 성적표

get a good report 좋은 성적표를 받다

club
[klʌb]

n. 클럽, 동아리

club activity 클럽활동

01 교육과 학교

class [klæs]
n. 수업
in class 수업중에

seminar [sémənà:r]
n. 세미나
a closed-door seminar 비공개 세미나

lesson [lésn]
n. 학과, 수업시간
attend an anatomy lesson 해부학 수업에 참석하다

experiment [ikspérəmənt]
n. 실험 *v.* 실험하다
a chemical experiment 화학 실험

examination [igzæmənéiʃən]
n. 시험
a midterm examination 중간고사

curriculum [kəríkjələm]
n. 교육과정
a school curriculum 학교의 교육과정

semester [siméstər]
n. (2학기제의) 학기
during the fall semester 가을 학기 동안에

term [tə:rm]
n. (3학기제의) 학기
at the end of a term 학기말에

course [kɔ:rs]
n. 과정
a course of study 연구 과정

subject [sʌ́bdʒikt]
n. 과목
a compulsory subject 필수 과목

credit
[krédit]

n. 학점

the credit system 학점제

elective
[iléktiv]

a. 선택의

elective subjects 선택 과목

required
[rikwáiə:rd]

a. 필수의

required reading 필독 서적

compulsory
[kəmpʌ́lsəri]

a. 의무적인, 필수의

compulsory education 의무 교육

essay
[ései]

n. 에세이, 수필

write an essay on poetry
시에 관한 에세이를 쓰다

diploma
[diplóumə]

n. 졸업장

a high school diploma 고교 졸업장

dictation
[diktéiʃən]

n. 받아쓰기

take dictation 받아쓰다

tuition
[tjuːíʃ-ən]

n. 수업료

remit the tuition fee 수업료를 면제받다

fail
[feil]

v. 실패하다

fail in an exam 시험에 실패하다

pass
[pæs]

v. 합격하다

pass the test 더 테스트에 합격하다

major
[méidʒəːr]

v. 전공하다

major in math 수학을 전공하다
(double major = 복수전공)

minor
[máinər]

v. 부전공하다

minor in history 역사를 부전공하다

preparation
[prèpəréiʃən]

n. 예습

go to school without doing one's preparation 예습하지 않고 학교에 가다

review
[rivjúː]

n. 복습

review exercises 복습용 연습 문제

■ 문구와 사무용품

pen
[pen]

n. 펜

write with a pen 펜으로 쓰다

pencil
[pénsəl]

n. 연필

a pencil case 필통

ballpoint pen
[bɔːl pɔint pen]

n. 볼펜

write with a ballpoint pen

eraser
[iréisər]

n. 지우개

a chalk eraser 칠판 지우개

correction fluid
[kərékʃən flúːid]

n. 수정액 (=whiteout)

Correction fluid for typing 사무용 수정액

fountain pen
[fáuntin pen]

n. 만년필

fill a fountain pen 만년필에 잉크를 넣다

highlighter
[hailàitər]

n. 형광펜

draw a line with a highlighter
형광펜으로 줄을 긋다

box
[baks]

n. 상자

a wooden box 나무상자

stapler
[stéiplə:r]

n. 스테이플러, 호치키스

stapled papers 호치키스로 철한 서류

brush
[brʌʃ]

n. 붓

the tip of a writing brush 붓끝

ink
[iŋk]

n. 잉크

write in red ink 붉은 잉크로 쓰다

envelope
[énvəlòup]

n. 봉투

a return envelope 반신용 봉투

scissors
[sízə:r]

n. 가위

cut (a thing) with scissors 가위로 자르다

rubber band
[rʌ́bə:r bænd]

n. 고무줄

stretch a rubber band 고무줄을 늘이다

ruler
[rú:lə:r]

n. 자

a graduated ruler 눈금자

glue
[gluː]
n. 풀
glue stick 딱풀

blackboard
[blǽkbɔ̀ːrd]
n. 칠판
wipe the writing off the blackboard
칠판에 쓴 글을 닦다

clip
[klip]
n. 클립
clasp papers with a clip 서류를 클립에 끼우다

chalk
[tʃɔːk]
n. 분필
chalk dust 분필 가루

notepad
[noutpæd]
n. 메모장
write on a notepad 메모장에 쓰다

scale
[skeil]
n. 저울
a point on a scale 저울의 눈금

compass
[kʌ́mpəs]
n. 컴퍼스
a beam compass
빔 컴퍼스(널빤지에 장치하는 큰 컴퍼스)

stamp
[stæmp]
n. 도장
a date stamp 날짜 도장

notebook
[nóutbùk]
n. 공책
copy into a notebook 공책에 베끼다

02 문화

■ 문화 일반

culture [kʌ́ltʃər]
n. 문화
mass culture 대중문화

civilization [sìvəlizéiʃən]
n. 문명
ancient civilization 고대문명

progress [prágrəs]
n. 진보
the progress of science 과학의 진보

language [lǽŋgwidʒ]
n. 언어
a foreign language 외국어

tradition [trədíʃən]
n. 전통
hand down a tradition 전통을 후세에 전하다

heritage [héritidʒ]
n. 유산
a culture heritage 문화유산

custom [kʌ́stəm]
n. 관습
preserve a custom 관습을 지키다

02 문화

habit [hǽbit]
n. 습관
break off a habit 습관을 없애다

race [reis]
n. 인종, 민족
race issues 인종문제

ethnic [éθnik]
a. 인종의, 민족의
the ethnic stereotype 민족 고유의 고정관념

tribe [traib]
n. 부족
rule over a tribe 부족을 지배하다

majority [mədʒɔ́(ː)rəti]
a. 다수의
an absolute majority 절대 다수

minority [minɔ́ːrəti]
a. 소수의
a minority opinion 소수의 의견

world [wəːrld]
n. 세계, 세간
a journey round the world 세계 일주 여행

society [səsáiəti]
n. 사회
human society 인간 사회

social [sóuʃ-əl]
a. 사회적인, 사회의
social skill 사회적 기능

public [pʌ́blik]
a. 공공의
public welfare 공공복지

private [práivit]
a. 사적인, 개인적인
one's private life 사생활

privacy
[práivəsi]

n. 프라이버시, 사생활

invasion of privacy 프라이버시의 침해

personal
[pə́ːrsənəl]

a. 개인적인

a personal favor 개인적인 호의

individual
[ìndəvídʒuəl]

a. 개인

the rights of the individual 개인의 권리

lifestyle
[láifstàil]

n. 생활양식, 생활

a healthy lifestyle 건전한 생활

liberty
[líbəːrti]

n. 자유

religious liberty 신앙의 자유

equality
[i(ː)kwáləti]

n. 평등

the equality of the sexes 남녀평등

discrimination
[diskrìmənéiʃən]

n. 차별

racial discrimination 인종 차별

class
[klæs]

n. 계급

the class struggle 계급투쟁

■ 예술·음악

art
[ɑːrt]

n. 예술/미술

an art critic 미술 평론가

painting
[péintiŋ]

n. 회화, 그림

a famous painting by Rembrandt 렘브란트의 유명한 그림

sketch
[sketʃ]

n. 소묘

make a sketch of a face 얼굴을 스케치하다

sculpture
[skʌ́lptʃəːr]

n. 조각

sculpture(s) by Rodin 로댕의 조각

masterpiece
[mǽstərpìːs]

n. 걸작

an immortal masterpiece 불후의 걸작

photo
[fóutou]

n. 사진

a colour photo 칼라 사진

picture
[píktʃər]

n. 그림, 사진

frame a picture 그림을 액자에 넣다

museum
[mjuːzíːəm]

n. 박물관, 미술관

a museum of natural history 자연사 박물관

gallery
[gǽləri]

n. 화랑, 미술관

an art-gallery 미술관

exhibition
[èksəbíʃən]

n. 전시회

a competitive exhibition 공진회, 품평회

movie
[múːvi]

n. 영화

a movie producer 영화 제작자

comedy [kámədi]	*n.* 희극	as good as a comedy 희극처럼 재미있는
tragedy [trædʒədi]	*n.* 비극	Shakespeare's tragedy of "Hamlet" 셰익스피어의 비극 「햄릿」
theater [θí(:)ətə:r]	*n.* 극장	a drive-in theater 드라이브인 극장(자동차 극장)
matinee [mæt-ənei]	*n.* 마티네(낮에 하는 연주회 등)	matinee performance 대낮의 흥행, 공연
seat [si:t]	*n.* 좌석	a reserved seat 예약석
audience [ɔ́:diəns]	*n.* 관객	an audience at a movie[theater] 영화관[극장]의 관객
appreciate [əprí:ʃièit]	*v.* 감상하다	appreciate art 예술을 감상하다
excitement [iksáitmənt]	*n.* 흥분	suppress one's excitement 흥분을 억누르다
enjoy [endʒɔ́i]	*v.* 즐기다	enjoy life 생활을 즐기다
intriguing [intrí:giŋ]	*a.* 흥미를 자아내는	an intriguing item of news 흥미를 끄는 뉴스

boring
[bɔ́:riŋ]
n. 지루한
a boring book 지루한 책

actor
[ǽktər]
n. 남자 배우
a tragic actor 비극 배우

actress
[ǽktris]
n. 여자 배우
a famous actress 유명한 여배우

director
[diréktər]
n. 감독, 연출자
a film director 영화감독

scenario
[sinέ-əriòu]
n. 대본, 각본
a scenario writer 시나리오 작가

role
[roul]
n. 역할, 역
play small roles 단역을 맡아 하다

music
[mjú:zik]
n. 음악
dance to music 음악에 맞추어 춤추다

sing
[siŋ]
v. 노래하다
sing a song 노래를 부르다

melody
[mélədi]
n. 멜로디, 선율
old Irish melodies 옛날 아일랜드 멜로디

rhythm
[ríð-əm]
n. 리듬
Latin-American rhythms 라틴아메리카의 리듬

rock
[rɑk]
n. 록
a rock band 록 밴드

jazz [dʒæz]	*n.* 재즈 jazz musicians 재즈 음악가들
classic music [klǽsik mjúːzik]	*n.* 고전음악 a lover of classical music 고전음악 애호가
opera [ápərə]	*n.* 오페라 hear operas by Verdi and Puccini 베르디와 푸치니의 오페라를 듣다
concert [kánsə(ː)ɹt]	*n.* 음악회 give a concert 음악회를 개최하다
recital [risáitl]	*n.* 독주회, 리사이틀 give a piano recital 피아노 독주회를 하다
stage [steidʒ]	*n.* 무대 a revolving stage 회전 무대
play [plei]	*v.* 상연하다, 공연하다 play a musical 뮤지컬을 공연하다
performance [pəɹfɔ́ːɹməns]	*n.* 연기, 공연 a musical performance 음악 연주
practice [prǽktis]	*n.* 연습 an hour's practice every day 매일 1시간의 연습
rehearsal [rihə́ːɹs-əl]	*n.* 시연, 예행연습 a public rehearsal 공개 시연

studio
[stjúːdiòu]

n. 방송실, 녹음실

a dance studio 무용 연습실

musician
[mjuːzíʃ-ən]

n. 음악가

a sensitive musician 감수성이 풍부한 음악가

band
[bænd]

n. 악단

a dance band 댄스용 밴드

orchestra
[ɔ́ːrkəstrə]

n. 관현악단

a symphony orchestra 교향곡 오케스트라

conductor
[kəndʌ́ktər]

n. 지휘자

a guest conductor 객원 지휘자

composer
[kəmpóuzər]

n. 작곡가

an idiomatic composer 개성 있는 작곡가

■ 취미

music
[mjúːzik]

n. 음악

listening to music 음악감상

movie
[múːvi]

n. 영화, 영화관

go to the movies 영화 보러 가다

play
[plei]

n. 연극

go to plays 연극을 보러 가다

concert
[kánsə(ː)rt]

n. 콘서트, 연주회

a rock concert 록 콘서트

musical
[mjúːzik-əl]

n. 뮤지컬

a musical performance 뮤지컬 공연

dance
[dæns]

n. 춤 *v.* 춤추다

social dance 사교댄스

cartoon
[kɑːrtúːn]

n. 만화

a Walt Disney cartoon 월트 디즈니 만화

animation
[ænəméiʃən]

n. 만화영화

mainline on TV animations
텔레비전 만화 영화에 푹 빠지다

collection
[kəlékʃən]

n. 수집, 수집물

a rich collection 풍부한 수집

stamp collecting
[stæmp kəléktiŋ]

n. 우표수집

a stamp-collecting craze 우표 수집열

coin collecting
[kɔin kəléktiŋ]

n. 동전수집

old coin collecting 오랜된 동전 수집

photography
[fətágrəfi]

n. 사진촬영

photography class 사진 수업

drive
[draiv]

n. 운전 *v.* 드라이브(운전)하다

go for a drive 드라이브 하러 가다

hiking
[háikiŋ]

n. 도보여행

hiking boots 하이킹용 신발

mountain climbing
[máunt-ən kláimiŋ]

n. 등산

a mountain-climbing expedition 등반대

fishing
[fíʃiŋ]

n. 낚시 해

fishing 낚시질하다

knitting
[nítiŋ]

n. 뜨개질

han-knitted gloves 손뜨개질한 장갑

sewing
[sóuiŋ]

n. 바느질

take sewing lessons 바느질을 배우다

embroidery
[embrɔ́idəri]

n. 자수

fine embroidery 섬세한 자수(cross stitch 십자수)

calligraphy
[kəlígrəfi]

n. 서예

learn calligraphy 붓글씨 연습을 하다

painting
[peintiŋ]

n. 그림 그리기

be good at painting 그림을 잘 그리다

pottery
[pátəri]

n. 도자기공예

bake pottery 도자기를 굽다

ski
[ski:]

v. 스키 타다

go skiing 스키 타러 가다

golf
[gɑlf]

n. 골프

play golf 골프하다

■ 오락

toy
[tɔi]
n. 장난감
a toy soldier 장난감 병정

playground
[pleigràund]
n. 놀이터
a children's playground 어린이 놀이터

game
[geim]
n. 게임, 경기
a game of chance 운으로 하는 게임

card
[kɑːrd]
n. 카드, 카드놀이
play cards 카드놀이하다

gamble
[gǽmbəl]
n. 도박 *v.* 도박하다
gamble on the horses 경마로 도박하다

lottery
[lɑ́təri]
n. 복권
win in a lottery 복권이 당첨되다

park
[pɑːrk]
n. 공원
amusement park 놀이공원
theme park 테마파크

ride
[raid]
n. 놀이기구 *v.* 타다
ride a roller coaster 청룡열차를 타다

cotton candy
[kɑ́tn kǽndi]
n. 솜사탕
buy a cotton candy 솜사탕을 사다

rest
[rest]
n. 휴식
take a rest 휴식을 취하다

admission ticket
[ædmíʃən tíkit]

n. 입장권

issue admission tickets 입장권을 발행하다

beach
[biːtʃ]

n. 해변

on a sandy beach 모래 해변에서

picnic
[píknik]

n. 소풍

go on a picnic 피크닉을 가다

horse race
[hɔːrs reis]

n. 경마

bet on horse races 경마에 돈을 걸다

hunt
[hʌnt]

n. 사냥 *v.* 사냥하다

go on a hunt 사냥하러 가다

hide-and-seek
[háid ənd síːk]

n. 숨바꼭질

playing hide-and-seek 숨바꼭질하다

kite
[kait]

n. 연

fly a kite 연을 날리다

03 스포츠와 레저

■ 스포츠

player
[pléiər]
n. 선수
reinforce a team with new players
신인 선수로 팀을 강화하다

coach
[koutʃ]
n. 코치
an armchair coach 실전 경험이 적은 코치

referee
[rèfərí:]
n. 주심, 심판
appeal to the referee 심판에게 항의하다

director
[diréktər]
n. 감독
be selected for a director 감독으로 발탁되다

exercise
[éksərsàiz]
n. 운동
do exercise 운동하다

match
[mætʃ]
n. 시합, 경기
win a match 시합에 이기다

athletics
[æθlétiks]
n. 운동 경기, 육상 경기
interscholastic athletics 학교 대항 운동 경기

baseball
[béisbɔ̀:l]

n. 야구

a baseball equipment 야구 장비

soccer
[sákə:r]

n. 축구

a soccer ball 축구공

football
[fútbɔ̀:l]

n. 미식축구

football hooligans 폭력적 축구광

volleyball
[válibɔ̀:l]

n. 배구

play volleyball 배구를 하다

basketball
[bǽskitbɔ̀:l]

n. 농구

play basket ball 농구를 하다

table tennis
[téib-əl ténis]

n. 탁구

play table tennis 탁구를 하다

bowling
[bóuliŋ]

n. 볼링

go bowling 볼링하러 가다

billiard
[bíljərd]

n. 당구

a billiard-cue 당구채

tennis
[ténis]

n. 테니스

tennis tournament 테니스 시합

hockey
[háki]

n. 하키

ice hockey 아이스하키

badminton
[bǽdmintən]

n. 배드민턴

play badminton 배드민턴을 하다

rugby
[rʌ́gbi]

n. 럭비

a rugby player 럭비선수

tie
[tai]

n. 무승부

end in a tie 무승부로 끝나다

draw
[drɔː]

n. 비김, 무승부

call it a draw 무승부로 하다

golf
[gɑlf]

n. 골프

play a round of golf 골프를 한 바퀴 치다

softball
[sɔ́ːftbɔ̀ːl]

n. 소프트 볼

a softball team 소프트볼 팀

swimming
[swímiŋ]

n. 수영

go swimming 수영하러 가다

swim
[swim]

v. 수영하다

swim the breaststroke 평영으로 헤엄치다
*freestyle 자유형, backstroke 배영
breaststroke 평영, butterfly stroke 접영

synchronized swimming
[síŋkrənàizd swímiŋ]

n. 수중발레

diving
[dàiviŋ]

n. 다이빙

sky diving 스카이 다이빙
scuba diving 스쿠버다이빙

yacht
[jɑt]

n. 요트

cruise in a yacht 요트를 타다

surf
[səːrf]

n. 파도타기 *v.* 서핑(파도타기)하다

go surfing 서핑하러 가러

sprint
[sprint]

n. 단거리 경주

a 100 meter sprint 100미터 단거리 경주

marathon
[mǽrəθən]

n. 마라톤

hold the world record for the marathon
마라톤에서 세계 기록을 보유하다

throw
[θrou]

n. 던지기

a discus throw 원반던지기

cycling
[sáikliŋ]

n. 사이클링, 자전거 경기

a cycling track 자전거 경주로

gymnastics
[ʤimnǽstiks]

n. 체조

a gymnastics competition 체조 경기

ski
[skiː]

n. 스키

go skiing 스키 타러 가다

snowboard
[snóubɔ̀ːrd]

n. 스노보드

go snowboarding 스노보드 타러 가다

skate
[skeit]

n. 스케이트

go for a skate 스케이트를 타러 가다
figure skating 피겨스케이팅

skateboard
[skéitbɔ̀ːrd]

n. 스케이트보드

ride a skateboard 스케이트보드를 타다

horseback riding
[hɔːrsbæk ráidiŋ]

n. 승마
go for a ride 승마하러 가다

ropejumping
[roup dʒʌ́mpiŋ]

n. 줄넘기
jump rope 줄넘기하다

martial arts
[máːrʃ-əl aːrts]

n. 무술, 격투기
practice martial arts 무예를 닦다

judo
[dʒúːdou]

n. 유도
a judo hall 유도장

Taekwondo
[táikwàndo]

n. 태권도
an instructor of Taekwondo 태권도 선생

boxing
[báksiŋ]

n. 권투
a boxing champion 권투 챔피언

wrestling
[résliŋ]

n. 레슬링
go to a wrestling match 레슬링 시합에 가다

weight lifting
[weit líftiŋ]

n. 역도
a weight lifter 역도선수

fencing
[fénsiŋ]

n. 펜싱
practice fencing 펜싱 연습을 하다

shooting
[ʃúːtiŋ]

n. 사격
a shooting gallery 실내 사격 연습장

sit-up
[sít ʌp]

n. 윗몸 일으키기

do 50 sit-ups every morning
매일 아침 윗몸 일으키기를 50회 하다

push-up
[púʃ ʌp]

n. 팔굽혀펴기

do fifty push-ups a day
하루 50번씩 팔굽혀펴기를 하다

chin-up
[tʃín ʌp]

n. 턱걸이

do twenty chin-ups 턱걸이를 20개 하다

jog
[dʒɑg]

v. 조깅하다

jog around the park 공원 주위를 조깅하다

finals
[fáinəlz]

n. 결승전, 파이널

run in the finals 결승전까지 올라가다

compete
[kəmpíːt]

v. 경쟁하다

compete against each other 서로 버티다

win
[win]

v. 이기다

win a game 게임에 이기다

lose
[luːz]

v. 지다

lose at cards 카드에서 지다

tie
[tai]

n. 무승부

end in a tie 무승부로 끝나다

draw
[drɔː]

n. 비김, 무승부

call it a draw 무승부로 하다

record [rékɔːrd]	*n.* 기록 *v.* 기록하다 set a new world record 세계 신기록을 세우다
overtime [óuvərtàim]	*n.* 연장전 lose in overtime 연장전에서 지다
championship [tʃǽmpiənʃip]	*n.* 우승, 선수권 the championship flag 우승기
participate [pɑːrtísəpèit]	*v.* 참가하다 participate in the Olympics 올림픽에 참가하다
join [dʒɔin]	*v.* 참여하다 join a team 팀에 들어가다
stadium [stéidiəm]	*n.* 경기장 a football stadium 축구 경기장
beat [biːt]	*v.* 치다, 이기다 beat down 때려눕히다
rule [ruːl]	*n.* 규칙 obey the rules 규칙을 준수하다
foul [faul]	*n.* 반칙 foul out of the game 반칙으로 퇴장당하다
penalty [pénəlti]	*n.* 반칙에 대한 벌칙 penalty kick 페널티 킥
cheering [tʃíəriŋ]	*n.* 응원 a cheering section 응원단

04 여행

■ 여행과 관광

leisure
[líːʒər]

n. 여가, 레저

have no leisure to travel 여행할 여가가 없다

travel
[trǽv-əl]

n. 여행 *v.* 여행하다

travel abroad 해외 여행을 하다

trip
[trip]

n. 여행

a trip around the world 세계 일주 여행

journey
[dʒə́ːrni]

n. 여행

a journey on foot 도보 여행

spend
[spend]

v. 보내다, 지내다

spend a week in New York
뉴욕에서 한 주일을 보내다

resort
[rizɔ́ːrt]

n. 휴양 리조트

a summer resort 여름 휴양지

honeymoon
[hʌ́nimùːn]

n. 신혼여행

go on a honeymoon 신혼여행을 떠나다

school excursion [skuːl ikskə́ːrʒən]	*n.* 수학여행	make a school excursion to Gyeongju 경주로 수학여행 가다
baggage [bǽgidʒ]	*n.* 짐	baggage handlers 수화물 취급자
map [mæp]	*n.* 지도	consult a map 지도를 살피다
reservation [rèzəːrvéiʃ-ən]	*n.* 예약	make reservations 예약을 하다
airport [ɛ́ərpɔ̀ːrt]	*n.* 공항	an international airport 국제공항
vacation [veikéiʃən]	*n.* 휴가	be on vacation 휴가 중이다
traveler [trǽvləːr]	*n.* 여행자	a traveler's check 여행자 수표
domestic [douméstik]	*a.* 국내의	domestic travel 국내여행
overseas [óuvərsíːz]	*a.* 해외의	overseas travel 해외여행
airlines [ɛərlàinz]	*n.* 항공사	a civil airlines 민간 항공사

jet lag
[dʒet læg]

n. 시차증

suffer from jet lag 시차증으로 고생하다

agency
[éidʒənsi]

n. 대리점, 취급점

travel agency 여행사

itinerary
[aitínərèri]

n. 여행일정

arrange the itinerary of the party
일행의 여정을 짜다

souvenir
[sùːvəníəːr]

n. 기념물

keep as a souvenir 기념품으로 갖고 있다

passport
[pǽspɔːrt]

n. 여권

apply for a passport 여권을 신청하다

visa
[víːzə]

n. 비자

extend a visa 비자를 연장하다

tourist information
[túːərist infərméiʃən]

n. 여행안내소

ask the toursist information for a map
여행안내소에 지도를 달라고 하다

sightseeing
[sáitsìːiŋ]

n. 관광

a sightseeing tour of the city 도시 순회 관광

tour
[tuəːr]

n. 관광 여행

package tour 패키지 관광 여행

tourist
[túːərist]

n. 관광객

a foreign tourist 외국인 관광객

tourist spot
[tú-ərist spat]

n. 관광지

Korea's most famed tourist spot
한국의 가장 유명한 관광지

hot spring
[hɑt spriŋ]

n. 온천

a hot-spring cure 온천 요법

city sightseeing
[síti sáitsìːiŋ]

n. 시내관광

go sightseeing the city 시내를 구경하다

cruise
[kruːz]

v. 선박여행하다

cruise in a yacht 요트를 타다

statue
[stǽtʃuː]

n. 동상

a bronze statue 청동의 상

exhibition
[èksəbíʃən]

n. 전시회

hold an exhibition 전시회를 열다

museum
[mjuːzíːəm]

n. 박물관, 기념관

the National Folklore Museum
국립 민속 박물관

palace
[pǽlis]

n. 궁전, 궁궐

ancient palace 고궁

memorial
[mimɔ́ːriəl]

n. 기념비

a war memorial 전쟁 기념비

festival
[féstəvəl]

n. 축제

a jazz festival 재즈 페스티발

seasick
[síːsìk]

a. 뱃멀미의

get seasick 뱃멀미하다

carsick
[káːrsìk]

a. 차멀미의

get carsick 차멀미 하다

infirmary
[infə́ːrməri]

n. 진료소, 양호실

the college infirmary 대학 양호실

■ 숙박

accommodations
[əkàmədéiʃənz]

n. 숙박시설

secure accommodations at the hotel
그 호텔에 숙소를 정하다

hotel
[houtél]

n. 호텔

a luxurious hotel 호화호텔

inn
[in]

n. 여관, 여인숙

run a country inn 시골 작은 여관을 경영하다

facilities
[fəsílətis]

n. 시설물

facilities for fire prevention 화재방지용 시설물

suite
[swiːt]

n. 스위트 룸

reserve a suite 스위트룸으로 예약하다

vacancy
[véikənsi]

n. 빈방

No vacancies 빈 방 없음

front desk
[frʌnt desk]

n. 안내 데스크

call the front desk 안내데스크에 전화하다

bellhop
[bélhàp]

n. 벨보이 (=bellboy)

tip a bellhop 벨보이에게 팁을 주다

check-in
[tʃek in]

n. 체크인

a check-in counter 체크인 프런트

check-out
[tʃek aut]

n. 체크아웃

a check-out clerk 체크아웃 안내계

room service
[ruːm sə́ːrvis]

n. 룸서비스

order from room service 룸서비스로 주문하다

wake up call
[weikʌpkɔːl]

n. 모닝콜

request a wake up call service at the front desk 프런트에 모닝콜 서비스를 부탁하다

stay
[stei]

v. 머무르다, 체류하다

stay at hotel for three days
호텔에 3일 머무르다

■ 쇼핑

shopping
[ʃápiŋ]

n. 쇼핑, 물건사기

do one's shopping 쇼핑하다

gift
[gift]

n 선물

a gift shop 선물 가게

gift wrapping
[gift rǽpiŋ]

n. 선물포장

gift wrapping counter 선물 포장 코너

souvenir
[sùːvəníːr]

n. 기념품

souvenir shop 기념품 가게

lost and found
[lɔ(ː)st ænd faund]

n. 분실물 센터

call for the lost and found
분실물 센터에 전화하다

snack bar
[snæk bɑːr]

n. 스낵바

eat sandwiches at the snack bar
스낵바에서 샌드위치를 먹다

department store
[dipáːrtmənt stɔːr]

n. 백화점

a year-end sale at a department store
백화점의 연말 세일

customer
[kʌ́stəmər]

n. 고객

have many customers 고객이 많다

consumer
[kənsúːmər]

n. 소비자

consumer prices 소비자 가격

clerk
[kləːrk]

n. 판매원, 점원

ask the clerk at the front desk
프론트 직원에게 물어보다

cashier
[kæʃíər]

n. 계산원

pay at the cashier 계산원에게 지불하다

shop
[ʃɑp]

n. 상점, 가게 (=store)

a flower shop 꽃집

mall
[mɔːl]

n. 대형 쇼핑센터

window shop at a mall 몰에서 아이쇼핑하다

supermarket
[súːpərmàːrkit]

n. 슈퍼마켓

go shopping at a supermarket
슈퍼마켓에서 물건을 사러 가다

convenience store
[kənvíːnjəns stɔːr]

n. 편의점

buy water at a convenience store
편의점에서 물을 사다

drugstore
[drʌgstɔːr]

n. 약국 (=pharmacy)

click over to the drugstore
황급히 약국으로 가다

grocery store
[gróusəri stɔːr]

n. 식품점

pick up some things at a grocery store
식품점에서 반찬거리를 사다

bookstore
[bukstɔːr]

n. 서점

browse some books at a bookstore
서점에서 책을 이것저것 구경하다

mail order
[meil ɔ́ːrdər]

n. 통신판매

a mail-order business 우편 주문 사업

goods
[gudz]

n. 상품

canned goods 통조림류

item
[áitəm]

n. 품목

a fast-selling item 잘 팔리는 품목

sale
[seil]

n. 판매

a sale for cash 현금 판매

bargain
[báːrgən]

n. 싼 물건, 특가품

good bargain 싸게 산 물건

price
[prais]

n. 가격

a fixed price 정가(定價)

cost
[kɔːst]

n. 비용, 원가

the prime cost 매입 원가

discount
[dískaunt]

n. 할인 *v.* 할인하다

give a discount 할인해주다

expensive
[ikspénsiv]

a. 비싼

an expensive car 고급차

cheap
[tʃiːp]

a. 싼 (=inexpensive)

cheap jewelry 싸구려 보석

reasonable
[ríːz-ənəb-əl]

a. 적정한

at a reasonable price 적당한 값으로

cash
[kæʃ]

n. 현금

pay in cash 현금으로 구입하다

credit card
[krédit kɑːrd]

n. 신용카드

put on a credit card 신용카드로 지불하다

change
[tʃeindʒ]

n. 거스름돈

small change 잔돈

receipt
[risíːt]

n. 영수증

sign a receipt 영수증에 서명하다

guarantee
[gæ̀rəntíː]

n. 보증

guarantee of quality 품질 보증

quantity
[kwántəti]

n. 양

a quantity of books 다량의 책

quality
[kwáləti]

n. 품질

goods of quality 양질의 상품, 고급품

compare
[kəmpéər]

v. 비교하다

compare two pieces of furniture 가구 2점을 비교하다

pay
[pei]

v. 지불하다

pay in installments 할부로 계산하다

refund
[rifʌ́nd]

n. 환불 *v.* 환불하다

ask for a refund on unused theatre tickets 사용 안 한 극장표에 대한 환불을 요청하다

exchange
[ikstʃéindʒ]

n. 교환 *v.* 교환하다

exchange a thing 물건을 교환하다

open
[óupən]

v. 개점하다

opening hours 개점 시간

closed
[klóuzd]

v. 폐점하다

Our shop will be closed at nine.
우리 상점은 9시에 폐점합니다

try on
[trai ɑn]

v. (한번) 입어보다

try on a skirt in a fitting room
피팅룸에서 치마를 입어보다

tight-fitting
[táit fítiŋ]

a. 꼭 끼는

a tight-fitting pants 꼭 끼는 바지

loose
[luːs]

a. 헐거운

a loose sweater 헐렁한 스웨터

stock
[stɑk]

n. 재고

out of stock 재고가 없는

display
[displéi]

v. 진열하다

display goods 상품을 전시하다

brand-new
[brǽnd njúː]

a. 신상품의

brand-new product 신상품

catalog
[kǽtəlɔ̀ːg]

n. 카탈로그, 목록

a catalog of articles for sale 판매품 목록

tag
[tæg]

n. 꼬리표

price tag 가격표

fixed price
[fikst prais]

n. 정가

sell at a fixed price 정가로 팔다

haggle
[hǽgəl]

v. 흥정하다

haggle over prices 값을 깎다

buy
[bai]

v. 사다

buy in bulk 대량으로 구입하다

warranty
[wɔ́(:)rənti]

n. 제품보증(서)

buy a car without a warranty
보증서 없이 차를 사다

price range
[prais reindʒ]

n. 가격대

Prices range between $7 and $10.
가격대가 7달러에서 10달러 사이이다.

down payment
[daun péimənt]

n. 계약금, 보증금

make a down payment 계약금을 치르다

PART 09

정치와
경제

01 정치

공명선거

■ 정치 일반

politics [pálitiks]
n. 정치(학)
party politics 정당 정치

political [pəlítikəl]
a. 정치적인
a political prisoner 정치범

authority [əθɔ́ːriti]
n. 권위
abuse one's authority 직권을 남용하다

legislature [lédʒislèitʃəːr]
n. 의회, 입법부
dissolve the legislature 의회를 해산하다

Assembly [əsémbli]
n. 의회
the National Assembly 국회

Congress [káŋgris]
n. (미)국회
lay a bill before the Congress
의안을 의회에 제출하다

Senator [sénətər]
n. 미 상원의원
Senator Edward Kennedy
에드워드 케네디 상원 의원

Parliament
[páːrləmənt]

n. 영국 의회

a Member of Parliamen 하원 의원

Diet
[dáiət]

n. 국회(일본 등에서)

Diet seats 국회 의석

convention
[kənvénʃən]

n. 당대회, 집회

hold an annual convention 연차 대회를 열다

session
[séʃ-ən]

n. 회기(會期)

extend the session 회기를 연장하다

committee
[kəmíti]

n. 위원회

a standing[special] committee
상임[특별] 위원회

party
[páːrti]

n. 정당, 당

join[leave] a party 입당[탈당]하다

representative
[rèprizéntətiv]

n. 대표자, 대리인

send a representative to the meeting
회의에 대표를 보내다

Congressman
[káŋgrismən]

n. 하원의원

a former Congressman 전 하원의원

White House
[hwait haus]

n. 미국정부, 백악관

cut the White House staff
백악관 직원을 줄이다

department
[dipáːrtmənt]

n. 부, 국, 청

the Department of the Environment 환경부

agency [éidʒənsi]	*n.* 청(廳), 국(局)	government agencies 여러 관청
official [əfíʃəl]	*n.* 공무원	government officials 정부 공무원
officer [ɔ́(:)fisər]	*n.* 공무원, 관리	a police officer 경찰관
bill [bil]	*n.* 법안, 의안	rush a bill 의안을 급히 통과시키다
proposal [prəpóuzəl]	*n.* 제안, 안	accept a proposal 제안을 수락하다
issue [íʃu:]	*n.* 문제, 안건	a political issue 정치적인 문제
adopt [ədápt]	*v.* 채택하다	adopt an idea 아이디어를 받아들이다
pass [pæs]	*v.* 가결되다, 통과하다	pass the National Assembly 국회를 통과하다
reject [ridʒékt]	*v.* 부결하다, 각하하다	reject an offer 제의를 거절하다
unanimous [ju:nǽnəməs]	*a.* 만장일치의	a unanimous vote 만장 일치의 표결

approval
[əprúːvəl]
n. 찬성, 승인
a nod of approval 찬성의 끄덕임

consensus
[kənsénsəs]
n. 동의, 일치
a consensus of opinion 의견 일치

resolution
[rèzəlúːʃ-ne]
n. 결의(안)
a New Year resolution 신년도 결의

statement
[stéitmənt]
n. 성명, 진술
an official statement 공식 성명

power
[páuər]
n. 권력
a struggle for power 권력 투쟁

policy
[páləsi]
n. 정책
a foreign policy 외교 정책

right
[rait]
n. 권리
the right to remain silent 묵비권

obligation
[àbləgéiʃən]
n. 의무
the obligation of tax 납세 의무

responsibility
[rispànsəbíləti]
n. 책임
avoid responsibility 책임을 회피하다

cooperation
[kouàpəréiʃən]
n. 협력
economic cooperation 경제 협력

ruling party
[rúːliŋ páːrti]
n. 여당
a member of the ruling party 여당의원

opposition party
[àpəzíʃən páːrti]

n. 야당

merger of the opposition parties 야당통합

faction
[fǽkʃən]

n. 당파, 파벌

faction fighting 파벌 투쟁

political power
[pəlítikəl páuər]

n. 정권

the lust for political power 정권에 대한 욕심

conservative
[kənsə́ːrvətiv]

a. 보수파, 보수적인

conservative policies 보수적인 정책

moderate
[má-d-ərèit]

a. 온건한

moderate groups 온건파

liberal
[líb-ərəl]

a. 자유주의의

a liberal democracy 자유민주주의

progressive
[prəgrésiv]

a. 진보적인, 혁신적인

a progressive political party 진보 정당

radical
[rǽdik-əl]

a. 급진적인, 과격한

a radical politician 급진적인 정치가

politician
[pàlətíʃən]

n. 정치가

a corrupt politician 부패한 정치가

statesman
[stéitsmən]

n. 정치가

a great statesman 위대한 정치가

■ 국가

country [kʌ́ntri]
n. 국가(가장 일반적인 의미)
a civilized country 문명국

state [steit]
n. 국가(정치적인 의미)
a welfare state 복지국가

nation [néiʃən]
n. 국민, 민족
the voice of the nation 국민의 소리, 여론

public [pʌ́blik]
a. 공공의, 대중의
public documents 공문서

sovereignty [sáv-ərinti]
n. 주권, 독립국
violate a contry's sovereignty
한 나라의 주곤을 침해하다

republic [ripʌ́blik]
n. 공화국
the Republic of Korea 대한민국

kingdom [kíŋdəm]
n. 왕국
the kingdom of Sweden 스웨덴 왕국

monarchy [mánərki]
n. 군주제
plans to abolish the monarchy
군주제 철폐를 위한계획

bureaucracy [bjuərákrəsi]
n. 관료제도(주의)
the government bureaucracy
정부의 관료주의

despotism
[déspətìzəm]

n. 독재정치

protest the despotism 독재주의에 항의하다

foreign country
[fɔ́(:)rin kʌ́ntri]

n. 외국

investment in foreign country 해외 투자

mother country
[mʌ́ðəːr kʌ́ntri]

n. 모국

separate from the mother country
모국으로부터 독립하다

President
[prézidənt]

n. 대통령

the vice President 부통령

Prime Minister
[praim mínistər]

n. 총리

the vice Prime Minister 부총리

secretary
[sékrətèri]

n. 비서, 서기관

a first secretary of the embassy
대사관 1등 서기관

minister
[mínistər]

n. 장관, 대신

the Minister for Defense 국방장관

governor
[gʌ́vərnər]

n. 지사

the state governor 주지사

diplomat
[dípləmæt]

n. 외교관

a ranking diplomat 상급 외교관

mayor
[méiəːr]

n. 시장

be elected as mayor 시장으로 선출되다

citizen
[sítəzən]

n. 시민

the citizens of Seoul 서울 시민

government
[gʌ́vərnmənt]

n. 정부

form a new government 신정부를 수립하다

cabinet
[kǽbənit]

n. 내각

form a new cabinet 새 내각을 조직하다

diplomacy
[diplóuməsi]

n. 외교

armed diplomacy 무력외교

embassy
[émbəsi]

n. 대사관

the British Embassy in Seoul
서울 주재 영국 대사관

patriotism
[péitriətìzəm]

n. 애국심

local patriotism 향토애

capitalism
[kǽpitəlìzəm]

n. 자본주의

financial capitalism 금융 자본주의

socialism
[sóuʃəlìz-əm]

n. 사회주의

the struggle to build socialism
사회주의 건설 투쟁

communism
[kámjənìzəm]

n. 공산주의

the last stage of communism
공산주의의 말기

communist
[kámjənist]

n. 공산주의자

go communist 공산주의자가 되다

democracy
[dimákrəsi]

n. 민주주의

grass-root democracy 풀뿌리 민주주의

democrat
[déməkræt]

n. 민주주의자

a liberal democrat 자유 민주주의자

legislation
[lèdʒisléiʃ-ən]

n. 입법(부)

the purpose of legislation 입법의 취지

judicature
[dʒúːdikèitʃər]

n. 사법(부)

the Supreme Court of Judicature (영국) 대법원

administration
[ædmìnəstréiʃən]

n. 행정, 정부

interview a top administration official 정부 고위 당국자를 취재하다

developed country
[divéləpd kʌ́ntri]

n. 선진국

leaders of the developed countries 선진국 수뇌

developing country 개발도상국
underdeveloped country 후진국

govern
[gʌ́vərn]

v. 다스리다, 통치하다

govern a state 국가[주]를 다스리다

 선거

election
[ilékʃən]

n. 선거

an election campaign 선거운동

run
[rʌn]

v. 출마하다, 입후보하다

run for the presidency 대통령후보에 출마하다

nominate
[námənèit]

v. 지명하다

be nominated for the Presidency
대통령 후보로 지명 추천되다

candidate
[kǽndidèit]

n. 입후보자

a candidate for the governorship
지사 후보

constituency
[kənstítʃuənsi]

n. 선거구

sweep a constituency
선거구에서 압도적 다수를 차지하다

violation
[vàiəléiʃən]

n. 위반

commit an election law violation
선거법 위반을 하다

suffrage
[sʌ́fridʒ]

n. 선거권, 참정권

woman suffrage 여성 참정권

ballot
[bǽlət]

n. 투표용지, 투표

elect by ballot 투표로 뽑다

voter
[vóutər]

n. 유권자, 투표자

recruit voters for the election
유권자를 동원하다

vote
[vout]

n. 투표 *v.* 투표하다

a secret vote 무기명 투표

poll
[poul]

n. 투표소, 투표결과

declare the poll 선거결과를 공표하다

turnout
[tə́ːrnàut]

n. 투표수, 투표율

expect a low voter turnout
낮은 투표율을 예상하다

resign
[rizáin]

v. 사임하다

resign from the Cabinet 내각을 물러나다

seat
[siːt]

n. 의석

hold[keep] a seat 의석을 보유하다

inauguration
[inɔ̀ːgjəréiʃən]

n. 취임(식)

an inauguration speech 취임사

02 법률

법과 재판

law [lɔː]
n. 법, 법률
break a law 법을 어기다

trial [trái-əl]
n. 재판
a criminal trial 형사 재판

constitution [kɑ̀nstətjúːʃən]
n. 헌법
establish a constitution 헌법을 제정하다

observe [əbzə́ːrv]
v. 지키다, 보존하다
observe good manners 예절을 지키다

forbid [fərbíd]
v. 금지하다
forbid smoking 흡연을 금지하다

valid [vǽlid]
a. 유효한
a valid marriage 정식 결혼

legislation [lèdʒisléiʃ-ən]
n. 입법, 법률 제정
passable legislation 가결 가능성이 있는 법안

legitimate
[lidʒítəmit]

a. 합법의, 합법적인

a legitimate claim 정당한 요구

legal
[líg-əl]

a. 합법적인

a legal act 합법적 행위

illegal
[illí:gəl]

a. 불법의

illegal immigrants 불법 이민

right
[rait]

n. 권리

All rights reserved. 불허복제, 판권 소유

justice
[dʒʌ́stis]

n. 정의, 공정

campaign for social justice
사회 정의를 위한 운동

suit
[su:t]

n. 소송

win a suit 승소하다 / file a suit 기소하다

charge
[tʃɑːrdʒ]

v. 고소하다, 고발하다

charge a person with theft
남을 절도죄로 고발하다

accusation
[æ̀kjuzéiʃən]

n. 고소, 고발

be under an accusation 고발당하고 있다

prosecution
[prɑ̀səkjú:ʃən]

n. 기소, 검찰당국

the witnesses for the prosecution
검찰측 증인

lawyer
[lɔ́ːjəːr]

n. 변호사

bring a case to a lawyer
소송사건을 변호사에게 의뢰하다

jury
[dʒúəri]

n. 배심(원단)

members of the jury 배심원

judgment
[dʒʌ́dʒmənt]

n. 평결, 판단

a judgment of acquittal[conviction]
무죄[유죄] 판결

approval
[əprúːvəl]

n. 찬성

with your kind approval 귀하의 찬성을 얻어

disapproval
[dìsəprúːvəl]

n. 반대

in disapproval 불찬성하여

court
[kɔːrt]

n. 법원

appear in court 출정하다
Supreme Court 대법원
family court 가정법원

counseling
[káunsəliŋ]

n. 상담

take counseling 상담을 받다

judge
[dʒʌdʒ]

n. 재판관, 판사

the presiding judge 재판장

prosecutor
[prásəkjùːtər]

n. 검사

state prosecutor's office 검사 사무실

defendant
[diféndənt]

n. 피고

the defendant company 피고측

plaintiff
[pléintif]

n. 원고

a plaintiff's lawyer 원고측 변호사

juror
[dʒúərər]

n. 배심원

select the jurors 배심원을 선출하다

verdict
[və́ːrdikt]

n. (배심원) 평결

a majority verdict of 8 to 4
8대 4의 과반수 평결

proof
[pruːf]

n. 증거, 증명

hard proof 확실한 증거

evidence
[évidəns]

n. 증거

gather evidence 증거를 수집하다

testimony
[téstəmòuni]

n. 증언

first-hand testimonies 직접 증언

acquit
[əkwít]

v. 석방하다

acquit a prisoner 죄인을 석방하다

convict
[kənvíkt]

v. 유죄를 선고하다

a convicted prisoner 기결수

innocent
[ínəsnt]

a. 무죄의

an innocent victim 무고한 죄를 덮어쓴 사람

guilty
[gílti]

a. 유죄의

be found guilty 유죄로 판결되다

interrogation
[intèrəgéiʃən]

n. 심문

ask in tone of interrogation 심문조로 묻다

misjudgment
[misdʒʌ́dʒmənt]

n. 오판

a misjudgment case 오판 사건

sentence
[séntəns]

v. 판결을 내리다

be sentenced to death 사형 선고를 받다

life imprisonment
[laif imprízənmənt]

n. 종신형

be sentenced to life imprisonment
종신형을 받다

appeal
[əpíːl]

v. 항소, 상고하다

appeal to the Supreme Court
대법원에 항소하다

capital punishment
[kǽpitl pʌ́niʃmənt]

n. 사형

abolish capital punishment 사형을 폐지하다

dismiss
[dismís]

v. 기각하다

dismiss an appeal 공소를 기각하다

03 국제관계

■ 외교

international
[ìntərnǽʃənəl]

a. 국제적인
international affairs 국제 문제

foreign
[fɔ́(:)rin]

a. 외국의
a foreign language 외국어

bilateral
[bailǽtərəl]

a. 쌍방의
a bilateral agreement 쌍방간의 합의

ambassador
[æmbǽsədər]

n. 대사
the U.S. Ambassador at Seoul
주한미국대사

summit
[sʌ́mit]

n. 정상, 수뇌부
a summit meeting 정상회담

cooperate
[kouápərèt]

v. 협력하다
cooperate with each other 서로 협력하다

partnership
[páːrtnərʃip]

n. 협력, 제휴
a successful partnership 성공적인 제휴

ally
[əlái]
v. 동맹하다
NATO allies 나토 동맹국들

reconcile
[rékənsàil]
v. 화해하다, 조정하다
reconcile a dispute 분쟁을 조정하다

compromise
[kámprəmàiz]
n. 타협 *v.* 타협하다
a life of compromise 타협의 생활

treaty
[tríːti]
n. 조약
a commercial treaty 통상 조약

pact
[pækt]
n. 협정, 조약
sign a non-aggression pact
불가침 협정에 서명하다

declaration
[dèkləréiʃən]
n. 선언, 발표
a declaration of war 선전 포고

sign
[sain]
v. 서명하다, 날인하다
sign and seal a paper 증서에 서명 날인하다

ratify
[rǽtəfài]
v. 승인하다, 비준하다
ratify a treaty 조약을 비준하다

border
[bɔ́ːrdəːr]
n. 국경
a border army 국경 경비대

colony
[káləni]
n. 식민지
a colony settlement 식민지

refugee
[rèfjudʒíː]

n. 망명자, 난민
political refugees 정치적 난민들

asylum
[əsáiləm]

n. 망명, 피난처
give asylum 피난처를 제공하다

■ 군사와 무기

military
[mílitèri]

n. 군, 군대
military training 군사훈련

troops
[truːps]

n. 군대, 병력
land troops 지상군

commander
[kəmǽndər]

n. 사령관
the commander in chief 최고 사령관

officer
[ɔ́(ː)fisər]

n. 사관, 장교
a military[naval] officer 육[해]군 장교

soldier
[sóuldʒəːr]

n. 군인
a soldier of fortune
(돈과 모험을 위해 일하는) 용병, 풍운아

army
[áːrmi]

n. 육군
army life 군대 생활

navy
[néivi]

n. 해군
join the navy 해군에 입대하다

air force
[εər fɔːrs]

n. 공군

strike an air force base 공군기지를 공격하다

Marine Corps
[məríːn kɔːrs]

n. 해병대

the U.S. Marine Corps 미 해병대

weapon
[wépən]

n. 무기

a deadly weapon 치명적인 무기

enemy
[énəmi]

n. 적

a natural enemy 천적

base
[beis]

n. 기지

an air base 공군 기지

camp
[kæmp]

n. 주둔지, 야영지

an army camp 군대 야영지

fighter
[fáitər]

n. 전투기

a fighter pilot 전투기 조종사

attack
[ətǽk]

v. 공격하다 *n.* 공격

attack an enemy 적을 공격하다

defend
[difénd]

v. 방어하다

defend a city against an attack
도시를 공격으로부터 지키다

rule
[ruːl]

n. 지배 *v.* 지배하다

majority rule 다수의 지배

independence
[ìndipéndəns]

n. 독립
the Declaration of Independence
(미국의) 독립 선언

battle
[bǽtl]

n. 싸움, 전투
the field of battle 전쟁터, 전장

victory
[víktəri]

n. 승리
lead the team to victory 팀을 승리로 이끌다

defeat
[difíːt]

n. 패배
admit defeat 패배를 인정하다

warship
[wɔ́ːrʃip]

n. 군함
convert a warship into a merchant ship
군함을 상선으로 개조하다

bomb
[bɑm]

n. 폭탄
an Atomic bomb 원자 폭탄

cannon
[kǽnən]

n. 대포
two 20-millimetre cannon
20 밀리미터 대포 두 대

missile
[mísəl]

n. 미사일
nuclear missiles 핵미사일

tank
[tæŋk]

n. 전차, 탱크
anti-tank missiles 대전차 미사일

aircraft carrier
[ɛərkræft kæriər]

n. 항공모함

an atomic-powered (aircraft) carrier
원자력항공모함

submarine
[sʌbməriː]

n. 잠수함

a nuclear submarine 핵 잠수함

war
[wɔːr]

n. 전쟁

a cold war 냉전 전쟁

battlefield
[bǽtlfiːld]

n. 전쟁터

the battlefield of life 인생이라는 싸움터

front
[frʌnt]

n. 전선

serve at the front 전선에서 복무하다

occupy
[ákjəpài]

v. 점령하다

the occupied territories 점령지

withdraw
[wiðdrɔ́ː]

v. 후퇴하다

withdraw troops from a position
진지에서 군대를 철수시키다

defense
[diféns]

n. 방어

Offense is the best defense.
공격은 최선의 방어이다

peace
[piːs]

n. 평화

a peace treaty 평화조약

security
[sikjú-əriti]

n. 안전

national security 국가 안보[안전]

stability
[stəbíləti]

n. 안정
social stability 사회의 안정

direction
[dirékʃən]

n. 방위
a sense of direction 방향 감각

injury
[índʒəri]

n. 부상
a knee injury 무릎 상처

terrorist
[térərist]

n. 테러리스트
terrorist attacks 테러공격

spy
[spai]

n. 간첩
military spy 군사 스파이

guerrilla
[gərílə]

n. 게릴라
guerrilla war 게릴라 전

coup
[kuː]

n. 쿠테타
a military coup 군사 쿠데타

ambush
[ǽmbuʃ]

n. 매복, 복병
fall into (an) ambush 복병을 만나다

surrender
[səréndər]

v. 항복하다
surrender to the enemy 적에게 항복하다

ceasefire
[síːsfáiər]

n. 휴전, 종전
negotiate a cease-fire 휴전을 협상하다

04 경제

■ 산업 일반

mining
[máiniŋ]

n. 광업
a mining village 광산촌

coal mine
[koul main]

n. 탄광
a coal miner 탄광부(夫)

fishing
[fíʃiŋ]

n. 어업
deep-sea fishing 원양 어업

fisherman
[fíʃərmən]

n. 어부
a seagoing fisherman 원양 어업자

fishing boat
[fíʃiŋ bout]

n. 어선
seize a fishing boat 어선을 나포하다

agriculture
[ǽgrikʌltʃər]

n. 농업
the Ministry of Agriculture and Forestry 농림부

farmer
[fá:rmər]

n. 농민
a dairy farmer 낙농업자

farm land
[fɑːrm lænd]

n. 농경지

fertile farmland 비옥한 농경지

harvest
[háːrvist]

n. 추수, 수확

rice harvest 벼 수확

rice planting
[rais plǽntiŋ]

n. 모내기

the rice-planting season 모내기철

fertilizer
[fɔ́ːrtəlàizər]

n. 거름, 비료

a bag of fertilizer 비료 부대

farm
[fɑːrm]

n. 농장

a mixed farm 다각 경영 농장

crop
[krɑp]

n. 농작물, 수확

gather a crop 농작물을 거둬들이다

forestry
[fɔ́(ː)ristri]

n. 임업

the Forestry Commission 임업 위원회

ranch
[ræntʃ]

n. 목장

a cattle ranch 소의 대방목장

livestock farming
[láivstɑ̀k fɑ́ːrmiŋ]

n. 축산, 목축

a livestock exhibition 축산 박람회

livestock
[láivstɑ̀k]

n. 가축

raise livestock 가축을 기르다

domestic animal
[douméstik ǽnəməl]

n. 가축

domestic animal species 가축 종류

seed
[siːd]

n. 종자

a handful of grass seed 한 움큼의 잔디 씨앗

breeding
[bríːdiŋ]

n. 사육, 번식

the breeding season 번식기

orchard
[ɔ́ːrtʃərd]

n. 과수원

apple orchards 사과 과수원

shipment
[ʃípmənt]

n. 출하

goods ready for shipment
선적 준비가 된 상품

industry
[índəstri]

n. 공업, 산업

manufacturing industry 제조업

factory
[fǽktəri]

n. 공장

a glass factory 유리 공장

process
[práses]

v. 가공(하다)

processed foods 가공 식품

log
[lɔ(ː)g]

n. 통나무

in the log 통나무 째로

05 직장과 일

■ 기업

business
[bíznis]
n. 사업
carry on business 사업을 하다

firm
[fəːrm.]
n. 회사
law firm 법률회사

company
[kʌ́mpəni]
n. 회사
establish a company 회사를 설립하다

enterprise
[éntərpràiz]
n. 회사, 기업
a government enterprise 공영기업

private
[práivit]
a. 민영의
a private sector 민간부문

competitive
[kəmpétətiv]
a. 경쟁의
a competitive power 경쟁력

conglomerate
[kənglámərət]
n. 복합기업
run a conglomerate 복합기업을 경영하다

joint venture
[dʒɔint véntʃər]

n. 합작사업

launch a joint venture 합작사업을 시작하다

found
[faund]

v. 설립하다

found a company 회사를 설립하다

establish
[istǽbliʃ]

v. 설립하다, 창립하다

establish a branch office 지점을 설립하다

merge
[mə:rdʒ]

v. 합병하다

merge the two companies together
두 회사를 합병하다

office
[ɔ́(:)fis]

n. 사무실

a lawyer's office 변호사 사무실

meeting
[mí:tiŋ]

n. 회의

hold a meeting 회의를 열다

factory
[fǽktəri]

n. 공장

a car factory 자동차 공장

agenda
[ədʒéndə]

n. 의제

the agenda of today's meeting
오늘 회의의 토의 사항

project
[prədʒékt]

n. 계획, 기획

realize a project 계획을 실현하다

estimate
[éstəmèit]

n. 견적

form a estimate 견적을 내다

sales
[seilz]

a. 판매(상)의

a sales department 판매부

work
[wəːrk]

n. 일

have some work to do 할 일이 있다

value
[vǽljuː]

n. 가치

market value 시장 가치

deficit
[défəsit]

n. 적자

a deficit in revenue 세입 적자액

surplus
[sə́ːrplʌs]

n. 흑자

a trade surplus of $400 million
4억 달러의 무역 흑자

sold out
[sould aut]

n. 매진

All sold out for today 금일 매진

bankruptcy
[bǽŋkrʌptsi]

n. 파산, 도산

go into bankrupt 파산하다

investment
[invéstmənt]

n. 투자

a company's investment plans
회사의 투자 계획

transaction
[trænsǽkʃ-ən]

n. 거래

cash transactions 현금 거래

supplier
[səpláiər]

n. 제조업자

a machine-parts supplier 기계공구점

distributor
[distríbjətər]

n. 유통업자

a major distributor of electrical goods
전기 제품의 주요 배급업자

debt
[det]

n. 부채

a funded debt 장기 부채, 이자부 공채

monopoly
[mənápəli]

n. 독점

the monopoly of the trade 장사의 독점

regular price
[régjələːr prais]

n. 정가 (=fixed price)

sell at a fixed price 정가로 팔다

high price
[hai prais]

n. 고가

high-priced article 고가품

employer
[emplɔ́iər]

n. 고용주, 사용자

refer to a former employer for a character 인적 사항을 전 고용주에게 문의하다

employee
[implɔ́iː]

n. 고용인, 종업원

hire employees 종업원을 채용하다

receipt
[risíːt]

n. 영수증

sign a receipt 영수증에 서명하다

system
[sístəm]

n. 제도

the double price system 이중 가격제

corporation
[kɔ̀ːrpəréiʃən]

n. 주식회사

a trading corporation 무역회사

product
[prádəkt]

n. 상품

launch a new product 새 상품을 시장에 내다

customer
[kʌ́stəmər]

n. 단골손님, 거래처

a prospective customer 사줄 것 같은 손님

■ 회사조직

headquarters
[hedkwɔ́ːrtərz]

n. 본사, 본부

relocate company headquarters
본사를 이전하다

branch
[bræntʃ]

n. 지사, 지점

an overseas branch 해외 지점

organization
[ɔ̀ːrgənizéiʃən]

n. 조직, 단체

a central organization 중앙 조직

structure
[strʌ́ktʃər]

n. 구조

management structure 경영 구조

post
[poust]

n. 직위, 지위

get a post as a teacher 교사직을 얻다

status
[stéitəs]

n. 신분, 지위

seek status and security
신분과 안전을 추구하다

president
[prézidənt]

n. 사장, 회장

a vice president 부사장

executive
[igzékjətiv]

n. 중역, 간부급

the Chief Executive Officer (=CEO)
최고경영책임자

manager
[mǽnidʒər]

n. 과장

assistant manager 대리

secretary
[sékrətèri]

n. 비서

a competent secretary 유능한 비서

meeting
[míːtiŋ]

n. 회의

a staff meeting 간부회의

merger
[mə́ːrdʒər]

n. 합병

the merger of three companies
3개 회사의 합병

stockholder
[stákhòuldəːr]

n. 주주

stockholders in a company 회사의 주주
labor union 노동조합
a member of a labor union 노동조합원
seniority system 연공서열
get promotion by seniority system
연공서열에 따라 승진하다

personnel
[pə̀ːrsənél]

n. 인사

work in the personnel department
인사과에서 일하다

department
[dipáːrtmənt]

n. 부, 부서

the sales department 영업부

division
[divíʒən]

n. 국, 사업부

the sales division of the company
회사의 판매부(문)

section
[sékʃ-ən]

n. 과

the section dealing with customer complaints 고객만족센터

advertising
[ǽdvərtàiziŋ]

n. 광고

an advertising agency 광고 대행사

accounting
[əkáuntiŋ]

n. 경리, 회계

the accounting department 경리부

public relations
[pʌ́blik riléiʃ-əns]

n. 광고, 선전활동

works in public relations 홍보 업무를 하다

supervise
[sú:pərvàiz]

v. 감독하다

supervise the building work
건축 작업을 감독하다

responsible
[rispánsəb-əl]

a. 책임 있는

a highly responsible position
대단히 책임감을 요하는 위치

subordinate
[səbɔ́:rdənit]

n. 부하

with five subordinates 부하 다섯을 거느리고

clerk
[klə:rk]

n. 평사원

a bank clerk 은행원

cooperate
[kouápərèit]
v. 협력하다, 협동하다
cooperate in harmony 동심협력하다

restructure
[riːstrʌ́ktʃəːr]
v. 재편성(조정)하다
restructure an organization
조직을 재조정하다

management
[mǽnidʒmənt]
n. 경영
a management course 경영 과정

■ 고용

job
[dʒɑb]
n. 일, 직업
get a job 취직하다

employ
[emplɔ́i]
v. 고용하다
be employed as a clerk
사무원으로 채용되다-정식, 계속적 고용

hire
[haiər]
v. 고용하다
hire a lawyer
변호사를 고용하다(임시, 한시적으로 개인이 고용)

interview
[íntərvjùː]
n. 면접
job interview 취직 면접

resume
[rèzuméi]
n. 이력서
submit a resume 이력서를 제출하다

qualification
[kwɑ̀ləfikéiʃən]
n. 자격
citizenship qualifications 시민권 취득 자격

ability [əbíləti]	*n.* 능력	diplomatic ability 외교적 수완
capable [kéipəbəl]	*a.* 유능한	a very capable woman 대단히 능력 있는 여자
overtime [óuvərtàim]	*n.* 시간외 근무, 잔업	work two hours overtime 두 시간 잔업을 하다
wage [weidʒ]	*n.* 임금	daily wages 일급
salary [sǽləri]	*n.* 봉급	a yearly salary 연봉
pension [pénʃən]	*n.* 연금	draw one's pension 연금을 타다
earn [əːrn]	*v.* 벌다	earn forty dollars a day 하루에 40달러 벌다
manage [mǽnidʒ]	*v.* 경영하다	manage a business 상사(商社)를 경영하다
layoff [léiɔ(ː)f]	*n.* (회사 사정으로) 일시해고	a layoff system 일시 해고 제도
fire [faiər]	*v.* (자신의 잘못으로) 해고 당하다	get fired 해고되다
business trip [bíznis trip]	*n.* 출장	go on a business trip 출장가다

day off
[dei ɔːf]
n. 휴가
take a day off 하루 휴가를 얻다

bonus
[bóunəs]
n. 보너스
a year end-bonus 연말 보너스

allowance
[əláuəns]
n. 수당
family allowance 가족 수당

promotion
[prəmóuʃən]
n. 승진
get promotion 승진하다

retirement
[ritáiərmənt]
n. 은퇴
enjoy retirement 은퇴 후의 생활을 즐기다

retire
[ritáiər]
v. 은퇴하다
retire under an age clause 정년퇴직하다

resignation
[rèzignéiʃ-ən]
n. 사직
a letter of resignation 사직서

reception desk
[risépʃ-ən]
n. 접수처
ask at the reception desk 접수처에 묻다

general affairs section
[dʒénərəl əféərs sékʃ-ne]
n. 총무과
the staff of the general affairs section 총무과 과원

discharge
[distʃáːrdʒ]
v. 해고하다
be honorably discharged 명예 퇴직 시키다

09

unemployment
[ʌnemplɔ́imənt]

n. 실업

an unemployment problem 실업 문제

strike
[straik]

v. 파업하다

strike work 파업에 들어가다

negotiate
[nigóuʃièit]

v. 협상하다

negotiate on equal terms
같은 조건으로 교섭하다

■ 직업

occupation
[ὰkjəpéiʃən]

n. 직업(정규직)

have a regular occupation
정직업을 가지고 있다

profession
[prəféʃən]

n. 직업(전문직)

the profession of a lawyer 변호사업

job
[dʒɑb]

n. 직업(일반적으로 쓰임)

seek a job as a secretary 비서직을 찾다

work
[wəːrk]

n. 일

after a day's work 하루의 일을 마치고

task
[tæsk]

n. 업무, 일

a laborious task 수고로운 일

duty
[djúːti]

n. 의무

a sense of duty 의무감

career
[kəríər]
n. 경력
a career in law 법률가로서의 경력

staff
[stæf]
n. 직원, 간부
the teaching staff of college 대학의 교수진

working conditions
[wɔ́ːrkiŋ kəndíʃəns]
n. 노동조건
the improvement of the working conditions 노동조건의 개선

contract
[kántrækt]
v. 계약(하다)
contract with a firm for the building 회사와 건축 계약을 맺다

free-lance
[fríː læns]
a. 자유계약제의 *n.* 프리랜서
a free-lance reporter 자유 계약제의 기자

shift
[ʃift]
n. 교대
an eight-hour shift 8시간 교대제

vacation
[veikéiʃən]
n. 휴가
the summer vacation 여름휴가

productivity
[pròudʌktívəti]
n. 생산성
high productivity 높은 생산성

efficiency
[ifíʃənsi]
n. 효율, 능률
promote efficiency 능률을 향상시키다

busy
[bízi]
a. 바쁜
busy hands 부지런히 일하고 있는 손

free
[fri:]

a. 한가한

have very little free time 여가가 없다

provide
[prəváid]

v. 지급하다

provide communication allowances
교통비를 지급하다

banker
[bǽŋkər]

n. 은행가

the Banker's Association 은행가 협회

accountant
[əkáuntənt]

n. 회계사

certified public accountant 공인 회계사

lawyer
[lɔ́:jə:r]

n. 변호사

consult a lawyer 변호사에게 상의하다

driver
[dráivər]

n. 운전사

taxi driver 택시 운전사

company employee
[kʌ́mpəni implɔ́ii]

n. 회사원

Furniture company employee
가구회사 근무자

businessman
[bíznismæ̀n]

n. 사업가

a smart business 수완있는 사업가

entertainer
[èntərtéinər]

n. 연예인

a well-known television entertainer
유명 텔레비전 연예인

comedian
[kəmí:diən]

n. 코미디언

a low comedian 저속한 희극 배우

singer
[síŋəːr]
n. 가수
an opera singer 오페라 가수

actor
[ǽktər]
n. 배우
a film actor 영화배우

actress
[ǽktris]
n. 여배우
the Oscar actress 아카데미상 수상 여배우

model
[mádl]
n. 모델
a fashion model 패션 모델

announcer
[ənáunsər]
n. 아나운서
a famous announcer 유명한 아나운서

pilot
[páilət]
n. 파일럿, 조종사
a fighter pilot 전투기조종사

designer
[dizáinər]
n. 디자이너
hair designer 미용사

worker
[wə́ːrkəːr]
n. 노동자
a temporary worker 임시 노동자

laborer
[léibərəːr]
n. 노동자
a day laborer 날품팔이 노동자

detective
[ditéktiv]
n. 형사, 탐정
employ a private detective
사설탐정을 고용하다

policeman [polismən]	*n.* 경찰	a policeman in plain clothes 사복 경관
professor [prəfésər]	*n.* 교수	visiting professor 객원 교수
part-time [páːrt tàim]	*a.* 파트타임의, 비상근의	work part-time 파트타임으로 일하다
fulltime [fúltáim]	*a.* 전시간제의	work fulltime 정규직으로 일하다
fireman [faiərmən]	*n.* 소방관	a firemen's convention 소방관 대회
athlete [ǽθliːt]	*n.* 운동선수	the best female athletes 최우수 여자 운동선수들
chef / cook [ʃef]/[kuk]	*n.* 요리사	a chef par excellent 아주 솜씨좋은 요리사
waiter [wéitəː]	*n.* 웨이터	shout for a waiter 큰소리로 웨이터를 부르다
waitress [wéitris]	*n.* 웨이트리스	remember the waitress 웨이트리스에게 팁을 주다
doctor [dáktər]	*n.* 의사	see a doctor 의사의 진찰을 받다

dentist
[déntist]

n. 치과의사

go to the dentist 치과에 (치료 받으러) 가다

pharmacist
[fá:rməmist]

n. 약사

a pharmacist's office (병원의) 약국

nurse
[nə:rs]

n. 간호원

a male nurse 남자 간호사

novelist
[návəlist]

n. 소설가

win fame as a novelist 소설가로서 고명하다

writer
[ráitə:r]

n. 작가

a fiction writer 소설가

author
[ɔ́:θər]

n. 작가

a rising author 신진 작가

journalist
[dʒə́:rnəlist]

n. 저널리스트

a free-lance journalist 프리랜서의 저널리스트

reporter
[ripɔ́:rtə:r]

n. 보도기자

a financial reporter 경제 기자

editor
[édətər]

n. 편집자

a general editor 편집장

interpreter
[intə́:rprətər]

n. 통역사

speak through an interpreter
통역을 통해서 말하다

musician [mjuːzíʃ-ən]	*n.* 음악가 a great musician 음악의 대가
composer [kəmpóuzər]	*n.* 작곡가 an idiomatic composer 개성 있는 작곡가
painter [péintər]	*n.* 화가 a painter in oils 유화 화가
sculptor [skʌ́lptəːr]	*n.* 조각가 a talented sculptor 재능있는 조각가
architect [áːrkitèkt]	*n.* 건축가 a naval architect 조선 기사
carpenter [káːrpəntər]	*n.* 목수 carpenter's shop 목공소
physicist [fízisist]	*n.* 물리학자 a nuclear physicist 핵물리학자
astronaut [ǽstrənɔ̀ːt]	*n.* 우주비행사 become an astronaut 우주비행사가 되다
engineer [èndʒəníər]	*n.* 기사, 기술자 a civil engineer 토목 기사
barber [báːrbər]	*n.* 이발사 go to the barber('s) 이발소에 가다

06 경제와 돈

■ 경제 전반

economy [ikánəmi] — *n.* 경제
a national economy 국민 경제

market [má:rkit] — *n.* 시장
the foreign market 외국 시장

invest [invést] — *v.* 투자하다
invest one's money in stocks
증권에 투자하다

budget [bʌ́dʒit] — *n.* 예산
a budget committee 예산 위원회

fiscal year [fískəl jiə:r] — *n.* 회계연도
carry over to the next fiscal year
내년도로 이월하다

revenue [révənjù:] — *n.* 세입
revenue and expenditure 세입 세출

outgo [áutgòu] — *n.* 지출, 출비
a record of income and outgo 수지 기록

expense
[ikspéns]

n. 비용

at public expense 공적 비용으로

cut
[kʌt]

v. 삭감하다

cut the budget 예산을 삭감하다

reduce
[ridjúːs]

v. 줄이다, 감하다

reduce expenses 비용을 줄이다

boom
[buːm]

n. 벼락경기

Business is booming. 경기가 아주 좋다

recession
[riséʃ-ən]

n. 불경기

a stagnating recession 침체하는 경기

stagnant
[stǽgnənt]

a. 불경기의

stagnant business 불경기

industry
[índəstri]

n. 산업

a growth industry 성장 산업

commerce
[kámərs]

n. 상업, 통상

domestic commerce 국내 무역

trade
[treid]

n. 무역

free trade 자유 무역

export
[íkspɔːrt]

n. 수출

the exports of Korea to America
한국의 대미(對美) 수출품

import
[impɔ́ːrt]

n. 수입

food imports 수입 식품

production
[prədʌ́kʃən]

n. 생산

mass production 대량 생산

sample
[sǽmp-əl]

n. 견본

buy by samples 견본을 보고 사다

order
[ɔ́ːrdər]

n. 주문 *n.* 주문하다

a mail-order catalogue 우편 주문 책자

price
[prais]

n. 가격

a cash price 현금 가격

cost
[kɔːst]

n. 비용

the cost of production 생산비

friction
[fríkʃ-ən]

n. 마찰, 알력

friction between two nations
두 나라 사이의 알력

fare
[fɛər]

n. 운임

a railroad fare 철도 요금

tax
[tæks]

n. 세금

an income tax 소득세

estimate
[éstəmèit]

n. 견적

a written estimate 견적서

confiscation
[kánfiskèiʃən]

n. 몰수

a confiscated article 몰수품

introduction
[ìntrədʌ́kʃən]

n. 도입

the introduction of foreign capital
외자 도입

commission
[kəmíʃən]

n. 수수료

get a commission of ten percent
10%의 수수료를 받다

shipping
[ʃípiŋ]

n. 선적

document of shipping 선적 서류

exchange rate
[ikstʃéindʒ reit]

n. 환율

stabilize exchange rates 환율을 안정시키다

offer
[ɔ́(:)fər]

n. 제의, 제안

a firm offer 확고한 제의

claim
[kleim]

n. 클레임, 청구

a claim for damages 손해 배상 청구

smuggling
[smʌ́g-əliŋ]

n. 밀수

a drug-smuggling operation 마약 밀수 작전

freight
[freit]

n. 화물

send goods by air freight
항공 화물로 물품을 보내다

sales
[seilz]

n. 매출(액)

the total sales 총매출

technology
[teknálədʒi]

n. 과학기술

recent advances in medical technology
최근의 의료 기술발전

demand
[dimǽnd]

n. 수요

the law of supply and demand
수요 공급의 법칙

supply
[səplái]

n. 공급

adequate supplies of raw materials
적절한 원자재 공급

consumption
[kənsʌ́mpʃən]

n. 소비

a daily consumption per head
1인당 1일 소비액

expenditure
[ikspénditʃər]

n. 지출

current expenditure 경상비

enterprise
[éntərpràiz]

n. 기업

private enterprise 민간 기업

depression
[dipréʃən]

n. 불경기

climb out of the depression
불경기 상태에서 벗어나다

prosperity
[prɑspérəti]

n. 호황

show signs of prosperity 호황을 보이다

profit
[práfit]

n. 이익

net profit 순이익

goods
[gudz]

n. 상품

essential goods 필수품

income
[ínkʌm]

n. 수입, 소득

an annual income 연수입

payment
[péimənt]

n. 지불

advance payment 선불

capital
[kǽpitl]

n. 자본

foreign capital 외자

discount
[dískaunt]

n. 할인 *v.* 할인하다

discount 10% for cash
현금 구매시 10% 할인하다

labor
[léibər]

n. 노동

physical labor 육체노동

quality
[kwáləti]

n. 품질, 질

goods of the highest quality
최고 품질의 상품

subcontract
[sʌbkántrækt]

n. 하청

a plumber doing subcontract work
하청 일을 하는 배관공

wholesale
[hóulsèil]

n. 도매

a wholesale dealer 도매 상인

retail
[rí:teil]

n. 소매

a retail price 소매가격

bargain
[bάːrgin]

n. 흥정 *v.* 흥정하다

bargain with a person about the price
…와 가격에 관해 흥정하다

deal
[diːl]

n. 거래 *v.* 거래하다

conduct a deal with …와 거래하다

compete
[kəmpíːt]

v. 경쟁하다

against other countries in trade
무역에서 다른 나라들과 맞서다

fail
[feil]

v. 실패하다

fail in business 사업에 실패하다

succeed
[səksíːd]

v. 성공하다

succeed in solving a problem
문제의 해결에 성공하다

produce
[prədjúːs]

v. 생산하다, 제작하다

produce cotton goods 면제품을 생산하다

waste
[weist]

n. 낭비 *v.* 낭비하다

a waste of time 시간낭비

■ 주식과 채권

stock
[stɑk]

n. 주식

a stock report 주식 기사

securities
[sikjú-əritiz]

n. (유가)증권

a securities company[firm] 증권 회사

government bond
[gʌ́vərnmənt band]

n. 국채

issue government bond 국채를 발행하다

stockholder
[stak hòuldə:r]

n. 주주

a general meeting of stockholders
주주총회 / **securities firm** 증권회사

stock market
[stak má:rkit]

n. 주식시장

speculating on the stock market
주식시장에 투기하다

stock exchange
[stak ikstʃéindʒ]

n. 증권거래소

companies listed on the stock exchange 증권거래소에 상장된 회사들

stock price
[stak prais]

n. 주가

stock prices rise 주가가 오르다

index
[índeks]

n. 지수

the composite stock exchange index
종합 주가 지수

volume
[válju:m]

n. 총액

trading volumes 거래총액

slump
[slʌmp]

n. (주가의) 폭락

a slump in stocks 주식의 급락

dividend
[dívidènd]

n. 배당(금)

declare a dividend 배당을 고시하다

금융(은행)

finance
[finǽns]
n. 금융, 재정
public[national] finance 국가 재정

financial
[finǽnʃəl]
n. 재무의, 재정의
be in financial difficulties
재정적 어려움에 처해 있다.

bank
[bæŋk]
n. 은행
a central bank 중앙은행

payment
[péimənt]
n. 지불
payment in full 전액 지급

money
[mʌ́ni]
n. 돈
send money 송금하다

bank account
[bæŋk əkáun]
n. 은행계좌
have a bank account of 200,000 won
은행에 20만원 저금이 있다

bank account number *n.* 계좌번호
[bæŋk əkáunt nʌ́mbəːr]

bankbook
[bæŋkbuk]
n. 통장
a post office-savings bankbook
우편 저금통장

remittance
[rimít-əns]
n. 송금(액)
promise a remittance 송금을 약속하다

savings
[séiviŋz]

n. 저금, 예금

savings deposits 저축성 예금

deposit
[dipázit]

n. 예금하다

deposit $500 in a bank
은행에 500달러를 예금하다

withdraw
[wiðdrɔ́ː]

v. 인출하다

withdraw money from the bank
돈을 은행에서 인출하다

balance
[bǽləns]

n. 잔액, 잔고

the balance at the bank 은행 예금 잔액

amount
[əmáunt]

n. 총액

the amount of money spent on one's clothes 옷에 들인 금액

salary
[sǽləri]

n. 봉급, 급료

a salary agreement 임금 협상

bonus
[bóunəs]

n. 상여금, 보너스

cost-of-living bonus
(물가 상승에 따른) 특별 수당

transaction
[trænsǽkʃ-ən]

n. 거래, 취급

cash transactions 현금 거래

overdue
[òuvərdjúː]

a. 지불기한이 지난

an overdue bill 지급 기한이 지난 어음

exchange rate
[ikstʃéindʒ reit]

n. 환율

fixed exchange rate 고정 환율

cash
[kæʃ]

n. 현금

convert into cash 현금으로 바꾸다

coin
[kɔin]

n. 동전

a 1-dollar coin 1달러짜리 동전

bill
[bil]

n. 지폐

a ten-dollar bill 10달러 지폐

loan
[loun]

n. 대출

pay off a loan 대출을 갚다

liability
[làiəbíləti]

n. 채무, 부채

assets and liabilities 자산과 부채

debt
[det]

n. 빚

a debt of ten dollars 10달러의 빚

credit
[krédit]

n. 신용

a credit condition 신용상태

security
[sikjú-əriti]

n. 보증, 증권

government securities 정부 유가 증권

installment savings
[instɔ́:lmənt séiviŋz]

n. 적금

save up by installments 적금을 붓다

check
[tʃek]

n. 수표

a check for one million won 100만원짜리 수표

09

draft [dræft]
n. 어음
pay by draft 어음으로 지불하다

currency [kə́:rənsi]
n. 화폐
currency depreciation 화폐의 가치저하

interest [íntərist]
n. 이자
a high rate of interest 높은 이자율

exchange [ikstʃéindʒ]
v. 환전하다
exchange won for dollars
원화를 달러로 환전하다

ATM [eiti:em]
n. 현금 자동 지급기 (=automatic teller machine)
withdraw money from an ATM
ATM기에서 현금을 인출하다

PIN number [pin nʌ́mbəːr]
n. 비밀번호
verify one's PIN number 비밀번호를 확인하다

money rate [mʌ́ni reit]
n. 금리
raise the rate of interest 금리를 인상하다

■ 세금

tax [tæks]
n. 세금
free of tax 세금 없이

taxpayer [tǽkspèiər]
n. 납세자
the right of taxpayers 납세자의 권리

tax rate
[tæks reit]

n. 세율

raise the tax rate 세율을 인상하다

tax increase
[tæks inkríːs]

n. 증세

enact a tax increase 증세를 입법화하다

tax cut
[tæks kʌt]

n. 감세

an income tax cut 소득세 감세

tax-exempt
[tæks igzémpt]

a. 비과세의

tax-exempt bonds 비과세 채권

tax-evasion
[tæks ivéiʒən]

n. 탈세

plead guilty to tax evasion
탈세에 유죄를 인정하다

tax-deductible
[tæks didʌ́ktəbl]

n. 과세공제

tax-deductible expenses 과세공제 비용

customs
[kʌ́stəmz]

n. 세관

go through customs 통관하다

duty-free
[djúːti friː]

a. 면세의

duty-free goods 면세품

tax reform
[tæks riːfɔ́ːrm]

n. 세제개혁

stage a full-court press for tax reform
세제 개혁을 위해 전면적인 노력을 하다

inhabitant tax
[inhǽbətənt tæks]

n. 주민세

pay an inhabitant tax 주민세를 내다

inheritance tax
[inhéritəns tæks]

n. 상속세

pay an inheritance tax in land
상속세를 토지로 대납하다

excise
[éksaiz]

n. 소비세

an excise on tobacco 담배의 소비세

tariff
[tǽrif]

n. 관세

a protective tariff 보호 관세

PART 10

언어
생활

01 부사적인 표현

■ 부사어

exactly
[igzǽktli]
ad. 정확하게
as exactly as I can 가능한 한 정확히

precisely
[prisáisli]
ad. 정확하게
at 2 o'clock precisely 정확히 2시에

certainly
[sə́:rtənli]
ad. 확실히, 틀림없이
most certainly 절대로 틀림없이

indeed
[indíd]
ad. 참으로, 실로
a very big parcel indeed 정말로 매우 큰 소포

really
[rí:-əli]
ad. 정말로, 실제로
a really charming person 정말 매력적인 사람

actually [ǽktʃuəli]
ad. 사실은, 실제로

clearly
[klíərli]
ad. 명확히, 분명히
to put it clearly 《문두에서》 분명히 말해서

almost
[ɔ́ːlmoust]

ad. 거의, 대략

almost every man 거의 모든 사람

nearly
[níərli]

ad. 거의

nearly finished 거의 끝난

generally
[dʒénərəli]

ad. 일반적으로

generally speaking 일반적으로 말하면

partly
[páːrtli]

ad. 부분적으로

be **partly** destroyed 일부 파괴되다

especially
[ispéʃəli]

ad. 특별히(=particularly)

especially important 특별히 중요한

absolutely
[ǽbsəlúːtli]

ad. 절대적으로

absolutely impossible 전혀 불가능한

extremely
[ikstríːmli]

ad. 극단적으로, 매우

extremely complicated 대단히 복잡한

practically
[prǽktikəli]

ad. 사실상, 실제로

practically impossible 거의 불가능한

naturally
[nǽtʃərəli]

ad. 본래, 당연히

a **naturally** gifted actor
천부적인 재능을 가진 배우

relatively
[rélətivli]

ad. 비교적으로

relatively speaking 비교해서 말하면

however [hauévər]	*ad.* 그렇지만	

always [ɔ́ːlweiz]
ad. 항상, 늘
almost always 대개, 거의 언제나

usually [júːʒuəli]
ad. 보통
more than usually late 여느 때보다 더 늦은

frequently [fríːkwəntli]
ad. 자주, 종종
write home frequently 집으로 자주 편지를 쓰다

often [ɔ́(ː)ftən]
ad. 흔히, 자주
often and often 몇 번이고

sometimes [sʌ́mtàimz]
ad. 때때로
come here sometimes 가끔 이리로 오다

seldom [séldəm]
ad. 좀처럼 ~않다, 드물게
not seldom 이따금, 흔히

scarcely [skɛ́ərsli]
ad. 간신히, 거의 ~않다
scarcely any 거의 없다

hardly [háːrdli]
ad. 거의 ~않다
hardly ever 좀처럼 …없다

never [névəːr]
ad. 전혀 ~않다
the habit of never speaking to strangers 낯선 사람과는 결코 말하지 않는 습관

once [wʌns]
ad. 한번
once a day 하루에 한 번

01 부사적인 표현

twice
[twais]
ad. 두 번
a twice-yearly event 년 2회 열리는 행사

again
[əgén]
ad. 다시
try again 다시 한 번 해보다

only
[óunli]
ad. 오직, 다만…뿐
only a little 아주 조금

probably
[prábəbli]
ad. 아마도
You're probably right.
당신이 아마 맞을 거예요.

perhaps
[pərhǽps]
ad. 아마도
Perhaps he's forgotten.
아마 그가 잊어버린 모잊어버린 모양이다.

maybe
[méibi]
ad. 아마도
You're right, maybe. 아마 그럴 겁니다.

ahead
[əhéd]
ad. 앞으로, 앞쪽으로
set a clock ahead 시계를 앞으로 돌리다

behind
[biháind]
ad. 배후에, 뒤쪽에
behind the house 집 뒤에

back
[bæk]
ad. 뒤로, 배후에
look back 뒤돌아보다, 회상하다

near
[niər]
ad. 가까이에
sit near 옆에 앉다

far [fɑːr]	*ad.* 멀리 wander far 멀리 방랑하다
away [əwéi]	*ad.* 멀리 떨어져 six miles away 6마일 떨어져서
gradually [grǽdʒuəli]	*ad.* 점차적으로, 차차 be getting better gradually 점차 나아지다
thoroughly [θə́ːrouli]	*ad.* 완전히, 철저히 know thoroughly 속속들이 알다
already [ɔːlrédi]	*ad.* 이미, 벌써<긍정문> It's already twelve o'clock. 벌써 12시다
yet [jet]	*ad.* 아직<부정문> I'm not ready yet. 난 아직 준비가 안 됐어.
still [stil]	*ad.* 여전히, 아직도 I'm still living in Seoul. 나는 아직 서울에 살고 있다
lately [léitli]	*ad.* 최근의(=recently) till lately 최근까지
immediately [imíːdiitli]	*ad.* 즉시, 곧 immediately after his death 그가 죽은 뒤 곧
quickly [kwíkli]	*ad.* 빨리 learn very quickly 아주 빨리 배우다
soon [suːn]	*ad.* 곧, 이내 as soon as possible 될 수 있는 대로 빨리

01 부사적인 표현

someday
[sʌ́mdèi]
ad. 언젠가, 훗날
someday soon 가까운 날에

suddenly
[sʌ́dnli]
ad. 갑자기
die suddenly 급살맞다

afterward
[ǽftərwərd]
ad. 후에, 나중에
long afterward 그후 쭉

forever
[fərévəːr]
ad. 영원히
last forever 영원히 계속되다

then
[ðen]
ad. 그때, 그다음에
till then 그때까지

■ 의태어와 의성어

laugh
[læf]
v. 웃다
laugh loudly 소리내어 웃다

smile
[smail]
v. 미소짓다
with a smile 웃는 낯으로

chuckle
[tʃʌ́kl]
v. 낄낄대다
chuckle with delight to oneself
혼자 신이 나서 낄낄거리다

giggle
[gígəl]
v. 킥킥 웃다
giggle away 계속 킥킥 웃다

grin
[grin]

v. 싱긋웃다

grin at a person 남을 보고 싱긋 웃다

cry
[krai]

v. 소리내어 울다

cry loudly 큰소리내어 울다

blubber
[blʌ́bər]

v. 엉엉 울다, 흐느껴 울다

stop blubbering 엉엉우는 것을 멈춰라

waul
[wɔːl]

v. 응애응애 울다, 울부짖다

a frightful din of wauling 울부짖는 무서운 소음

sob
[sɑb]

v. 흐느껴 울다

sob one's heart out 가슴이 메이도록 흐느껴 울다

say
[sei]

v. 말하다

say carefully 조심스레 말하다

mutter
[mʌ́tər]

v. 중얼중얼거리다

mutter to oneself 중얼중얼 혼자 말하다

grumble
[grʌ́mbəl]

v. 투덜대다, 불평하다

grumble out a protest 투덜투덜 항의하다

fluently
[flúːəntli]

ad. 술술, 줄줄

speak very fluently 청산유수로 이야기하다

whisper
[hwíspəːr]

v. 속삭이다

talk in whispers 소곤소곤 이야기하다

02 동작 표현

■ 동작을 나타내는 말

clean
[kliːn]
v. 청소하다, 깨끗하게 하다
clean one's teeth 이를 깨끗이 닦다

wipe
[waip]
v. 닦다, 치우다
wipe a desk with a cloth 걸레로 책상을 훔치다

sweep
[swiːp]
v. 쓸다, 털다
sweep the floor 마루를 쓸다

remove
[rimúːv]
v. 제거하다, 없애다
remove a polish from one's nails
메니큐어를 지우다

burn
[bəːrn]
v. 태우다, 불사르다
burn up the rubbish 쓰레기를 소각하다

paint
[peint]
v. 그리다, 페인트칠하다
paint the walls white 벽을 하얗게 칠하다

attach
[ətǽtʃ]
v. 붙이다
attach a label to a parcel
소포에 꼬리표를 붙이다

fix [fiks]	*v.* 고정시키다 fix a mirror to the wall 거울을 벽에 고정시키다
bend [bend]	*v.* 구부리다 bend a wire up 철사를 구부려 올리다
saw [sɔː]	*v.* 톱질하다 *n.* 톱 saw a branch off 나뭇가지를 톱질해서 자르다
drill [dril]	*v.* 꿰뚫다 *n.* 드릴 drill a hole in the wall 벽에 구멍을 뚫다
punch [pʌntʃ]	*n.* 펀치 *v.* 구멍을 뚫다 punch a ticket 표에 구멍을 뚫다
pierce [piərs]	*v.* 꿰찌르다, 관통하다 have one's ears pierced 귀고리를 하려고 귀에 구멍을 뚫다
stir [stəːr]	*v.* 휘젓다, 뒤섞다 stir vinegar into salad oil 식초를 샐러드오일에 넣어 저어서 섞다
change [tʃeindʒ]	*v.* 바꾸다, 교환하다 change gear (자동차의) 기어를 바꿔 넣다
manage [mǽnidʒ]	*v.* 관리하다, 운영하다 manage a company 회사를 경영하다
protect [prətékt]	*v.* 보호하다, 지키다 protect the interests of labor 노동자의 권익을 보호하다

fold
[fould]
v. 접다
fold a handkerchief in four
손수건을 넷으로 접다

spread
[spred]
v. 펴다, 펼치다
spread out the newspaper 신문을 펼치다

limit
[límit]
n. 한계 *v.* 제한하다
limit one sentence to 15 words
한 문장을 15단어로 제한하다

cause
[kɔːz]
v. 초래하다, 일으키다
cause a fire 화재를 일으키다

treat
[triːt]
v. 취급하다, 치료하다
treat like a child 어린아이 취급하다

become
[bikʌ́m]
v. ~이 되다
become a great man 훌륭한 사람이 되다

let
[let]
v. ~하게 해주다
let things take their own course
추세에 맡기다

lead
[liːd]
v. 인도하다, 안내하다
lead the young generation 후진을 이끌다

cover
[kʌ́vər]
v. 덮다, 감싸다
cover one's face with one's hands
손으로 얼굴을 감싸다

share
[ʃɛəːr]

v. 나누다

share the profit 이익을 나누다

separate
[sépərèit]

v. 분리하다

separate church and state
종교와 정치를 분리하다

split
[split]

v. 쪼개다, 분할하다

split a log into two 통나무를 둘로 쪼개다

deserve
[dizə́ːrv]

v. ~할 만하다

deserve attention 주목할 만하다

solve
[sɑlv]

v. 풀다, 해결하다

solve a riddle 수수께끼를 풀다

lack
[læk]

n. 부족 *v.* 부족하다

lack all sense of responsibility
책임감이 없다

need
[niːd]

v. 필요하다 *n.* 필요

be in need of help 도움을 필요로 하고 있다

hide
[haid]

v. 숨기다, 숨다

hide one's feeling 감정을 드러내지 않다

add
[æd]

v. 첨가하다, 추가하다

add sugar to tea 홍차에 설탕을 타다

fall
[fɔːl]

v. 떨어지다, 내리다

fall out of a car 차에서 떨어지다

miss
[mis]

v. 놓치다, 빗맞히다
miss the mark 표적을 벗어나다

mistake
[mistéik]

v. 잘못 알다 *n.* 잘못
make a mistake 실수하다

03 수량

■ 수와 양을 나타내는 표현

many
[méni]

a. 많은

many years ago 여러 해 전에

plenty
[plénti]

a. 많은, 충분한   *n.* 많음, 가득

a plenty of time 충분한 시간

much
[mʌtʃ]

a. 많은

have much rain 비가 흠뻑 오다

enough
[inʌ́f]

a. 충분한

enough money to buy a house
집을 사기에 충분한 돈

sufficient
[səfíʃənt]

a. 충분한, 족한

a necessary and sufficient condition
필요 충분 조건

numerous
[njúːm-ərəs]

a. 다수의, 수많은

the numerous voice of the people
국민 다수의 목소리

several
[sév-ərəl]

a. 몇몇의

after several days 수일 후에

some
[sʌm]

a. 약간의

need some bread and milk
빵과 우유가 좀 필요하다

few
[fjuː]

a. 거의 없는, 다소의

a man of few words 말수가 적은 사람

narrow
[nǽrou]

a. 좁은, 가까스로의

by a narrow margin 겨우, 아슬아슬하게

wide
[waid]

a. 폭넓은

have one's eyes open wide
눈이 휘둥그레져서

broad
[brɔːd]

a. 폭이 넓은, 광대한

this broad land of ours 이 넓은 우리나라

low
[lou]

a. 낮은

be low in price 값이 싸다

high
[hai]

a. 높은

a house 40 feet high 높이 40피트의 집

shallow
[ʃǽlou]

a. 얕은, 천박한, 얄팍한

a shallow idea 얄팍한 생각

deep
[diːp]

a. 깊은

a pond 5 feet deep 깊이 5피트의 연못

thin [θin]	*a.* 얇은, 가는 a thin finger 가는 손가락
thick [θik]	*a.* 두꺼운 thick lips 두툼한 입술
count [kaunt]	*v.* 세다 count one by one 물건을 점점이 세다
calculate [kǽlkjəlèit]	*v.* 계산하다 calculate the speed of light 빛의 속도를 계산하다
sum [sʌm]	*n.* 합계 figure out a sum 합계를 내다
average [ǽvərid ʒ]	*n.* 평균, 보통 strike an average 평균을 내다
standard [stǽndəːrd]	*a.* 표준의, 수준의 elevate the standard of living 생활수준을 향상시키다
equal [íːkwəl]	*a.* 같은, 동등한 equal pay for equal work 동일 노동에 동일 임금
total [tóutl]	*a.* 전체의 the sum total 총액
whole [houl]	*a.* 전부의, 모두의 taken as a whole 전체적으로 볼 때

entire
[entáiər]
a. 전체의, 전부의
the entire staff 직원 전체

extra
[ékstrə]
a. 여분의, 추가의
pay extra 별도로 돈을 치르다

part
[pɑːrt]
n. 일부, 부분
an underlined part 밑줄 친 부분

unit
[júːnit]
n. 단위
a monetary unit 화폐의 단위

piece
[piːs]
n. 조각
fall to pieces 떨어져서 박살이 나다

heavy
[hévi]
a. 무거운
heavy eyes 졸린 눈

light
[lait]
a. 가벼운
as light as air 매우 가벼운

weigh
[wei]
v. 무게를 달다, ~의 무게가 나가다
weigh 60 kilograms 체중이 60kg이다

big
[big]
a. 큰
a big voice 큰 목소리

large
[lɑːrdʒ]
a. 넓은
a large family 대가족

huge
[hjuːdʒ]
a. 거대한, 막대한
a huge man 거인

long
[lɔːŋ]

a. 긴
have long legs 다리가 길다

short
[ʃɔːrt]

a. 짧은
a short walk 단거리의 보행

small
[smɔːl]

a. 작은
a small quantity 적은 분량

fine
[fain]

a. 가는, 미세한
fine rain 가랑비

compact
[kəmpǽkt]

a. 소형의
rent a compact car 소형차를 빌리다

04 물건에 관한 표현

물건에 관한 표현

thing
[θiŋ]
n. 것, 물건
all things 만물, 모든 것

object
[ábdʒikt]
n. 물건, 사물
object in view 보이는 것들

old
[ould]
a. 늙은, 오래된
old brandy 오래된 브랜디

used
[juːst]
a. 중고의
a used car market 중고차 시장

antique
[æntíːk]
a. 골동품의, 고대의
an antique shop 골동품점

new
[njuː]
a. 새로운
a new book 신간 서적

up-to-date
[ʌp tu deit]
a. 최신의
an up-to-date hotel 최신식 호텔

fresh
[freʃ]
a. 신선한
fresh fruit 신선한 과일

modern
[mádəːrn]
a. 현대의, 현대적인
modern city life 현대의 도시 생활

contemporary
[kəntémpərèri]
a. 현대의, 동시대의
contemporary literature 현대문학

weak
[wiːk]
a. 약한
be week in math 수학에 약하다

strong
[strɔ(ː)ŋ]
a. 강한, 힘센
be strong in English 영어에 강하다

powerful
[páuərfəl]
a. 강력한, 유력한
a powerful speech 힘찬 연설

intense
[inténs]
a. 격렬한, 심한
intense cold 혹한

severe
[sivíəːr]
a. 맹렬한, 혹독한
a severe shock 심한 충격

effective
[iféktiv]
a. 유효한, 효과적인
effective against polio 소아마비에 효과적인

moderate
[má-d-ərèit]
a. 알맞은
take moderate exercise 적당히 운동하다

considerable
[kənsídərəbəl]

a. 꽤 많은, 상당한

a considerable sum of money
상당한 액수의 돈

enormous
[inɔ́ːrməs]

a. 거대한, 막대한

a enormous profit 막대한 이익

tremendous
[triméndəs]

a. 굉장한

a tremendous propaganda effect
대단한 선전 효과

extraordinary
[ikstrɔ́ːrdənèri]

a. 대단한, 비상한

have extraordinary talent 출중한 재주가 있다

ultimate
[ʌ́ltəmit]

a. 최후의, 궁극의

the ultimate end of life 인생의 궁극적인 목적

maximum
[mǽksəməm]

a. 최대한, 최고의

maximum temperature 최고 기온

minimum
[mínəməm]

a. 최저의, 극소의

the minimum amount of effort 최소한의 노력

dark
[dɑːrk]

a. 어두운

a dark night 어두컴컴한 밤

shade
[ʃeid]

n. 그늘

take a rest in the shade 그늘에서 쉬다

shadow
[ʃǽdou]

n. 그림자

cast a shadow on the wall
벽에 그림자를 던지다

dull
[dʌl]

a. 밝지 않은, 칙칙한

dull-looking hair 칙칙한 색깔의 머리

shabby
[ʃǽbi]

a. 초라한

look shabby 꼴이 초라하다

bright
[brait]

a. 밝은

a bright color 밝은 색깔

light
[lait]

a. 밝은, 연한

a light brown sweater 연한 갈색 스웨터

brilliant
[bríljənt]

a. 찬란하게 빛나는

brilliant jewels 번쩍거리는 보석

vivid
[vívid]

a. 선명한, 생생한

a vivid description 생생한 묘사

shine
[ʃain]

v. 빛나다

shine brilliantly 찬연히 빛나다

flash
[flæʃ]

v. 빛나다, 번쩍이다

flash a mirror in the sun
햇빛에 거울을 반짝이다

PART 11

감정과 화술

01 성질과 상태

모습과 체격

dark [dɑːrk]
a. 검은
dye dark hair 검은머리로 염색하다

fair [fɛər]
a. 살결이 흰, 금발의
have a fair complexion 살결이 희다

bald [bɔːld]
a. 대머리의
go bald 대머리가 되다

long-haired [lɔːŋ hɛərd]
a. 긴머리의
long-haired, dope-smoking dropouts
장발에, 마리화나를 피우는 낙오자들

physique [fizíːk]
n. 체격
a man of strong physique 체격이 강건한 사람

tall [tɔːl]
a. 키가 큰
a tall girl 키가 큰 소녀

short [ʃɔːrt]
a. 키가 작은
a short man 키가 작은 사람

sturdy
[stə́:rdi]

a. 강건한, 튼튼한

a sturdy child 튼튼한 아이

fat
[fæt]

a. 살찐, 뚱뚱한

get fat 뚱뚱해지다

slender
[sléndə:r]

a. 날씬한, 호리호리한

a slender girl 몸매가 호리호리한 소녀

slim
[slim]

a. 가는, 가냘픈

have a slim waist 허리가 가늘다

thin
[θin]

a. 마른, 여윈

get thin 수척해지다

beautiful
[bjú:təfəl]

a. 아름다운

a beautiful flower 아름다운 여인

pretty
[príti]

a. 예쁜, 귀여운

a pretty little child 귀여운 아이

handsome
[hǽnsəm]

a. (남자가) 잘생긴

a handsome boy 잘생긴 소년

attractive
[ətrǽktiv]

a. 매력적인

an attractive waman 매력적인 여성

homely
[hóumli]

a. 못생긴

a homely but good-natured student
못생겼지만 성격이 좋은 학생

alike
[əláik]

a. 비슷한, 서로 같은

look-alike 매우 흡사한 사람[것]

■ 도형

shape
[ʃeip]

n. 모양, 꼴

take shape 형태를 갖추다[구체화되다]

circle
[sə́:rkl]

n. 원, 동그라미

in a circle 원형으로

square
[skwɛəːr]

n. 네모, 정사각형

a square of carpet 정사각형의 융단

rectangle
[réktæŋg-əl]

n. 직사각형

Semiotic rectangle 기호학적 사각형

triangle
[tráiæŋg-əl]

n. 세모, 삼각형

an inverted triangle 역삼각형

figure
[fígjər]

n. 도형

a plane figure 평면 도형

diamond
[dáiəmənd]

n. 마름모꼴

diamond-shaped 마름모꼴의

cube
[kju:b]

n. 정육면체

A cube has six faces. 정육면체는 6면이다

rectangular parallelepiped
[rektǽŋgjələːr pæ̀rəlèləpáid]

n. 직육면체

trigonal pyramid
[trígən-əl pírəmìd]

n. 삼각뿔

fan-shape
[fænʃeip]

n. 부채꼴

fan shape nozzle 부채꼴형 노즐

dot
[dɑt]

n. 점

put a dot on a piece of paper 종이에 점을 찍다

dotted line
[dátid lain]

n. 점선

draw a dotted line 점선을 긋다

parallel line
[pǽrəlèl lain]

n. 평행선

draw a line parallel 평행하게 선을 긋다

acute angle
[əkjúːt ǽŋgl]

n. 예각

be at an acute angle to …와 예각을 이루다

obtuse angle
[əbtjúːs ǽŋgl]

n. 둔각

most-obtuse-angle 최둔각

line
[lain]

n. 줄, 선

the line of life (손금의) 생명선

curve
[kəːrv]

n. 곡선

learning curve 학습 곡선

straight line
[streit lain]

n. 직선

draw a straight line 직선을 긋다

angle
[ǽŋgl]

n. 각도

measure[take] an angle 각도를 재다

02 감정과 감각

■ 감정을 나타내는 명사

feeling
[fíːliŋ]

n. 감정(가장 일반적인 말)
appeal to feelings 감정에 호소하다

emotion
[imóuʃən]

n. 감정(강하게 나타내는 감정)
weep with emotion 감정에 복받쳐 울다

sentiment
[séntəmənt]

n. 감정(이성적인 사고에 입각한 감정)
express a sentiment 감정을 표현하다

sensation
[senséiʃən]

n. 감각, 지각
keen sensation 예리한 감각

heart
[hɑːrt]

n. 마음
a warm heart 따뜻한 마음

mood
[muːd]

n. 기분, 분위기
a dreamy mood 꿈꾸는 듯이 황홀한 기분

pleasure
[pléʒər]

n. 즐거움
pleasure and pain 고락

excitement
[iksáitmənt]

n. 흥분

shout in excitement 흥분하여 소리지르다

happiness
[hǽpinis]

n. 행복

achieve true happiness 진정한 행복을 얻다

cheerfulness
[tʃíərfəlnis]

n. 유쾌함

assume an air of cheerfulness
쾌활한 체하다

amusement
[əmjúːzmənt]

n. 즐거움, 재미, 오락

watch a TV program with amusement
재미있게 TV 프로를 보다

kindness
[káindnis]

n. 친절

kindness to a stranger 낯선 사람에 대한 친절

love
[lʌv]

n. 사랑

a love song 사랑의 노래

imagination
[imæ̀dʒənéiʃən]

n. 상상

a stretch of imagination 상상의 날개를 펼치기

hope
[houp]

n. 희망

have hope 희망을 갖다

relief
[rilíːf]

n. 안심

a sense of relief 안도감

comfort
[kʌ́mfərt]

n. 편안함, 위안

relax in cool comfort 아주 편안하게 쉬다

sympathy
[símpəθi]

n. 동정, 연민

feel a deep sympathy for the poor
가난한 사람들에게 깊이동정하다

fear
[fiər]

n. 두려움

turn white with fear 무서워서 파랗게 질리다

worries
[wɔ́ːriz]

n. 걱정

household worries 가정의 고민

anxiety
[æŋzáiəti]

n. 불안

anxiety about the future 미래에 대한 불안

agony
[ǽgəni]

n. 고민

agony of mind 마음의 번민

nervousness
[nə́ːrvəsnis]

n. 긴장, 초조함

try to hide one's nervousness
초조함을 감추려 애쓰다

sadness
[sǽdnis]

n. 슬픔

be filled with deep sadness
비통한 생각에 잠기다

anger
[ǽŋgər]

n. 화, 노여움

in a moment of anger 화가 난 김에

shame
[ʃeim]

n. 부끄러움, 수치

feel shame at having told a lie
거짓말 한 것에 부끄러움을 느끼다

hatred
[héitrid]

n. 미움

sow the seeds of hatred 증오의 씨를 뿌리다

envy
[énvi]

n. 부러움

become an object of envy
선망의 대상이 되다

jealousy
[dʒéləsi]

n. 질투

driven by jealousy 질투한 나머지

disappointment
[dìsəpɔ́intmənt]

n. 실망

have a severe disappointment
크게 실망하다

misunderstanding
[mìsʌndəːrstǽndiŋ]

n. 오해

by a gross misunderstanding 심한 오해로

impression
[impréʃən]

n. 인상, 감명

create a favourable impression
좋은 인상을 주다

reaction
[riːǽkʃ-ən]

n. 반응, 반발

action and reaction 작용과 반작용

temper
[témpəːr]

n. 기질, 성질

a calm temper 차분한 성미

■ 감정을 나타내는 동사와 형용사

feel
[fiːl]

v. 느끼다

feel pain 아픔을 느끼다

regret
[rigrét]

v. 후회하다

regret the past 과거를 후회하다

admire
[ædmáiər]

v. 감탄하다

admire the beautiful scenery of Korea
한국의 경치를 탄미하다

amaze
[əméiz]

v. 몹시 놀라게 하다

be amazed at …에 깜짝 놀라다

annoy
[ənɔ́i]

v. 성가시게 굴다

annoy a person with frequent questioning 자주 질문을 해서 남을 괴롭히다

excite
[iksáit]

v. 흥분시키다

get excited over the news
그 뉴스를 듣고 흥분하다

hate
[heit]

v. 미워하다, 증오하다

hate cockroaches 바퀴벌레는 질색이다

impress
[imprés]

v. 인상을 주다, 감동시키다

impress a person favorably
사람에게 좋은 인상을 주다

irritate
[írətèit]

v. 짜증나게 하다, 화나게 하다

be irritated at the thought of it
그것을 생각만 해도 짜증이 나다

laugh
[læf]

v. 웃다, 비웃다

laugh(out) aloud 큰 소리로 웃다

please
[pliːz]

v. 기쁘게 하다

a dress that pleases me
내 마음에 드는 드레스

disappoint
[dìsəpɔ́int]

v. 실망시키다

be disappointed in a person
어떤 사람에 실망하다

satisfy
[sǽtisfài]

v. 만족시키다

satisfy the conditions 조건을 충족시키다

offend
[əfénd]

v. 성나게 하다

offend national susceptibilities
국민 감정을 상하게 하다

ashamed
[əʃéimd]

a. 부끄러워하는, 수줍어하는

an ashamed look 부끄러워하는 얼굴

afraid
[əfréid]

a. 두려워하는, 걱정하는

be much afraid of snakes
뱀을 아주 무서워하다

angry
[ǽŋgri]

a. 화난, 성난

angry protesters 성난 시위자들

sad
[sæd]

a. 슬픈

a sad look 슬픈 표정

anxious
[ǽŋkʃəs]

a. 걱정하는, 열망하는

anxious cares 걱정거리

stressed [strest]	*a.* 압박을 받는	
	feel stressed 압박감을 느끼다	

stressed [strest] — *a.* 압박을 받는
feel stressed 압박감을 느끼다

calm [kɑ:m] — *a.* 침착한
a calm voice 차분한 목소리

glad [glæd] — *a.* 기쁜
glad news 기쁜 소식

happy [hǽpi] — *a.* 행복한, 기쁜
a happy smile 행복한 미소

horrible [hɔ́:rəbəl] — *a.* 무서운, 끔찍한
a horrible sight 무서운 광경

awful [ɔ́:fəl] — *a.* 무서운, 대단한
an awful accident 무서운 사고

funny [fʌ́ni] — *a.* 재미있는, 웃기는
funny stories 우스운 이야기

lonely [lóunli] — *a.* 외로운
a lonely exile 외로운 유랑자

blue [blu:] — *a.* 우울한
a blue mood 우울한 기분

gloomy [glú:mi] — *a.* 우울한
a gloomy atmosphere 울적한 분위기

sensitive [sénsətiv] — *a.* 민감한
a sensitive skin 섬세한 피부

mental
[méntl]

a. 정신의, 마음의

mental hospital 정신병원

like
[laik]

v. 좋아하다

like playing tennis 테니스를 좋아하다

favorite
[féivərit]

n. 가장 좋아하는

my favorite song 내가 가장 좋아하는 노래

bother
[báðə:r]

v. 귀찮게 하다

bother one's parents 부모를 성가시게 하다

hard
[hɑ:rd]

a. 엄한, 냉혹한

a hard heart 냉혹한 마음

offensive
[əfénsiv]

a. 불쾌한

a sight offensive to the eye
눈에 거슬리는 광경.

violent
[váiələnt]

a. 격렬한, 흥분한

violent passions 격정

embarrass
[imbǽrəs]

v. 당황하게 하다

be embarrassed with responsibility
책임을 지게 되어 쩔쩔매다

scared
[skɛə:rd]

a. 겁먹은

a scared look 겁에 질린 표정

frightened
[fráitnd]

a. 깜짝 놀란

be frightened to death 놀라서 까무러칠 정도다

great
[greit]

a. 굉장한, 매우 좋은

a great man 위대한 인물

marvelous
[máːrv-ələs]

a. 놀라운, 신기한

a marvellous idea 놀라운 생각

fantastic
[fæntǽstik]

a. 환상적인

fantastic dreams 기상천외한 꿈

overwhelming
[òuvərhwélmiŋ]

a. 압도적인

an overwhelming victory 압도적인 승리

touch
[tʌtʃ]

v. 감동시키다

The story touched his heart.
그 이야기는 그를 감동시켰다.

grateful
[gréitfəl]

a. 고마워하는

a grateful letter 감사의 편지

miserable
[mízərəbəl]

a. 비참한, 불쌍한

lead a miserable life 비참한 생활을 하다

pitiful
[pítifəl]

a. 가엾은, 한심한

a pitiful plan 한심한 계획

despair
[dispéər]

v. 절망하다, 단념하다

despair of success 성공을 단념하다

upset
[ʌpsét]

v. 당황하게 하다

upset a person's mind 남을 당황하게 하다

02 감정과 감각

crazy
[kréizi]
a. 미친, 흥분해 있는
a crazy guy 미친 놈

mad
[mæd]
a. 분노한, 미친
go mad 미치다

surprised
[sərpráizd]
a. 놀란
a surprised look 놀란 표정

nervous
[nə́:rvəs]
a. 긴장한
get nervous 조마조마하다, 흥분하다

confused
[kənfjú:zd]
a. 혼란스러운
a confused statement 애매한 진술

■ 감각

touch
[tʌtʃ]
v. 만지다
touch (a person) on the shoulder
어깨를 만지다

soft
[sɔ(:)ft]
a. 부드러운
as soft as velvet 벨벳같이 부드러운

hard
[hɑ:rd]
a. 단단한, 딱딱한
a hard knot 견고한 매듭

smooth
[smu:ð]
a. 매끄러운
smooth skin 매끈한 피부

rough [rʌf]	*a.* 거칠거칠한, 껄껄한 **rough hands** 거친 손
sharp [ʃɑːrp]	*a.* 날카로운, 예리한 **a sharp knife[edge]** 잘 드는 칼
hot [hɑt]	*a.* 더운, 뜨거운 **a hot day** 더운 날
warm [wɔːrm]	*a.* 따뜻한, 온난한 **a warm climate** 온난한 기후
lukewarm [lúːkwɔ̀ːrm]	*a.* 미적지근한 **adopt a lukewarm attitude** 미적지근한 태도를 취하다
cold [kould]	*a.* 추운, 찬 **cold bath** 냉수욕
chilly [tʃíli]	*a.* 차가운, 쌀쌀한 **chilly weather** 쌀쌀한 날씨
cool [kuːl]	*a.* 시원한, 서늘한 **store food in a cool place** 서늘한 장소에 음식을 보관하다
smell [smel]	*v.* 냄새나다 **smell good** 좋은 냄새가 나다
odor [óudər]	*n.* 냄새, 향기 **an odor of cigar smoke** 담배 연기 냄새

stink
[stiŋk]

v. 고약한 냄새가 나다

stink of rotten fish 생선 썩은 냄새가 물컥 나다

■ 성격과 태도

liar
[láiər]

n. 거짓말쟁이

a poor liar 거짓말이 서툰 사람

coward
[káuərd]

n. 겁쟁이

play the coward 비겁한 짓을 하다

idler
[áidlər]

n. 게으름뱅이

a group of idlers gathered on the corner 모퉁이에 모여있는 한 무리의 게으름뱅이들

cold
[kould]

a. 냉정한, 냉담한

cold in manner 태도가 냉담한

openminded
[óupənmáindid]

a. 편견이 없는, 허심탄회한

an open-minded person 도량이 넓은 사람

talkative
[tɔ́ːkətiv]

a. 수다스러운

a very talkative child 아주 말이 많은 아이

moody
[múːdi]

a. 변덕스러운

a moody and unpredictable man
변덕스럽고 예측 불가능한 남자

patient
[péiʃənt]

a. 인내심이 많은

be patient with others 남에게 짜증을 내지 않다

jealous
[dʒéləs]

a. 질투심이 많은

a jealous husband 질투심 많은 남편

stubborn
[stʌ́bəːrn]

a. 고집 센, 완고한

a stubborn child 고집이 센 아이

responsible
[rispánsəb-əl]

a. 책임감 있는

a responsible position 책임 있는 지위

outgoing
[áutgòuiŋ]

a. 사교적인, 활발한

a warm and outgoing person
마음씨가 따스하고 외향적인 사람

brave
[breiv]

a. 용감한

a brave act 용감한 행동

wise
[waiz]

a. 슬기로운, 현명한

a wise choice 현명한 선택

careful
[kéərfəl]

a. 주의 깊은, 조심성 있는

a careful man 조심성 있는 사람, 신중한 사람

curious
[kjúəriəs]

a. 호기심이 강한

a curious look 호기심이 많은 표정

diligent
[dílədʒənt]

a. 근면한, 부지런한

a diligent worker 성실한 일꾼

lazy
[léizi]

a. 게으른

a lazy fellow 게으름뱅이

02 감정과 감각

honest [ánist]
a. 정직한
an honest opinion 솔직한 의견

gentle [dʒéntl]
a. 점잖은, 예의바른
a gentle manner 점잖은 태도

stupid [stjúːpid]
a. 어리석은
a stupid mistake 어리석은 실수

silly [síli]
a. 어리석은
a silly little boy 어리석은 꼬마 녀석

foolish [fúːliʃ]
a. 어리석은
a foolish decision 어리석은 결정

modest [mádist]
a. 겸손한, 정숙한
quiet and modest man 조용하고 겸손한 남자

polite [pəláit]
a. 공손한
a polite refusal 정중한 거절

shy [ʃai]
a. 수줍은, 부끄럼타는
a shy whisper 수줍어하는 작은 목소리

rude [ruːd]
a. 무례한
say rude things 버릇없는 말을 하다

selfish [sélfiʃ]
a. 이기적인
selfish behaviour 이기적인 행동

bold [bould]
a. 대담한
a bold attack 대담한 공격

timid
[tímid]

a. 소심한

as timid as a hare 몹시 수줍어하는, 소심한

positive
[pázətiv]

a. 긍정의, 적극적인

a positive reply (그렇다고) 긍정하는 대답

negative
[négətiv]

a. 부정의, 소극적인

take a negative attitude 소극적 태도를 취하다

flexible
[fléksəbəl]

a. 적응력 있는

a flexible mind 유연한 정신(의 소유자)

optimistic
[àptəmístik]

a. 낙천적인

have an optimistic view of life
낙관적인 인생관을 갖다

pessimistic
[pèsəmístik]

a. 비관적인

be pessimistic about the future
미래에 대해 비관적이다

unique
[ju:ní:k]

a. 독특한

a unique aroma 일종의 독특한 향기

ordinary
[ɔ́:rdənèri]

a. 보통의

ordinary people like you and me
당신과 나와 같은 보통 사람들

cheerful
[tʃíərfəl]

a. 쾌활한

a smiling cheerful man
생글생글 웃는 명랑한 사나이

humorous
[hjúːmərəs]

a. 유머 있는

a humorous situation
우스꽝스러운[유머러스한] 상황

quiet
[kwáiət]

a. 조용한

a quiet person 얌전한 사람

easygoing
[íːzigóuiŋ]

a. 태평한, 안이한

an easygoing fellow 마음편한 녀석

persistent
[pəːrsístənt]

a. 완고한

persistent resistance 완강한 저항

kind
[kaind]

a. 친절한, 상냥한

a kind heart 상냥한 마음

nice
[nais]

a. 좋은, 훌륭한

a nice evening 기분 좋은 저녁

friendly
[fréndli]

a. 다정한

a friendly greeting 다정한 인사

helpful
[hélpfəl]

a. 유용한

a helpful suggestion 도움이 되는 제안

calm
[kɑːm]

a. 침착한

a calm voice 차분한 목소리

generous
[dʒénərəs]

a. 관대한

a generous mind 너그러운 마음

straight [streit]	*a.* 솔직한, 직선적인	straight speech 직언
pure [pjuər]	*a.* 순수한	pure in heart 마음이 순수한
reliable [riláiəb-əl]	*a.* 믿음직한	a reliable source 믿을만한 소식통
independent [ìndipéndənt]	*a.* 독립적인	an independent spirit 독립적 기상
graceful [gréisfəl]	*a.* 우아한	a graceful dancer 우아한 무용수
vulgar [vʌ́lgər]	*a.* 천박한	a vulgar fellow 야비한 사람
sincere [sinsíəːr]	*a.* 진실한, 성실한	a sincere well-wisher 진심으로 행운을 비는 사람

03 화술

■ 의사소통

spelling
[spéliŋ]
n. 철자법
a spelling mistake 철자상의 오류

word
[wəːrd]
n. 단어, 말
new words 새로운 단어

accent
[ǽksent]
n. 악센트
a stress accent 강약악센트

intonation
[ìntənéiʃən]
n. 억양
intonation patterns 억양 형태

pronunciation
[prənʌ̀nsiéiʃən]
n. 발음
English pronunciation 영어의 발음

standard language
[stǽndəːrd lǽŋgwidʒ]
n. 표준어
use the standard language
표준어를 사용하다

dialect
[dáiəlèkt]
n. 방언
a local dialect 지역 방언

slang [slæŋ]
n. 속어
overuse slang 비속어를 남발하다

translation [trænsléiʃ-ən]
n. 번역
free translation 의역

interpretation [intə̀ːrprətéiʃən]
n. 통역, 해석
interpretation of a treaty 조약의 해석

proverb [právəːrb]
n. 속담
as the proverb says 속담에 있듯이

gender [dʒéndər]
n. 성별
gender issues 성 논의의 쟁점들

topic [tápik]
n. 화제, 주제
a topic of conversation 대화 화제

introduction [ìntrədʌ́kʃən]
n. 소개
make an introduction to …에게 소개하다

conversation [kànvərséiʃən]
n. 대화
a private conversation 사사로운 이야기

gesture [dʒéstʃər]
n. 제스처, 몸짓
facial gesture 표정

discussion [diskʌ́ʃən]
n. 토론
have a lively discussion 활기찬 토론을 하다

argument [áːrgjəmənt]
n. 언쟁
a heated argument 열띤 논쟁

meaning
[míːniŋ]

n. 의미

a remark full of meaning 의미심장한 말

foreigner
[fɔ́(ː)rinəːr]

n. 외국인

an ignorant foreigner 무지한 외국인

opinion
[əpínjən]

n. 의견

public opinion 여론

speech
[spiːtʃ]

n. 연설

a very boring after-dinner speech
만찬 후의 아주 따분한 연설

joke
[dʒouk]

n. 농담

tell a joke 농담을 하다

quotation
[kwoutéiʃən]

n. 인용

a quotation from Shakespeare
셰익스피어 작품의 인용구

look
[luk]

v. 보다(정지된 것)

look aside 옆을 보다

watch
[wɑtʃ]

v. 보다(움직이는 것)

watch a football game 축구 시합을 보다

see
[siː]

v. 보다, 보이다

see over <집 등을> 둘러보다

stare
[stɛəːr]

v. 응시하다, 빤히 쳐다보다

stare a person up and down
아무를 빤히 위아래로 훑어보다

show
[ʃou]

v. 보이다, 보여주다

show the ticket at the gate
입구에서 표를 보이다

hear
[hiə*r*]

v. 듣다, 들리다

hear a loud voice 큰 소리가 들리다

listen
[lísən]

v. 듣다(주의하여)

listen to a lecture 강연을 듣다

speak
[spi:k]

v. 말하다

speak clearly 똑똑히 말하다

say
[sei]

v. 말하다

say a few words 몇 마디 말하다

tell
[tel]

v. 이야기하다

tell him a story 그에게 이야기를 들려주다

talk
[tɔ:k]

v. 대화하다

talk over a cup of coffee
커피를 마시면 서 이야기하다

chat
[tʃæt]

v. 잡담하다, 담소하다

chat with a friend 벗과 담소하다

mention
[ménʃən]

v. 언급하다

as I mention ed before
전에 말씀드린 바와 같이

03 화술

explain
[ikspléin]

v. 설명하다

explain how a computer works
컴퓨터가 어떻게 작동하는가를 설명하다

describe
[diskráib]

v. 묘사하다

describe something to a person
남에게 어떤 일을 설명하다

write
[rait]

v. 쓰다

write an application 신청서에 기입하다

read
[ri:d]

v. 읽다

read a book 책을 읽다

ask
[æsk]

v. 묻다

ask the way 길을 묻다

question
[kwéstʃən]

n. 질문 *v.* 질문하다

ask a lot of questions 많은 질문을 하다

answer
[ǽnsər]

n. 대답 *v.* 대답하다

write an answer 답장을 쓰다

reply
[riplái]

n. 응답 *v.* 응답하다

reply to a question 질문에 답하다

respond
[rispánd]

v. 응답하다

briefly respond to a question
질문에 간단히 답하다

suggest
[səgdʒést]

v. 제안하다

suggest a plan 일책을 내놓다

lie
[lai]

n. 거짓말 *v.* 거짓말하다

tell a lie 거짓말을 하다

pardon
[páːrdn]

v. 용서하다, 허락하다

pardon a fault 과실을 용서하다

promise
[prámis]

n. 약속 *v.* 약속하다

make a promise 약속하다

cancel
[kǽnsəl]

v. 취소하다

cancel permission 허가를 취소하다

insist
[insíst]

v. 주장하다

insist on working late 밤늦게까지 공부하겠다고 우기다

order
[ɔ́ːrdər]

n. 명령 *v.* 명령하다

receive orders to do …하라는 지시를 받다

refuse
[rifjúːz]

v. 거절하다

refuse an offer 제의를 거절하다

shout
[ʃaut]

v. 소리치다

shout at a girl 소녀에게 큰소리치다

protest
[prətést]

v. 항의하다, 이의를 제기하다

protest a decision 결의에 반대하다

get
[get]

v. 얻다, 입수하다

get a victory 승리를 얻다

take
[teik]

v. 취하다

take a wife 아내를 맞이하다

obtain
[əbtéin]

v. 손에 넣다, 획득하다

obtain information 정보를 얻다

gain
[gein]

v. (이익, 혜택을) 얻다

gain a reputation 명성을 얻다

acquire
[əkwáiər]

v. 취득하다

acquire property 재산을 취득하다

receive
[risíːv]

v. 받다

receive a letter from a friend
친구로부터 편지를 받다

inherit
[inhérit]

v. 상속하다

inherit a strong constitution from one's mother 어머니로부터 튼튼한 체질을 물려받다

give
[giv]

v. 주다

give a birthday present 생일 선물을 주다

present
[prizént]

v. 증정하다

present a message 메시지를 주다

award
[əwɔ́ːrd]

v. 수여하다, 상을 주다

award a prize to a person 아무에게 상을 주다

grant
[grænt]

v. 수여하다

grant a degree 학위를 수여하다

offer
[ɔ́(:)fər]
v. 제공하다
offer her a job 그녀에게 일자리를 제공하다

donate
[dóuneit]
v. 기부하다
donate large sums to relief organizations 구제기관에 거금을 기부하다

hand
[hænd]
v. 전해주다
hand him the pen back 그에게 펜을 돌려주다

distribute
[distríbju:t]
v. 배포하다
distribute magazines to subscribers 잡지를 구독자에게 발송하다

lend
[lend]
v. 빌려주다
lend a book 책을 빌려주다

borrow
[bɔ́(:)rou]
v. 빌리다
borrow books from the library 도서관에서 책을 빌리다

return
[ritə́:rrn]
v. 돌려주다
return the borrowed money 빌린 돈을 갚다

exchange
[ikstʃéindʒ]
n. 교환 *v.* 교환하다
exchange teachers 교환 교사

■ 토론

thought
[θɔ:t]
n. 생각, 사고, 사상
after much[serious] thought 잘 생각한 뒤에

03 화술

opinion
[əpínjən]

n. 의견, 견해

public opinion 여론

idea
[aidíːə]

n. 착상, 아이디어

man of ideas 아이디어가 풍부한 사람

think
[θiŋk]

v. 생각하다

think about a new plan
새로운 계획에 대해서 생각하다

consider
[kənsídər]

v. 숙고하다, 고려하다

consider the feelings of others
남의 감정을 고려하다

regard
[rigáːrd]

v. …으로 여기다, 간주하다

regard the artist as a genius
그 예술가를 천재로 여기다

mean
[miːn]

v. 의미하다

What does this mean? 이것은 무슨 뜻인가?

reflect
[riflékt]

v. 반성하다, 곰곰이 생각하다

reflect on one's virtues and faults
자기의 장단점을 곰곰이 생각하다

concentrate
[kánsəntrèit]

v. 전념하다, 집중하다

concentrate upon a problem
어떤 문제에 전념하다

attitude
[ǽtitjùːd]

n. 태도, 마음가짐

a gentlemanly attitude 신사적 태도

attention
[əténʃən]

n. 주의, 주목

call a person's attention
…의 주의를 환기시키다

---

understand
[ʌ̀ndərstǽnd]

v. 이해하다

understand each other 서로 이해하다

---

guess
[ges]

v. 추측하다

guess the woman's age at 25
그 여자의 나이를 25세로 추측하다

---

suppose
[səpóuz]

v. ~라고 가정하다

suppose (that) it is true
그것이 사실이라고 생각하다

---

imagine
[imǽdʒin]

v. 상상하다

imagine passing the exam
시험에 합격하는 것을 상상하다

---

wonder
[wʌ́ndəːr]

v. …이 아닐까 생각하다

wonder if it is true 그것이 사실일까 생각하다

---

suspect
[səspékt]

v. …이 아닌가 의심하다, 의심쩍게 여기다

suspect a person as the theft
…에게 도둑의 혐의를 걸다

---

doubt
[daut]

v. 의심하다

doubt one's eyes 자기의 눈을 의심하다

---

realize
[ríːəlàiz]

v. 깨닫다

realize one's mistake 자기 실수를 깨닫다

recognize
[rékəgnàiz]

v. 인정하다, 인식하다

recognize that it is important
그것이 중요하다는 것을 인식하다

believe
[bilíːv]

v. 믿다, 생각하다

have no reason to believe 믿을 이유가 없다

convince
[kənvíns]

v. 납득시키다

It is difficult to convince him.
그를 설득하기는 어렵다.

emphasize
[émfəsàiz]

v. 강조하다

emphasize the point 중점을 역설하다

know
[nou]

v. 알다, 알고 있다

know oneself 자신을 알다

find
[faind]

v. 알아내다

find[work out] a solution 해법을 찾다

experience
[ikspíəriəns]

n. 경험 *v.* 경험하다

learn by experience 경험으로 배우다

intend
[inténd]

v. …할 작정이다

intend to study abroad 유학할 작정이다

decide
[disáid]

v. 결정하다

decide against …하지 않기로 결정하다
decide for …하기로 결정하다

determine
[ditə́:rmin]

v. 결의하다

determine to launch a new project
새 프로젝트에 착수하기로 결의하다

indicate
[índikèit]

v. 나타내다

indicate that the price is negotiable
가격이 협상할 여지가 있음을 나타내다

remember
[rimémbə:r]

v. 생각해 내다

remember one's name …의 이름을 생각해내다

memorize
[méməràiz]

v. 암기하다

memorize a poem 시 한 편을 암기하다

forget
[fərgét]

v. 잊어버리다

forget and forgive (원한 등을) 깨끗이 잊다

controversial
[kàntrəvə́:rʃəl]

a. 논쟁의

discuss the controversial issue
논쟁의 여지가 있는 문제에 대해 토론하다

subjective
[səbdʒéktiv]

a. 주관적인

take a subjective view of 주관적으로 보다

objective
[əbdʒéktiv]

a. 객관적인

an objective report of the accident
사고에 대한 객관적인 보도

logical
[ládʒikəl]

a. 논리적인

reach a logical conclusion
논리적인 결론에 도달하다

agree
[əgríː]

v. 동의하다

agree to the proposal 제안에 동의하다

deny
[dinái]

v. 부정하다

deny the report 보도를 부정하다

give up
[givʌp]

v. 포기하다

give up studying abroad 유학을 포기하다

■ 판단

common
[kámən]

a. 보통의

lack common sense 상식이 결여되어있다

general
[dʒénərəl]

a. 일반적인

as a general rule 일반적으로, 보통은

universal
[jùːnəvə́ːrsəl]

a. 보편적인

universal rules 보편적 법칙

typical
[típik-əl]

a. 전형적인

the typical businessman 전형적인 실업가

interesting
[íntəristiŋ]

a. 재미있는, 흥미 있는

read an interesting book 재미있는 책을 읽다

chief
[tʃiːf]

a. 주된

his chief merit 그의 주된 장점

necessary
[nésəsèri]

a. 필요한

have the necessary talent
필요한 재능을 갖추고 있다

trivial
[tríviəl]

a. 하찮은, 사소한

argue about a trivial matter
사소한 일로 언쟁하다

important
[impɔ́ːrtənt]

a. 중요한

carry out an important mission
중요한 임무를 수행하다

precious
[préʃəs]

a. 귀중한

precious metals 귀금속

particular
[pərtíkjələr]

a. 특정의, 특수한

in this particular case
특히 이 경우는 (딴 것과 달라)

strange
[streindʒ]

a. 이상한

have a strange sensation 이상한 기분이 들다

peculiar
[pikjúːljər]

a. 기묘한, 특유의

an expression peculiar to Canadians
캐나다인 특유의 표현

basic
[béisik]

a. 기초의, 근본적인

sic principles 근본 원리

same
[seim]

a. 같은

wear the same dress as mine
나와 같은 옷을 입고 있다

similar
[símələːr]
a. 비슷한
similar tastes 비슷한 취미

different
[dífərənt]
a. 다른
different people with the same name 동명이인

simple
[símp-əl]
a. 단순한, 간단한
a simple question 단순한 질문

complicated
[kámplikèitid]
a. 복잡한, 뒤얽힌
a complicated relationship 복잡한 관계

concrete
[kánkriːt]
a. 구체적인
a concrete example 구체적인 예

abstract
[æbstrǽkt]
a. 추상적인
an abstract idea 추상적 개념

rational
[rǽʃ-ənl]
a. 합리적인, 이성적인
make a rational decision 합리적인 결정을 내리다

suitable
[súːtəbəl]
a. 적절한
arrange a suitable time to meet 만나기에 적절한 시간을 정하다

terrific
[tərífik]
a. 굉장한, 훌륭한
enjoy a terrific view 절경을 즐기다

splendid
[spléndid]
a. 뛰어난, 눈부신
splendid talents 뛰어난 재능

incredible
[inkrédəbəl]

a. (믿기 어려울 만큼) 굉장한, 대단한

an incredible memory 굉장한 기억력

remarkable
[rimáːrkəb-əl]

a. 주목할 만한, 두드러진

a remarkable discovery 주목할 만한 발견

perfect
[pə́ːrfikt]

a. 완벽한

achieve the perfect score 만점을 받다

accurate
[ǽkjuərit]

a. 정확한

file an accurate report 정확한 보도를 하다

exact
[igzǽkt]

a. 정확한

the exact time 정확한 시간

rough
[rʌf]

a. 대강의, 개략적인

a rough estimate 개산(槪算)

right
[rait]

a. 옳은, 선량한

right conduct 선행

just
[dʒʌst]

a. 올바른, 공정한

a just decision 공정한 판결

fair
[fɛər]

a. 공정한, 공평한

a fair decision 공정한 결정

good
[gud]

a. 좋은

exhibit good behavior 좋은 행동을 보여주다

true
[truː]

a. 정말의, 참된

tell a true story 참된 이야기를 하다

bad
[bæd]
a. 나쁜
break a bad habit 나쁜 습관을 고치다

false
[fɔːls]
a. 거짓의, 허위의
give false evidence 허위 진술을 하다

terrible
[térəb-əl]
a. 무서운, 무시무시한
present a terrible sight 참상을 나타내다

ridiculous
[ridíkjələs]
a. 터무니없는
ridiculous claim 어처구니없는 주장

wrong
[rɔːŋ]
a. 틀린, 그릇된
take the wrong way 길을 잘못 가다

evil
[íːvəl]
a. 사악한
evil conduct 악행

practical
[præktikəl]
a. 실제적인, 실용적인
practical English 실용 영어

convenient
[kənvíːnjənt]
a. 편리한
a convenient appliance 편리한 기구